W9-BEG-292

Missionary
Principles and Practice

Books by Harold Lindsell

ABUNDANTLY ABOVE
THE THING APPOINTED
A CHRISTIAN PHILOSOPHY OF MISSIONS
PARK STREET PROPHET
A HANDBOOK OF CHRISTIAN TRUTH
(WITH CHARLES J. WOODBRIDGE)

Missionary
Principles and Practice

BY

HAROLD LINDSELL

FLEMING H. REVELL COMPANY

Westwood, N.J.—316 Third Avenue
London E.C. 4—29 Ludgate Hill
Glasgow C. 2—229 Bothwell Street

To Lawrence and Dagmar Andreson, beloved friends in Jesus Christ, devoted soldiers of the cross, and free givers of their substance for the work of His kingdom this book is affectionately dedicated.

Contents

8 CONTENTS

Preface

EVERY BOOK IS WRITTEN FOR A PURPOSE HOWEVER ILL-DISGUISED that purpose may be. Some write because of an inner compulsion which finds expression only by the written word. Some write for fame and fortune. Still others write for reasons they do not understand themselves.

This volume was undertaken for a variety of reasons. Not the least in the gamut of these reasons was the need for a textbook in this field. Like all textbooks it was inevitably subjected to tensions which could not be resolved. Being general in character it could not treat any one subject exhaustively. Due to problems of publishing costs it could not be as long as the author might have made it were no consideration given to costs.

A second reason for the writing of this volume was a sense of compulsion derived from a personal interest and concern for missionary endeavor. In a changing world one must be almost blind to escape seeing the gross spiritual maladjustment of mankind. And when the sense of that maladjustment is combined with a deep conviction that the gospel of Jesus Christ is the only remedy for sin and for sinners, one is constrained to use his influence and employ his efforts in attempting to rectify conditions. Thus the work has been a labor of love for the Lord of the church and for the progress of His gospel.

The material in the book is elementary. It is also basic to an understanding of the missionary task. For the reader whose interest is stimulated, the bibliography will enable him to pursue that interest in detail. By no means is the bibliography thought to be exhaustive, but it is large enough to open the door to further inquiry and should enable any reader to go on from there to the limits of his ability.

Some acknowledgements are due individuals who have helped to make this volume possible. First among them is Dr. R. Pierce Beaver and the staff of the Missionary Research Library in New York City. The west coast possesses no research facilities comparable to those found in this library, and the church owes a great deal to those who have made this center of missionary material available. The friendliness and genuine interest of the entire staff is exemplary. Dr. & Mrs. Lawrence Andreson of Lexington, Massachusetts, made available a cottage at Camp Brookwoods on Lake Winnepesaukee in New Hampshire. By the shores of this lake, in a room overlooking the blue waters, a good deal of the writing was done. Fuller Theological Seminary in the interests of faculty writing inaugurated a system of sabbatical leaves which made possible a period of six months without administrative and teaching responsibilities. This period of time allowed for the completion of the manuscript. And last, but not least, the author acknowledges his profound gratitude to Miss Lossie Brown whose secretarial competence has helped incalculably, and whose keen eye has caught many errors.

HAROLD LINDSELL

Pasadena, Calif.
December 1954

Missionary
Principles and Practice

CHAPTER I

Missions Today

~~~~~~

ON EVERY HAND MEN ARE SAYING THAT MISSIONS ARE AT THE crossroads. The characteristic of our age is the "crossroads" philosophy. Thus every day the newspapers proclaim that democracy is at the crossroads. They say that the free world is at the crossroads, and that it is engaged in a death struggle with the totalitarianism of Russia in its monolithic communistic structure.

Cultures are in crisis, and vast changes are being wrought in our day. The convulsive cataclysm into which western culture has been thrust has all but engulfed that culture and all other cultures. But there is one great difference between the situation of missions and the gulf into which western culture, democracy, and the free world have been thrown. That difference is so profound that, from the outset, it must be elaborated and kept distinct from the tensions in which western culture and democracy operate.

Missions are always at the crossroads. Democracy, totalitarianism, and western culture may come to a crossroad occasionally, and they may be faced with moments of great decision in the vortex of revolutionary movements. But in between these convulsions they may have periods of rest and freedom from danger. But with missions it is not so. Missions from the beginning have been in crisis, and they shall ever be in crisis because the very nature of missions from within its own genius presupposes a crisis component.

The world today is in transition. The changing world is undergoing alterations which, in their relationship to missions, appear to place missions at the crossroads. But missions have always been at the crossroads, and today's world simply makes this more apparent. Furthermore, it serves to awaken those who are interested in missions to a perceptive awareness of the peculiar nature and relevancy of missions to the world in which they live.

The church of Jesus Christ needs to re-orient itself and to re-appraise and re-evaluate its functions, its methods and its usefulness. It must ask itself the question whether it has fulfilled its obligation in giving clear and unequivocal answers to the questions which have been forged in the fires of conflicting ideologies. But even before it has tried to do this, it must ask itself questions about its own nature and function in terms of its basic obligation to the world.

The church itself stands in the midst of unusual world situations and problems. These are quite disturbing because of their dynamic and soul-shaking implications. But the church cannot begin to minister to this age until it develops an acute consciousness of the problems it is expected to attack, and until it understands and is able to fit into a synthetic picture the individual strands which make up the complexity of our day.

The first and most obvious fact today is that the whole world is on the march. Everywhere there is unrest, disaffection, and dislocation. In the aftermath of two world wars which have rocked the entire earth, every area has felt the impact of these struggles. Giants which have long slept are now awakened and in motion. One cannot suppose that the two world wars were in themselves the total causes for this new situation. Certainly the industrial revolution has helped to bring it about. Increased means of communication via wireless, radio, telephone, and telegraph have made the world smaller. The turbine engine and the airplane have brought

Bombay, Manila, Tokyo, Rio de Janeiro, and Moscow too close for comfort. Whereas men used to wait several months to hear of revolutions which had come and gone, the world is briefed daily in advance of the revolts and gets a blow-by-blow description during and following the encounter. Every diplomatic station is a listening post bringing to the home base daily accounts of international intrigue and domestic happenings.

2. The second great fact of our day is the diminishing size of the world which has produced a geographic unity. Localism and regionalism have been all but destroyed. In a sense never known before the world has become one world. Nations are confronted daily with each other and are having to live together as never before. But in the midst of this geographic unity there has been a discordant note. Rising nationalisms have created a disunity in the midst of a geographic unity. Slogans of "Asia for the Asians" have appeared over and over again. Opposition to the dominance of the white man, hatred of imperialism and colonialism, the bankruptcy of the colonial policies of France and England have all added fuel to the fires of discordancy. Within areas new forces have arisen to do battle with each other. The Arab world stands poised against the people of Israel; Pakistan stands opposed to India proper. The Mohammedan and the Hindu are at each other's throat. Communists have been boring from within in every nation, and conflicts have raged in Guatemala, Costa Rica, Italy, India, Indonesia and other nations of the world. And with it all there is great likelihood that the unrest will continue undiminished for at least another full generation.

3. In the midst of the marching world and the unity and disunity, other important factors bearing on the world situation have become obvious. Not the least of these has been the disappearance of absolutes and the consequent reign of relatives. In the eastern world relativism has always reigned supreme, while in western culture the absolute has held sway for two

thousand years. But in recent years the dominance of absolutism in western culture has given way to relativism to such an extent that there has been the practical disappearance of the absolute. Life has been stripped of its significance in terms of absolutes, and ethics, morality, religion, standards, and spiritual values have succumbed to relativism. The capstone of this change has been signified by recent decisions of the Supreme Court of the United States in which the relativistic philosophy of Oliver Wendell Holmes has been made a cornerstone of jurisprudence. The court has held that what was true in other days is not true today. That morals and ethics change, being grounded in sociological concepts, and that since ethics and morality are governed by sociological concepts, the change of these concepts of necessity validates changes in ethics and morality.

When the church of Christ understands that it faces a hostile western culture based upon relativism, it perceives that its very life is threatened because the church has always been built upon the rock of the absolute. It then becomes the business of the church to examine the alternatives and to demonstrate to man where the reign of the relative will lead him. The danger of relativism is its threat to man in his totality. For man is rooted and grounded in God who is the Absolute, and when the absolute is destroyed by man, he destroys himself because he is rooted and grounded in the absolute.

Relativism has its twin devil, which is secularism. When man declares God to be irrelevant to life (because relativism does precisely this), then the secular spirit takes over. Man has become enthroned instead of God, and God is left out of the picture. One of the causative factors which has produced both relativism and secularism has been scientism. Scientific progress has enabled man to find solutions and to master his environment by his wits without reliance upon religion.

In a relativistic culture man has not changed himself, and

the same devils which beset him a thousand years ago continue to plague him today. Because of the way he is made, man continues to seek for absolute truth and ultimate reality. Modern man does not always perceive that he has declared the ultimate to be ineffable in relativism (although it may be said that the insistence upon relativism makes for the absolute of the relative so that the relativist ultimately must forego relativism or agree to the relativism of relativism which in turn is circular and leads him back where he was in the first place), and so he is faced with the vexing dilemma of the inner urge which seeks for an ultimate while he declares that there is none. And when absolutes are divorced from life, man supposedly becomes a free or autonomous spirit with the power of intellectual and moral judgment. This makes man rather than God the measure of all things.

The misfortune of man is that he cannot create absolutes as much as he may wish to for the simple reason that absolutes would be his human creation. Sooner or later he discovers that the law which comes from within him is not absolute and that if he is to find one that is suitable it must come from without and from above. But God is dead, and so man is left with a split personality, bedeviled by the desire for that which he knows he needs, but refusing the only source which can supply it for him.

The evidence that man has left God may be found in man's turning to competing alternatives for his answer. These answers have been fascism of the Italian brand, nazism of the German stripe, communism with the Russian trademark, and in America man has also turned to the state not in a totalitarian pattern but in a social service one.

Fascism and nazism have been nullified by World War II. Yet seeds of these totalitarian systems linger beneath the surface. But the chief totalitarian system which threatens the world today is that of communism. Already half of the world has been engulfed by it, and the mass of land areas controlled by Russia either directly or indirectly is staggering. The penetrating ability of Communist sympathizers in scores of countries defies the efforts even of missionaries to equal it. Willing to suffer physically, socially, and materially for this ideology thousands of men and women have engaged in legal, extra-legal, and illegal activities for the furtherance of the system. No nation has been exempt from the pressures of communism and the democratic world cannot forget too easily what happened in Indo-China and Korea.

Besides communism, Romanism exists as a menace to historic Protestantism. It is a competing option which has a subtle attractiveness. Totalitarian like communism, fascism and nazism, men cannot help admiring its monolithic structure. When men seek for religious certainty, the Roman church openly claims that they can find it within the fold of Romanism. Protestantism has succumbed in many directions to the lure of relativism, but Romanism stands without apology for absolutism in a dogmatic fashion. It is true that its absolutism has been at variance with Protestantism historically even when Protestantism was solidly grounded in an absolutistic framework. The absolutism of Protestantism was found in the sovereignty of God and evidenced in the priesthood of all believers. But in Romanism the sovereignty of God was expressed in a sovereignty supposedly granted to Peter and by Peter to the popes of Rome in episcopal succession. Romanism consistently has proclaimed an authority both religious and secular, and to this hour the Roman See has never denied these exorbitant claims. With an absolutism which amazes the average Protestant, Romanism has not ceased to profess that he who does not have the church (the Roman church) for his mother cannot have God for his father. This group must be reckoned with as a force which has significance and which has persistently resisted the pressures of communism.

The church of Jesus Christ lives in this kind of world. It has

made concessions to the world which have undermined the
structure of the church and which call the church to a recon-
sideration of its biblical nature and witness. Formerly Christianity has been closely allied to the idea of a Christian state
and a Christian culture and a Christian society. Gradually the
church has come to see that this is an illusory vision which has
neither biblical warrant nor historical foundation. To speak
of America as a Christian nation or of Britain as a Christian
empire is an error. The church must accustom itself to this indisputable fact and realize that it is a minority group swim-
ming upstream and not a majority group going with the tide.
Perhaps the reason the church today is not so powerful is its
supposition that the church should be of the world as well as
in the world, and it has made concessions to science and in
morals and ethics which it never should have made. These
concessions have come from the larger denominations and
particularly those in the United States which have been tied
in with the National Council of Churches. Smaller groups and
independent or "fundamentalist" segments of Christianity
have not made the same error, but they have not been guiltless
either for they have fallen into still another pitfall. If the
churches in the National Council grouping have been
tempted in the direction of making concessions to the world
and of being incorporated in the structure of the world, the
other groups have isolated themselves carefully from the
world in conformity to the idea that they are in the world but
not of the world. In the one case, it has been a total divorce
from the world and in the other, identification with the world.
The one in witnessing to the world tended to become part of
it; the other in withdrawing from the world lost its contact
with it and its witnessing power to it. One can hardly suppose
that either is the correct solution but that, somewhere between, the church is to be in contact with the world as a witness without being caught in its web.

The church must first rediscover its nature. It is a fellowship of believers who are rooted and grounded in God through redemption. Redemption is unto a relationship with God in which worship, fellowship and service are expressions. The church is a society of redeemed people who worship God, who live in fellowship not only with God but also with all other believers who are members of the same great fellowship, and who have been redeemed by God to serve Him and His interests in His divine redemptive order. The church and each believer is committed to the service and the salvation of men, and they exist as witnesses who are opposed to the evil of this world and who identify themselves with the sufferings and needs of the world as agents of Jesus Christ. This identification of believers with the sufferings and needs of the world is not in itself redemptive, but it is a result of God's redemption in the hearts of men which causes them to suffer for the sake of the world without becoming partakers of the sins of the world.

In every day and every age the nature and function of the church remain the same. It is rooted in the absolute and does not change. Whatever pressures may impinge upon the church from without and however history may seem to deny it, the church must sense anew its unchanging purpose and know that it is called upon to render the same witness in any age and under any circumstances, be the times turbulent, revolutionary, evolutionary or quiescent.

One of the greatest weaknesses of the church has been its parochialism, its regionalism, or its isolation. The church has failed to comprehend the concept of the New Testament that it lives in one world and that the field is the world. Consistently, missionary ideology has embraced the idea that missionaries are reaching the "heathen" with the gospel and are performing a colonizing job on them. Anything outside their national boundaries is "foreign." This parochialism is utterly disastrous and must go. Perhaps there was some excuse for thinking this way one hundred years ago, but there is no excuse for this kind of misunderstanding today. The Christian faith now cuts across all societies with a few exceptions. If the term "heathen" is to be employed at all, it must be employed correctly. Then "heathenism" runs horizontally through all religions, nations, and cultures without exception. It runs through American religions, and culture too. There are tens of thousands of highly-educated "heathen" in the United States. They occupy high places in government, in the schools, in industry, and in the scientific field. But they are just as much "heathen" as the lowliest African in the bush. The synonym for "heathen" is "pagan," and the antipathy which arises when cultured and educated but unregenerate people are called "heathen," suggests that the word itself be dropped in favor of one which will accomplish the same result without giving offense. Christians are to be all things to all men, and since the objective of the church is to secure commitment of life to Jesus Christ and not to antagonize needlessly they do well to bear this in mind.

Another great weakness of the church is its compartmentalism in which the distinction between clergy and laity has been sharpened beyond biblical recognition. The result of this false antithesis has been the feeling on the part of the laity that the responsibility for the onward progress of the church belongs to the clergy. That professional class of worker is supposed to do what God has ordained shall be done by all believers. Today the appalling demands made on the church are being met by a small minority. The vast majority have no interest, understanding, or a sense of responsibility. Yet they are members of one body and each member has equal responsibility. If the weakness is great, the need for proper education is greater. Somehow believers must be made conscious of their duties and responsibilities. The goal of this education is to convince the church that *all* must support the program financially, that *all* must pray, that *all* must be willing to do the will of God, and that *all* are obligated to be witnesses for Jesus Christ wherever they are.

Compartmentalism helps to encourage the development of a hierarchy and ecclesiasticism in which one segment of the church becomes the overlord of God's flock. This incipient evil is one of the permanent tensions of the church, and Romanism has succumbed quite easily to this evil. The correction of such abuses is not the elimination of the offices of bishop and deacon. Once again there are two extremes: one is ecclesiasticism, the other is anarchy without visible organization. We must steer a course between Scylla and Charybdis, the twin dangers, and find a *via media* in which ecclesiasticism does not secure control of the organization and in which the correction of the abuses of ecclesiasticism does not lead to anarchy. God has ordained that His church shall have officers to guide His people, but they are *pares inter pares* whose leadership is spiritual and which leadership is derived from the consent of the people. The people in turn grant recognition to this leadership as the gift of God and know that certain men have been called of God to devote themselves to vocational full-time service in the interests of the Kingdom and for the glory of God.

Still another weakness of the church has been its failure to distinguish between western culture and the Christian faith. Unquestionably this error arose out of a false eschatology which posited the Christianization of the world and the advent of a golden age introduced by the permeation of the gospel as a leaven throughout the world. Lamott recently asked the same question which alert missionary statesmen have been asking for some time. "Is it actually, we inquire, a part of our missionary purpose to Christianize the world? Is there not some more clearly defined goal, less open to criticism, less vague and general, to which we may address ourselves in the years ahead?"* The answer to this question is patent to all

* Willis Church Lamott, *Revolution in Missions* (New York, The Macmillan Co., 1954), p. 16.

who study the Bible. Christianization of the world is not the biblical goal, and all men will not be saved.

The idea of Christianization of the world has been further complicated by identifying the Christian faith with western culture so that missionaries have somehow been left with the idea that western culture is an integral part of the gospel. Nothing could be further from the truth. Western culture is a product which has its roots in the Hebrew-Roman-Greek-Christian tradition. Some parts of that culture are distinctly Christian; others are sub-Christian and some parts are purely pagan. It is an amorphous creature of questionable origin, and the quicker the church divorces the faith from it the better it will be.

Western culture has been identified also with enlightenment and freedom. Enlightenment has often meant bathtubs, electricity, and modern conveniences. And when the people, to whom missionaries have gone, have come around to their way of life in its external manifestations they felt that they had succeeded. Of course it is true that some people take baths three or four times a day and regard the people of the western world as virtually unclean because they bathe one or twice a week. Perhaps their standards should be adopted instead of those of the western world. With the bathtub has gone democracy. And democracy means freedom. Normally the western world equates freedom with the gospel and assumes again its integral relation to the gospel. This is not so.

Once and forever believers should grasp the proposition that the Christian faith was made to exist in any environment and under any circumstances. It is valid in a totalitarian structure as well as in a democratic one. Historical occasions arise which force the church to be a church of persecution, or a church of the catacombs, or a church of the underground. But never does persecution or anything else change the nature of the witnessing church or relieve the church of its responsibilities. It may have to operate differently than it would in a totally free environment, but operate it must even though the price be death. Fortunately, the church can work with the reasonable certainty that its labor will not be in vain but that God will accomplish through its ministry His eternal purposes.

One of the final problems which has always vexed the church is its tendency to promise men more than the church can produce. For some decades the church has suffered the obloquy which comes from the failure to perform according to generous promises. The failure to live up to sweeping promises has been due to making promises which the church could not fulfil if it wished to do so. Missionaries have confused the invariables of the gospel with the variables and have mistakenly linked them inextricably so that the failure of missions to make good all of the promises of the variables has led men to question the validity of the invariables. The hard central core of missionary work is the gospel, and this the church must cling to, realizing that all else, however much the western world may prize it, is not directly relevant to missionary labor and thus is peripheral. Missionaries need to define carefully their goal and outline more clearly their objectives. It will be good both for the missionary and for the person to whom he witnesses to know this. The one will not then promise more than he can produce, and the other will not expect more than he ought to expect from the limited promises.

Communism has for one of its significant slogans the idea of "pie in the sky." It promises men the impossible. This approach may lead to the triumph of communism in many lands and even perhaps all over the world. But communism is ultimately doomed for the same reason. It cannot possibly produce what it promises, and sooner or later its unfulfilled promises will be the very stone over which the back of the ideology will be broken. At best communism and all other "isms" are temporal and shall perish from the earth. But the Christian gospel is eternal because it is rooted and grounded in God. It behooves Christianity to be conservative in its promises and to remember that time is on the side of God's people. True believers know what Christianity can and ought to do. Let them proclaim to the fullest measure all that the gospel promises, but let them not go one step beyond this.

A final problem so vexing to the church of Christ has been its disappointment that the Christian faith has not swept the globe and brought all men and nations to the foot of the cross. Somehow the number of converts has been smaller than it anticipated, and it has looked for "success" in the typical western sense which means "big, bigger, biggest," and which is less concerned with solidness than it is with size. It is about time that the church grew up and gained some insight into the proper philosophy of the Christian mission. Numbers will not reveal either the worth or the permanency of its labor. Nor will it determine the success of the venture. All true missionaries are neither disillusioned nor broken if their message is not received. They continue to work apace regardless of hardship, difficulty or reception—good or bad. It is the duty of the witnesses to be God's voice and servants, and they must leave the rest to God. The chief reason they are to persevere amid every failure and success is not either the failure or the success, but their obligation to God.

At long last the church has begun to envision dimly a truth which it should have known a hundred years ago. This error of the church has been associated with the error of Christianization and the "white man's burden." The church begins to see that Christians from the western world cannot evangelize the world unaided. In the late nineteenth century the church constantly sounded forth the cry "the evangelization of the world in our generation." This objective was excellent, but the proponents were surely wrong in their ideas of fulfilling that ambition. They thought that white men were going to do the job, and that they could enlist the personnel and collect the money to do it. But the church at the crossroads today is weakening at this level, for it senses its inadequacy and sees more clearly that it can aid in the task but that finally the great push must come from the nationals of every nation themselves.

Part of the disillusionment derives from the inability of the church to challenge its finest young people or to recruit sufficient men or to raise enough money. Since more than sixty per cent of all missionaries today are women, one can perceive how great has been the change from the day when most of the missionary personnel were male. The inability of the church to enlist men may be one of the chief factors in the missionary revolution which is going on today.

We return to the place we began. Missions are at the crossroads. They have always been at the crossroads, and this is a cause for rejoicing. More than anything else the church must understand the times in which it lives, and it must comprehend vitally the fact that missions are relevant to every age and particularly to the age today. It needs to understand missions in their present operation and make full use of every device and strategy at its command in this hour. In a sinful world the ideal is always a dream toward which the church strives, but reality demands that it make the best of what it has and move forward toward the ideal through the employment of the present means, agencies and human instrumentalities which it is able to command.

Never in the history of mankind has the outlook for the furtherance of missions been ideal. Competing forces have always pressed in and down on missionary endeavor. But the hope of the church derives not so much from either the good or the bad circumstances of the moment as from the Lord of the church in Whose service it is engaged and under Whose banner it marches and for Whose glory it labors. It moves in the consciousness of His presence, His power, and His promise of ultimate victory. And its undying persuasion is that the church of Jesus Christ shall some day cease to be the church militant, becoming the church triumphant and the church at rest. The day shall come (and who knows how soon that shall be) when missions will no longer be at the crossroads but will enter into its destination of eternal rest, the job completed and its warfare ended forever.

The Missionary Motive and Imperative

~~~~~~

WHY SHOULD ANYONE TAKE THE CHRISTIAN RELIGION TO OTHER men and women in the world? The answer to this question is basic to all Christian missionary endeavor. Any missionary work which has not faced and answered this question is not properly grounded nor has it established for itself a philosophy and a rationale which will enable it to endure when shocks and tests come, and cataclysms engulf it.

The problem at this juncture is not that which answers the question, "What constitutes a missionary call?" or "How can I know whether I should be a missionary?" The problem here precedes that of the missionary vocation and call to the individual life, and seeks to answer the question whether *any* person ought to be a missionary; not which ones should heed the call. It asks the basic question, "Should anyone be a missionary?" and when this is satisfactorily resolved, the question "Which ones should be missionaries?" will be ripe for discussion and solution.

Some years ago when the Student Volunteer Movement had reached its height, a famous slogan was developed which captivated the minds and hearts of a generation. This slogan was "Evangelize to a finish." It presupposed the necessity of evangelizing. Its main burden was to finish the work. It never asked whether Christians ought to evangelize; this was taken for granted. It only urged upon them the necessity for completing the work of evangelization. The question the leaders of the Student Volunteer Movement took for granted must be discussed and answered before the problem of finishing the task can be taken into account.

For centuries since the Reformation men have referred to the Great Commission, and have accepted this Commission (which is also spoken of as being a commandment of our risen Lord) as the final ground for the missionary motive and imperative. So it was that the Student Volunteer Movement really based its slogan for finishing the work of evangelization on the ground of the Great Commission. But the Great Commission itself is not final. It rests upon another pillar which, for the Christian, is the ultimate ground on which the case for missionary endeavor rests. The Great Commission is found in the Word of God, the Bible. This brings us logically to the biblical and theological basis of missions.

In the final analysis missionary endeavor is grounded in the Word of God. When we speak of the gospel of Jesus Christ, the only gospel we know is that one which is delineated in the pages of the Sacred Book. When we speak of Jesus Christ, the Son of God incarnate, the historical Jesus is the One who is found within the confines of the same Book. When we speak of the Great Commission, that Commission is found within the covers of the Word of God.

In recent years men have turned increasingly to the study of biblical theology, not alone for their understanding of Christology and anthropology, but also for missions in its biblical and theological orientation. This trend is markedly evidenced among the older denominations in the United States which are banded together in the organization known as the Foreign Missions Conference of North America which is a department of the National Council of the Churches of Christ in the U.S.A. No one should overlook the apparent effort which these denominations and the Foreign Missions Conference of

North America are making to recapture what so many of them lost when liberalism was ascendant a few decades ago.

Fundamentalists, on the other hand, did not depart from the Word of God theologically or in missionary endeavor. They took it for granted that missionary work is based upon the Scriptures and yet, except for fleeting efforts by a small minority, very little of a significant nature has come from the pens of fundamentalists to undergird biblically and eventually philosophically the missionary enterprise. One notable exception was the late Robert Hall Glover of the China Inland Mission who tackled the problem in his work *The Biblical Basis of Missions*.

Early in 1952 the Committee on Research in Foreign Missions of the Division of Foreign Missions and the Central Department of Research and Survey of the National Council of the Churches of Christ in the U.S.A. produced a mimeographed report in five sections under the general heading "The Missionary Obligation of the Church." The report of Commission I dealt with the question "Why Missions?" and it considered the biblical and theological basis of missions. Throughout this and other sections of the report there are quotations from the Scriptures which speak eloquently of a bias in the direction of recognition of the authority of the Word of God on the subject of Christian missions. Whether all of the leadership and the constituencies at large would approve of this "biblicism" is unknown, but the membership of this commission was committed in principle to the authority of the Word of God as the ground for the missionary motive and imperative. All parties in the Christian church might not be satisfied *en toto* with all this commission has said. But the commission has taken its work seriously, and it has said some things which the most extreme fundamentalist should consider seriously.

The conclusion may be drawn from what has been said that ultimately all missionary endeavor is rooted and grounded in the Word of God. Even aberrations like liberalism and the social gospel are traceable to deductions derived from the Bible. Missionary activity, both good and bad and at its best and worst, can be explained at last only by recourse to the revelation of God. Directly or indirectly the final explication for missionary activity returns us to the Holy Scriptures.

The Bible is a missionary book, and the source of its missionary zeal lies in the heart of God Himself. Jesus Christ is God's missionary to a lost and dying world, and the entire sacred canon is a description of God reaching down and reaching out toward sinful man for the purpose of redeeming him. Who can deny what Peter has so wonderfully declared that Christ is the Lamb of God slain from before the foundation of the world? Before the creation of man and when, in the world of man as we know it, no sin existed, God in covenant with the Son planned the redemption of a lost creation not yet created.

The Petrine declaration that Christ is the Lamb slain from before the foundation of the world is in a sense a mystery, but there is no mystery in the truth that before God asked any man to become a missionary, He was in the Person of Jesus Christ a missionary. He reached out His hand toward sinful men, and all history points in a forward direction to Calvary just as all history since that time points back to it.

The Old Testament is not always thought of as being a missionary book. But it is. The Pentateuch discloses that God had the entire world in His plan, and the choice of a chosen race was not designed to exclude some or to limit the favor of God to the few. Rather, the choice of Israel provided a channel of blessing, not for that race alone, but for the entire world. The people of Israel were a channel through which the promise of a Redeemer should become a reality; and through this people God's divine revelation was given and preserved. It was no accident of birth that Jesus the Christ was born of the tribe of Judah and thus came from the loins of Abraham. For the Son of God to become incarnate, some human being and some race among men had to be chosen. The finger of God was evident through Israel and Jesus Christ fulfilled those prophecies which foretold long ago that the Messiah should be a Hebrew.

Still the impression is oftentimes generated that little or no missionary emphasis may be found in the Old Testament. All will grant that God was working among the Hebrews, but they question whether He was then working among the Gentiles. His interest, they feel, did not commence until after the advent of Jesus when the way should be opened to the Gentiles. This is a serious misapprehension, for the Old Testament is just as much a missionary document as the New Testament. The Jews fell into this error. They believed that God was exclusively interested in them. This error was derived from a narrow and bigoted viewpoint that they and they alone were worthy of God's attention. But the Bible itself demonstrates that God has ever been concerned for all men and not just for a chosen few.

Who can escape the extent of God's concern when Isaiah cries out that ". . . The God of the whole earth shall he be called." The Psalmist was not mistaken when he affirmed "Declare his glory among the heathen, his wonders among all people. . . . Say among the heathen that the Lord reigneth! . . . for . . . he shall judge the world with righteousness, and the people with his truth."

The Book of Jonah testifies to the love of God for the Gentiles. Jonah was called by God and commissioned to take the divine message of repentance to Nineveh. God promised that genuine repentance would result in the withholding of divine judgment which was imminent because of Nineveh's sins. As a Hebrew missionary to the Gentiles of Nineveh, Jonah was the instrumentality used by God to win for the city a reprieve. Here was a Jew sent by God to save a city of Gentiles.

Joseph was a missionary in Egypt, by life and by precept manifesting the power, the mercy, and the goodness of God.

Moses likewise was a missionary in the court of the Pharaoh both as a young man and also when he came as the servant of God to seek the release of his people from their bondage. Esther, in the court of Ahasuerus with Mordecai, was a missionary. Daniel, without equivocation and in the sight of all men, witnessed to the keeping power of his God and found deliverance from the lion's den as did the three Hebrews in the fiery furnace. Here were captives who yet were missionaries unto God. And all were among Gentiles.

The line from which Jesus Christ sprang gives further evidence of God's desire toward the Gentiles as well as toward the Israelites. Rahab, a harlot once, is listed among the forebears of the Christ; Ruth, a Moabitess, faithful to her mother-in-law Naomi, found a permanent heritage in the lineage of David and thus of Jesus Christ.

However dull may have been the awareness of men of the vision of God reaching out for the whole lost world; however His people Israel may have failed to understand what God had in mind; however the idea of God in search for all men everywhere may not have been fully developed so far as progressive revelation bears on the matter—this much is clear: the Old Testament is a missionary book, and God cares for Jew and Gentile alike.

If the Old Testament can be called a missionary book, and if from that section of the Scriptures one may discern a missionary motive and imperative, how much more is this true of the New Testament. From beginning to end, from Matthew to the Revelation of John the panorama of missions is unfolded before the eyes of every Christian. The Gospels unfold the life of Jesus, and they record His statements of the Great Commission. The Acts of the Apostles is the historical record of the early church working out obediently the terms and obligations of the Commission. The Epistles record the history of missionary activity as churches were formed and as the Apostles wrote letters to these churches to help them solve their pressing problems. Every church in the Apostolic age derived its life from missionary sources, and the churches through two thousand years of missionary history originated as missionary churches. The oldest churches were at some time "younger churches," "infant churches," established by the impetus of missionary endeavor which has never died out.

The whole atmosphere of the New Testament breathes out the missionary spirit; it can be found in the warp and woof of the book; it is the peculiar genius of its message. The first message given to men by the angels at the birth of Jesus was a missionary message. ". . . behold, I bring you *good* tidings of great joy, which shall be to *all* people." This message was not directed to the people of Israel alone; it was not limited in its scope. How wonderfully the angels proclaimed that the good tidings were to *all* people. When Jesus began His public ministry, John records for us the conversion experience of one named Andrew. The part of this story which pertains to missionary endeavor is the immediate witnessing efforts of Andrew who promptly became a missionary and who brought his brother Simon Peter to Jesus Christ. So far as we know Andrew was the first convert, and the first convert became the first missionary. Salvation led to witnessing; it was an automatic reflex rising from the depths of a tremendous religious experience.

In the Sermon on the Mount wherein Christ enunciates permanent principles for life, He also teaches His disciples what has been called the Lord's Prayer. This prayer is, in part, a missionary prayer. We are encouraged to pray for the coming of His kingdom and the petition, ". . . thy will be done in earth, as it is in heaven" cannot be understood apart from the truth that it is not the will of God that any man should perish. It is, however, the will of God that all men should come to the knowledge of truth. This missionary emphasis rarely receives attention from the best expositors of this Scripture.

The first command of the risen Lord to His disciples following His death and resurrection was a missionary command. John tells us that Jesus stood in the midst of the disciples after the resurrection and showed them His hands and His side. He said, ". . . as my father hath sent me, even so send I you." So also the last message of the risen Jesus prior to His ascension into heaven was the command to evangelize the world. Luke in the Acts of Apostles leaves us with the final words of Jesus, "But ye shall receive power, after that the Holy Ghost is come upon you: and ye shall be witnesses unto me both in Jerusalem and in all Judæa, and in Samaria, and unto the uttermost part of the earth."

Pentecost came ten days after the Ascension. At this time the Holy Spirit was poured out upon the disciples and followers of Jesus. Fearful, frightened Peter became a man of holy boldness preaching the first Apostolic sermon. Here he did not limit his message to the Jew, but under the inspiration of the Holy Spirit testified to the world outreach of the gospel and to the intention of God to include all men everywhere in the benefits of Christ's atoning work. Peter told his audience that ". . . the promise is unto you, and to your children, and to all that are afar off, even as many as the Lord our God shall call." And what Peter proclaimed at Pentecost God intended from the beginning, and the church reiterates today—the gospel is for men of every color, race, and creed.

The missionary character of the Word of God is indisputable, and it constitutes the ground on which the whole cause of missions rests. Because the Bible is itself a missionary book and because the Bible professes to make missions the unalterable obligation for those who profess faith in Christ, it may be seen that the motivation for missionary work is derived from the Bible and any imperative which makes missions a *sine qua non* can alone find justification in the Scriptures.

In more specific terms, an examination of several biblical concepts—again noting that what shall be said is derived from the Scriptures which are the real and final ground for missionary motivation—will throw further light on the subject of the motive and imperative of missions.

Men speak of the church of Jesus Christ, and beneath the surface of this name lie truths so profound and implications so vast that if those who profess to be Christians were to utilize these truths to their fullest extent, the world would be shaken for God to its foundations and men would behold in action dynamistic forces so insuperable that the citadels of evil would crumble before their attack. If the church of Jesus Christ were to be the church—what God intended it to be—changes more radical than the world has seen to this hour would ensue.

In the New Testament the mystery of the church, which was not fully revealed before this time, is made much plainer. The church is said to be the "body of Christ" "the bride" belonging to the bridegroom. This church has both its visible and invisible aspects. Many saints now buried in graves are members of the same body. At the end of the age in the resurrection, all who are members of the body, who are in the church of Jesus Christ, will be resurrected and will live and reign together.

The church of Christ is not sectarian. It knows no barriers of denominational attachment. In it will be found men and women who are Baptists, Presbyterians, Methodists, Lutherans, Episcopalians, yes, and even some who are Roman Catholics in name. This church of Christ which is a spiritual body, includes the communion of saints, and is invisible. It is never to be equated with a visible church or churches for in the membership of the invisible church are found only those who have truly been regenerated. Not all who associate themselves with a visible church or churches will actually be regenerated people. But the existence of the invisible church which has in it all true members of the body of Christ does not lessen the importance nor diminish the functional usefulness of the visible church or churches.

Considerable impairment of the New Testament doctrine of the visible church has come about through misunderstandings which have exalted the invisible church and left Christians with the impression that the institutional or visible church is of no importance and of little value. A solitary Christianity and a multitudinous fragmentation has vitiated and dissipated the strength of the visible churches and led to a disunity which has shocked the unbelieving world and often rendered ineffectual the witness of truly Christian, but, nonetheless, highly sectarian and competitive groups.

Not all fragmentation is psychological in origin or the consequence of aberrations in individuals. Some of it stems from a sincere belief in the distinctives which the group holds. Distinctives automatically divide one group from another. They render the diverse groups incompatible and make cooperation and unity impossible without compromising the distinctives held to be vital. This issue will be considered in another connection. All that must be made plain immediately is that the New Testament does not depreciate the visible church or churches and they, like the true invisible church, are the creation of God and exist for a purpose. They cannot be overlooked nor underestimated. And the missionary motive and imperative are intertwined inextricably with the biblical doctrine of the visible church as constituted by God in terms of its real nature and function.

The church visible is a community of the redeemed who are in the world yet not of the world. The members are called out ones who have been regenerated and who have received the gift of the Holy Spirit. At least in theory the membership of this visible body should include only those who have experienced the grace of God in Christ and whose membership in the body of Christ is assured. Not all who are members of the true body will be found in visible churches although they should be; and not all who are found in visible churches will be true members of the body although they should be.

A visible church, then, brings into focus and fellowship people who have an allegiance to Jesus Christ and who pro-

fess Him to be the Lord or the King of their lives. Such a
church has for its head no human king but the Son of God.
It is His church and He is the head. It belongs to Him by creation and by purchase in redemption as its king. Its rules are
His rules; its objectives His objectives; its life His life. While
such a church is not identical with, nor co-extensive with, the
invisible church, yet in some measure it distinctly overlaps
with the invisible church and is related to it. Filled with
members who are not yet fully sanctified and living in a world
wherein even the members of this church can err and sin it is
like unto the ultimate reality and is a token and manifestation of that perfection which shall be at last the living reality.

This church which includes in its composition truly regenerated people has a twofold function, for it exists neither
as a freak of nature nor is it an accident. Its twofold function
deals first with the believer for whom the church is just as
much a necessity as he is a necessity to it. Second, it deals with
the world of men for whom the church is a vital necessity just
as they are a vital necessity to the church. We shall examine
further these functions.

When regeneration occurs in the heart and life of a man,
he does not exist in a saving relationship to God in a solitary
framework. He becomes a member of a body, a fellowship
which transcends both space and time relationships—space
because he is immediately related to all other believers in this
present physical world, and time because he is immediately
related to all believers of ages past and of ages to come. As a
believer who is part of a body, he engages in worship. The
church exists for purposes of worship, and worship is more
perfectly comprehended in corporate fashion. Worship in its
highest sense is corporate and reflects the truism that one of
the functions of the church for believers is the corporate worship of God. Common usage of the term church has confused
the thinking of believers with respect to the non-physical nature of the church. A building is not a church and to say, "You

are going to church" is erroneous when what is meant is that you are going into a building where a group of believers meet. This creates a more intelligent apprehension of the nature of a church. You can meet in a stable or a home or a building constructed exclusively for purposes of worship, but one is no more of a church than another. None of them is a church, for a church is an assembly of believers irrespective of the building in which they meet.

If the church exists for corporate worship where two or three are gathered together in Christ's name, so does it exist for fellowship. This fellowship is not simply that which binds men together in the exercise of religion. It is not to be confused with a club which may bring together men of diverse backgrounds and interests for one special stratum of life. A church does bring men together for common worship, but it also includes fellowship in its broadest and widest sense. A community of interest develops with social, educational and other implications so that the orbit of one's life revolves around the church, and the pursuit of the world and its vain attractions do not allure nor distract. Common interests bind all phases of life and make of the church and the Christians a community within a community.

For the believer the church also exists for edification. Through a preaching and a teaching ministry, each believer is to be built up in the most holy faith. He is to learn the basic doctrines of the faith along with their applications to human life. He shall obtain instruction which will enable him to make decisions in matters ethical and moral as well as in social, political, and business concerns.

God gave the sacred ordinances or sacraments of the church for a help or aid in the nurture of the Christian. The celebration of these ordinances is a help to those of like faith and is intrinsic in the nature of true worship. Active participation in these ordinances of baptism and the Lord's table is obligatory, and they are necessary for growth in grace and the fullest understanding and appreciation of the Christian's heritage. These all refer to the life of the believer, and the church was created to preserve, protect and enlarge the new life which, through regeneration, came to him when first he encountered Christ in an experience of salvation.

The second major function of the church and rationale for its existence is its service to lost mankind. The church exists in and for the service of the world. It must go to the depths in its identification with the world in the presentation of Jesus Christ. The field it serves is the world. The church is not a reservoir for the storage of spiritual energy. It is only a channel through which blessings are to be conveyed. As a channel its purpose is to bring the water of life from the wellspring which is Jesus Christ to lost men at the other end of the channel. The failure of the church to be usable as a channel *per se* means its failure in the fulfillment of its divine function.

Biblical theology attests to the existence of a church militant; i.e. a church at war. Some day the church will be the church triumphant; i.e. the church at rest. But so long as evil exerts its power and until sin has been conquered forever, the church remains the church militant. The objective of the "fighting" church is to present to men everywhere the gospel of Jesus Christ.

From the vantage point of the nature and function of the church, the missionary motive and imperative takes clearer shape. The church was created to be a fellowship for believers, but it was also created to be a witnessing fellowship to all men about Jesus Christ. In its basic nature, then, the church is missionary having been created for missionary purposes and finding its perfect expression in submission to the Lord of the church who has ordained this to be His instrument through which the divine will of God for the world shall be accomplished. There is no second method or way through which the will of God for the world shall become a reality. If the church does not do it, it will not be done. Lost mankind needs the church and needs it desperately; so the church just as desperately needs lost mankind for from among them shall come those who will constitute the members of the church in the days ahead. The moment the church ceases to reproduce itself in the lives of others through a regenerating experience that soon shall the church die. The measure in which the church is truly the church can be determined by the work of the church in its divinely appointed task outside the church; i.e. in its divine mission to the world.

What the characteristics of an obedient church will be may be discovered from an appraisal of the early church whose characteristic marks disclose the reasons for its mighty power and success. The early church was a separated church. Not in a negative sense alone was this so, although the church was detached from the world. But positively the church had a real and a dynamic attachment to Jesus Christ which so outweighed the allurement and enticements of the world that the one was no competition for the other. Believers were so busy doing what they should be doing that they had no time for the things which would detract from what they ought to be doing. In today's world the margin which separates the church from the world is so thin that it is difficult to know which side of the fence the average Christian is on. Even where there is a positive separation from the things of the world this separation is often purely negative, and it is not supplemented by a dynamic attachment to Christ in a positive sense. This condition may be likened to that described by John when he denounces the church at Ephesus—a church which has left its first love and is lukewarm.

The early church understood the biblical concept of Christian discipleship. It believed that all Christians were missionaries and that all believers were obligated to tell others—to be witnesses of those things which God had done in their lives. Sometimes this regnant passion has been called a "high conception" of Christian discipleship as though it were possible to have other lower concepts. Only one concept of discipleship is advanced in the New Testament, and any deviation from this removes believers from the only ground and position which satisfies the demands of the Scriptures. The early church knew what Christian discipleship was—but more than this they approximated the standard in their own lives with the result that they manifested a holy boldness, a divine unction, and a mighty power.

The Apostolic church held to a series of sharply defined biblical doctrines. These constituted an imperative and demanded of them haste because men were perishing without Christ and His truth. They preached Christ and Him crucified; son of God, risen, ascended, coming again; prophet, priest and king. Nowhere do the disciples parade their intellectual doubts. They affirmed to men that which they held to be true, and they were neither ashamed of Jesus Christ nor of their supernatural and miraculous faith. Their holy zeal was unbounded; their perseverance unquenchable; their tenacity unyielding; and their convictions unshaken. In other words, the early church was the church—what a real church ought to be.

Whatever the church is supposed to be each individual should be too. The church comprises individuals and ultimately what the church itself is will be determined by what the individuals are who make up the church. The church is the composite of all its members, and to the extent the members are yielded and dedicated servants of the Lord to that degree it will be the church. Contrariwise, to the extent or degree that the church adherents depart from the ideal to that degree will the church not be the church. Fortunately, it is not an "either-or" proposition since at all times and in all ages there have been those devoted and consecrated souls who have been what they ought to be, although huge majorities in the church have been careless, unconsecrated, and far from the ideal.

Whether the individuals who comprise the church become what they ought to be will finally determine whether the church is the church. And the individuals will make their decisions in the framework of their personal relationship to the Lord of the church, Jesus Christ. Granted that Christ commanded His church to evangelize the world because He wished it to be evangelized, and He wanted it to be evangelized because He knew it needed to be evangelized. The constant reiteration of the command of Christ in itself will never produce the result; the goal is as far away as ever. Whether men obey the command of the Head of the church will depend on their personal relationship to Him.

One's personal relationship may be determined by the way he answers the question, "Does Christ mean anything to me?" If he means nothing, then why should the believer feel constrained to obey Him or to spend his life in obedience to His command? But if Christ means everything to him, the Christian will be driven by an overmastering desire to make known to all the glad tidings of so great salvation. The church (and this would obviously mean individual believers) which does nothing to extend the knowledge of Christ to the pagan world admits by this that Christ means little to it which no amount of amiable piousness or declarations of devotion can extinguish.

The relationship of the average believer has been defective and is defective today. Two thousand years of missionary history proves this contention. For 1900 years China and other nations were without the gospel while the members of the Christian churches enjoyed the benefits of the gospel without fulfilling the obligations attendant upon the acceptance of the blessings. What judgment must be passed on the ethics of those who have had the good news of eternal life and who have been commanded to take the news to every creature yet have not obeyed? Can the strictures of judgment be too severe or is the indictment too heavy against the discipleship of those who have kept back from their fellowmen the benefits of the gospel?

Bishop Westcott aptly remarks that "the claim to the knowledge of God without obedience and the claim to the love of God without action involve not only the denial of what is known to be true, but falseness of character." Thus missions become not only an expression of the believer's interest in the world but also an evidence of his love of the church's Lord, and the proof of the integrity and honor of his own personal life and relationship to the Head of the church.

If the follower of Jesus does not fulfill his divine function as a member of the church on whom the commission is binding, God is not at fault. The want is in the will of the individual. When the want of will is reflected in actual hostility to missions, it discloses a lack of a high and scrupulous sense of common honesty. Indifference denotes a serious lack in the spiritual life and, like hostility, it is a symbol of unorthodoxy since the tenor of the Bible is so completely in favor of missions.

Ancillary to the missionary bias of the Bible, the nature and function of the church, and the personal relationship of the believer to Jesus Christ is the eschatology of the Scriptures. Prominent in eschatology is the return of Jesus Christ, His second advent. Some aspects of this advent have been realized and some have not. The Scriptures teach that Christ shall be king. This truth has both a present and future bearing on the Christian faith. That Christ will be king in the future does not mean that Christ is not king now. Affirming that Christ will set up an earthly kingdom in the millennium is not to say that Christ is not truly king now. He is king now, but the full measure of that kingship and final goal will not be attained until the end of the age. Today two kingdoms exist in the world and in the hearts of men; these kingdoms are in opposition to each other. One kingdom is temporary and one eternal; one is comprised of cohorts of the devil and one of the adherents of Christ; one has *already* conquered, the other *is* conquered. The devil, no matter how hard he tries and with what force he assails the followers of Christ, cannot win. For Jesus Christ victory is sure because the victory has *already* been won.

The coming of Jesus Christ and the establishment of His millennial kingdom will signify His victory and will be the token of it. His coming is organically linked to the missionary nature of the Scriptures and the church. The second advent will be the index demonstrating that the church has, at last, fulfilled its function relevant to the world, and has completed its primary job of witnessing to the world by finishing the task given to it by its Lord—the evangelization of the world.

In the New Testament the second coming of Jesus Christ is frequently connected with the Great Commission. The task enunciated in the Great Commission is for the church to witness "unto the uttermost part of the earth." How extensive and how intensive this witness must be before the job is finished the Bible does not state, but the coming of the king will be the announcement of its completion and the tarrying of the king can only mean that the job is still uncompleted. The consummation of the age and the advent of Christ will coincide with the preaching of the gospel to the uttermost part of the earth.

Many earnest believers will not agree that the coming of Jesus Christ will coincide with the completion of the Great Commission. Many hold that the evangelization of the world will be completed following the rapture of the church before the great tribulation. But, increasingly, biblical scholars insist that the second coming of Christ awaits the completion of the task of evangelization and that when this task is finished, Christ will come. For those who hold the view that the completion of the task of evangelization and the second advent will coincide, this eschatology gives life and urgency to the missionary motive and imperative.

Thoughtful students of the Bible note that the Great Commission was given to the church of Christ. They sense that the Commission is the evangelization of the world. If this can never occur, Christians are dupes. If it can and will occur as Christians believe, then the completion of that task must signify something. That something which it obviously must signify is the goal of history or the end of history leading to the suprahistorical when ". . . The kingdoms of this world are become the kingdoms of our Lord, and of His Christ; and he shall reign for ever and ever."

A realistic eschatology must ever give impetus to missionary response and missionary reflex. The sure knowledge that the coming of the king awaits the fulfillment of the Commission to the church gives men hope to believe that this generation will hasten the coming of the Lord, providing the church becomes the church and by a mighty act of will combines its energies and pours out its life sacrificially and in devotion to the common task of witnessing unto the uttermost part of the earth.

Last in our consideration of the motive and imperative for missions is the need of the non-Christian world. The spiritual, physical and moral condition of the pagan world are comprehended under this title. Perceptive observers do not always assent to the proposition that the need of the non-Christian world rightfully deserves consideration as a legitimate motive for missions. They assert that the Bible, the command of Christ, and a right relationship of the believer to His Lord are the bedrock on which the motive and imperative rest and that these items are extraneous to the problem.

The foregoing may have a large measure of truth in it, but the need of the non-Christian world should be weighed in the light of one fact. If we did not have the book we call the Bible, and if Christ did not give us a command to evangelize, yet the simple possession of divine truth as over against the darkness of heathendom would still place the Christian under a bond and obligation to share with his less fortunate brothers the light and truth which he possesses. When any Christian notes the spiritual, physical and moral morass of the pagan world, all of which he knows to be the consequences of sin, and when he realizes that he himself has been delivered from this bondage and corruption without works and by grace, constraint, of necessity, is laid upon him to bring to others the same opportunity for deliverance which has been his. The nature of the Christian faith apart from a written revelation and the commandment of Christ, when it sees the urgent need of the world, must react reflexively to that need and meet it through the preaching of the gospel.

The spiritual darkness of the pagan world (and one need not depart from his own country to behold such darkness) makes the Christian witness an imperative. The knowledge that all men without Christ are doomed to an eternal death and that there is no second chance beyond the probation of this life ought to move believers to action. Assured that unbelievers cannot work their way into heaven by merit, and that neither their morality nor their good intentions will suffice to satisfy God, Christians who are truly Christian cannot help reacting instinctively to this need.

Spiritual darkness is most frequently combined with undesirable physical and moral conditions. But the Christian must guard against the assumption that such is ever true. In the western world today, in which the Christian faith has exercised its most beneficent influence, physical and moral conditions are immeasurably better than in India, Africa, and other places. Many have inherited the legacy of the Christian faith in these things, but they are as spiritually bankrupt and as hopelessly lost as the aborigines whose total existence in all phases of life has been corrupted. Good men do not get to heaven; moral men or men who do not practice the fearfully corrupt and licentious ways of the worst pagans do not get to heaven. The best and the finest with wealth, education, ethics, and intentions still require regeneration for admission to Christ's kingdom.

Besides the spiritual condition of the heathen, the physical situation of the lost world presses for attention. Poverty, dis-

ease, and famine lurk abroad each year. Words never can re-
count the indescribable suffering which is the lot of the
greater portion of the people living on this earth. These conditions often spring out of ignorance. Many do not know
the basic laws of sanitation; they are without medical aid or
they have not benefited from the advances in medical science.
Just one sight of the Ganges River in India will illustrate this
point. In a short stretch of a mile, one can behold multitudes
of Indians bathing in the river, washing their clothes in the
same river, drinking of the water of that river, dumping into it
their sewage, burning on the shore the bodies of the dead,
and performing their religious rites of cleansing in the waters.

Christianity can and does do something about physical conditions. One of its most important by-products is that humanitarian concern which corrects these tragic anomalies through
education, example, and Christian zeal. Many conditions can
never be corrected without the help of regeneration which
first cuts through the binding cords of superstition, ignorance,
and human credulity. Missionary administrators today regret
the false antithesis created by titles given to distinguish one
type of missionary from another whose approach to paganism
came through diverse means. Thus to call one a physician,
another an educator, and another an evangelist served to give
credence to the idea that a physician and an educator were
not sent to do evangelistic work. All missionary work, if it is
faithful to the Lord of the church, must be evangelistic. But
growing out of that evangelism comes the application of modern knowledge and understanding to all phases of life, for the
Christian faith is not simply a transcendental religion covering the life after death. Redemption is present as well as future, and Christ is the Lord of life on earth *and* in heaven.

The social gospel of yesterday was "another gospel" not because the gospel does not have social applications, but because
it was an end in itself and was removed from that preaching
which demanded the new birth. If the liberal was guilty of

perverting the gospel, the arch conservative was often guilty of failing to recognize that there are social applications of the gospel and that the Christian faith is designed to do something about conditions in this life as well as about a future life. Properly oriented, the drive to ameliorate evil physical conditions moves the Christian to bring the gospel which in turn generates and sets in operation forces which change the structure of physical life in addition to bringing salvation.

The moral dilemma of the pagan world challenges the Christian to action too. When he perceives the position of women in heathen society; when he sees child marriage in all of its unloveliness; when he sees the brutalities and devilishness of slavery; when witchcraft, polygamy, the propitiation of evil spirits, prostitution, lying, treachery, and a thousand moral evils are flung before his eyes daily, the Christian should find in them a challenge to missionary action. Christ came to redeem men from this, and their very existence presents a constant indictment against the Christian church if it does not arise to fight them. Those who make these practices their delight and who find pleasure in doing them are spiritually dead in trespasses and sins and know not the gravity of their sins nor can they rejoice in the Christian faith of which they have no knowledge. Knowing that Christ can redeem them and that ". . . he by the grace of God should taste death for every man," even apart from an express commandment, the Christian should be ready to bring to others what God by His grace has brought to him. So the moral as well as the spiritual condition of the pagan world cries out night and day to Christian men and women, and the hands which are stained with the blood of heathen sacrifices are potential material for the church of Christ if someone tells them the old, old story.

The believer who is not moved by any of these arguments, and whose spirit remains cold to the motivation and imperative as expressed here might do well to ask himself a searching and penetrating question: "If my heart remains unmoved have I really encountered God in Jesus Christ? Does the Holy Spirit indwell my heart? Do I know experientially Father, Son and Holy Ghost?" If the answer to this question is "Yes," then that Christian needs to examine his personal relationship to Christ as the Lord of his life. The failure to be moved for missions can mean either that the person in question has not met God face to face, or that he has a defective Christian experience which, while he is a Christian, implies that he needs a work of grace in his heart by way of sanctification.

Missions is a passion with the minority in the church in our day. If it is to become the passion of the majority or all of the church, the arguments presented here must be relayed to Christians everywhere. The Sunday School, the pulpit, the discussion groups, the prayer meeting, and the societies of each church must be springboards for the inculcation of missionary zeal. Those who educate men to their nature in Christ as witnesses, and to their obligations as recipients of divine grace, must first be aflame with a holy zeal for missions, and they must have dedicated their own lives, fortunes, and hearts to this holy cause. To convince, one must first be convinced; to move others, one must first be moved himself; to secure consecration for missions, one's own life must first be consecrated.

CHAPTER III

Call and Preparation for Foreign Missionary Service

~~~~~~

I

THROUGHOUT THE CHRISTIAN WORLD THE CHURCH HAS STRESSED missions in a more positive way in the last decade. Christians are being urged to support missions with their means and with their prayers. The revival of a positive missionary emphasis has included an appeal for personnel to replace old and dying missionaries and for additional personnel in the constant struggle to evangelize the world.

The answers to the renewed appeal for money, prayer, and personnel, have varied. The appeals for money and prayer have met with some measure of success. "Faith" missions report increasingly higher annual incomes for their work. The reports of the International Missionary Council (not including "faith" missions) reveal substantial increases financially during the last decade for denominational mission boards. This has been a reversal of a trend which began around 1930 when missionary giving slumped, until 1940 when it was still more than one-third less than it had been in 1930.

So Christians have responded and more money has been raised in and out of denominations, for denominational and faith work. More Christians have been made conscious of their duty to pray for the onward progress of this work and for the individual missionaries laboring all over the world. Few, if any, Christians have questioned the rightness of the appeals for money and prayer. Some of the people have been neglectful, and others may have been miserly, but none can find ground for dissent.

While the appeals for money and prayer have met with some success, the call for adequate, trained personnel has not brought forth a sufficient response. Multitudes who give freely of money and prayer take an entirely different attitude toward the supply of the manpower on which those other items are spent. All too frequently there is a puzzled and perplexed attitude toward actual missionary service. It is an attitude which is not found about money and prayer.

The perplexity of Christians, particularly younger ones, concerns guidance and light on the missionary call. Recognizing the validity of their obligations to give and to pray, many are searching desperately for an adequate answer to the questions: "What constitutes a call to the foreign field?" "How can I know whether I ought to be a foreign missionary?"

Oftentimes perplexity about the missionary call exists because Christians are uninformed. They lack information about the fields of the world as well as biblical understanding. Thus when Christians are told that there is only one missionary for every 360,000 people in some fields, they are amazed and amazement gives way to a Godly concern. So also when Christians understand that the Great Commission is binding on *all* Christians (see Matthew 28:18–20; Mark 16:15; Luke 24:45–48; Acts 1:8; and John 20:21 to mention some of the verses on missions), the acquisition of this information changes the picture. Those who lack *only* information are more easily won for missions. At least they rarely have a bias against missions but are neutral or just careless. It is highly probable that most Christians are in this class—missions are far removed from their thinking. When they become conscious of the facts and come to grips with them, many will be enlisted to a vigorous support of foreign missions.

Beyond the uninformed are the remainder of the believers. Some of these walk in the fullness and center of God's will for their lives. Others are either openly disobedient or grossly misinformed. The misinformed usually "know" a great deal about foreign missions and have definite ideas of their own regarding their responsibility. They have an antipathy for missions based upon misleading information. Included in this group of the misinformed are those who believe that God will save the heathen apart from the missionary labors of His children. There are others who believe that somehow God will not condemn those who never hear of Christ or will give them a second chance in the world to come.

The openly disobedient are those who know the will of God and know the facts of the case but who, in spite of this knowledge, refuse to heed the voice of God and do what they are commanded to do. Still others have a directive, but are lethargic and careless to the point where they never fulfill their high calling in Christ Jesus.

Among the people who have a bias against the foreign field, whether it is an unconscious one or one with which they are well acquainted, catch phrases are common. These phrases are used by the misinformed, the careless, and the recalcitrant. In fact, even the uninformed find them to be part of the current terminology of the churches, and they employ them effectively. Without exaggeration the free use of these phrases does much to create a bias in the hearts and minds of younger and less mature Christians who assume that the users of the phrases are representing gospel truth.

Possibly you have heard these phrases recently among Christians: "God needs Christian businessmen," "The need at home is great," and "If God wants me on the foreign field, He will show me." Now God does need and use Christian businessmen, the need at home is always great, and God does promise to lead and guide men and women to the foreign field. What then is the objection to such expressions? The objection in each case is the same. Each phrase represents a state of mind which posits a bias against the foreign field. Always the assumption is that the first choice is to remain at home, and what appears to be a suitable excuse is offered to justify that desire.

A believer ought not criticize a Christian businessman, a home worker, or any other person who is in the will of God. The businessman who rests in the assurance that he has the will of God for his life need not be ashamed to acknowledge it, nor ought he apologize for it. A man on the foreign field who should have remained at home as a businessman is as much a misfit as the businessman who should have been a missionary. Unfortunately the suspicion lingers that there are more men in business who should have been missionaries than there are missionary misfits who should have been businessmen.

All sham and pretense must be done away with and the problem approached with unprejudiced minds as far as that is possible. An objective view of the matter will do much to clarify difficulties which spring out of human subjectivism. Truth is ever an asset and never a liability. With this in view we come to grips with the problem that perplexes so many of our Christian young people, "What constitutes a missionary call?"

II

The correct approach to the problem of the missionary call revolves around a basic biblical principle. This principle is expressed in the Word of God by the Apostle John. ". . . he that doeth the will of God abideth for ever" (I John 2:17). Inherent in this Scripture are several key thoughts. One is that there is a will of God. The second is that human beings may or may not do that will. Last there is the assurance that there is an adequate reward for those who do the will of God.

Christians are prone to reason from a naturalistic viewpoint about doing the will of God. They presume that God should reveal this will, and then give them the choice of accepting or rejecting that will. With the average Christian, the will of God constitutes the presentation of a concrete situation or choice involving a specific type of endeavor or even geographic location for service. Somehow in man's finiteness he cannot get away from "things" and "objects." Thus a man faces the concrete challenge to be a medical doctor, or lawyer, or missionary and makes a choice when faced with the concrete situation. He wills to do or not to do. And he believes that God has revealed His will and has given him the choice. Christians generally assume that God will somehow confront a man with a challenge to the specific field, the individual assuring himself that when God does this he will accept that will. The absence of a specific concrete call to a field or form of service is taken to mean that God does not want the individual to be anything He has not specifically and categorically asked him to be.

The absence of some form of a specific call for which Christians look keeps too many true believers from being what God wants them to be. God may call one with an outward challenge to a particular work to which the individual may respond affirmatively or negatively. But it can generally be demonstrated that this "call" frequently comes to those who are "ready" for the call. And this readiness is not a bolt out of the blue, but it is a prior submission of the individual to the will of God.

The Bible is full of examples of men who were willing to do God's will whatever that will might entail. Jeremiah's commitment occurred before the revelation of the various phases of service. The first chapter of Jeremiah tells how God commissioned this man who laid his life upon the altar of sacrifice, not knowing that this commitment meant imprisonment and distress for many years. And thus it was that when Jeremiah was subjected to severe persecution he wished to draw back from his original commitment. In Jeremiah 20:9, the Scripture says, "Then I said, I will not make mention of him, nor speak any more in his name. But his word was in mine heart as a burning fire shut up in my bones, and I was weary with forbearing, and I could not stay."

Moses, likewise, made a commitment at the burning bush (Exodus 3) indicating his willingness to do God's will, little knowing that it should include all of the trials, tribulations, and difficulties which were to be his lot. But he did not turn back from that vision. Surely Joshua also reflects that willingness to do God's will in the face of bitter opposition. He and Caleb withstood all of their people in Numbers 14:6, willing to trust God in their commitment and to enter the promised land despite the power of the enemies holding that land. Long before he became Moses' actual successor he had proved his consecration and demonstrated his trust and faith in God. The willingness of Caleb and Joshua to enter the promised land is full evidence of their desire to do God's will.

Paul, too, was committed to Christ before the challenge of the evangelization of Europe came to him. In Galatians 1, Paul states that he was called of God who revealed His Son in him "that I might preach him among the heathen; . . ." From the day his eyes were opened, his commitment was an established fact although the consequences of that commitment, and his ultimate imprisonment, were not fully known to him. Does he not also indicate in Romans 1, that his life was so controlled by God that the will of God was preeminent for him? For he says to the Romans that ". . . oftentimes I purposed to come to you, (but was let hitherto,). . . ." Thus even his deepest longings in the gospel to preach redemption to a lost people were controlled by God.

Before any man can assuredly know the specific will of God as to the field and nature of his service, surrender to the general will of God must occur. Perhaps this can happen in an experience where both take place simultaneously, but logically it ought to happen before the will of God as to the place and field of service is known. The first question relative to a missionary or any other "call" is "Are you willing to do the will of God?"

III

Assuming that there has been a life commitment and a recognition of the Lordship of Jesus, the problem of discovering the specific will of God as to field and place of service follows. Discovering this will is not as simple as might appear on the surface.

All believers could wish for a means of guidance that would be immediate, definite, and without any complexity—something which would give them what they needed at any time and in such a manner that they could not be deceived. One of the best illustrations of the type of guidance many believers have in mind comes from some of the native tribes in Africa. In particular, the Azande people get their guidance in what is an amazingly simple fashion. Theirs is a kind of Ouija Board.

This is a miniature table, carved out of wood, which has two straight legs and a sort of curved tail, together with another piece of wood the size of the table top, which is slid around on the latter by means of an upright handle. The juice or soft meat of a certain fruit is put on the table top, and the opposite part is moistened and put down over it, and pushed back and forth. Such is the quality of the juice and the two pieces of wood that the upper piece either goes gliding smoothly over the lower, or else it soon sticks to it quite tightly so that it cannot be pushed back and forth and has to be pulled off. This is all there is to it, and the worker simply asks the board a question, telling it to stick for a yes and slide for a no. It usually leaves no doubt as to what it is doing, either sliding smoothly or sticking promptly, and so it gives the impression that it knows what it is saying and has no doubt in its mind. The occasions on which it misbehaves by getting only partially stuck or not sliding readily, are easily interpreted as caused by a question being asked wrongly or stupidly, or by the board seeing complications which have escaped the questioner. It is a useful and well-liked oracle, and one that the Azande use all the time because it can be referred to readily. They are continually demanding things of it, wanting to know if they should build a house here or plant a garden there, if a witch is after them, if they will die this year.*

For the Christian who has willed to do God's will the Azande system of guidance is hardly enough. Nor does it fit the biblical idea of God's methods of dealing with His children. Perhaps he might like to have such a simple system which is equally foolproof, but it would not befit the relationship he has with his Father. The simplicity of the Azande method arises out of the simpleness of the people who use it. Thus if the Azande discovers from his board that evil will befall him if he takes a trip, he does not make the trip. The Apostle Paul knew that evil would befall him if he went to Jerusalem, but he went anyway. (Acts 21:11 ff.). In the first case the personal interest of the individual is ever the center of the guidance; in the latter case the will of God transcends all else. For Paul and for the Christian the question is not how a certain act will affect the individual, but whether that act is the will of God, regardless of the effect. Furthermore, every Christian will know instinctively that there are many decisions in life in which God expects him to use his sanctified common sense. It is unquestionably far more accurate than the willy-nilly consultation with a board as to whether he should plant a garden here or there.

Nonetheless, God has not left men without help in securing guidance for the affairs of life. Generally the Christian can ascertain the will of God via three media: ¹through the Word, ²through circumstances, and ³through the inward per-

---

* William Howells, "Oracles and Omens," *Atlantic Monthly*, January, 1948. Taken from E. E. Evans-Pritchard, *Witchcraft, Oracles and Magic Among the Azande.*

suasion of the Holy Spirit Who is our Guide. Of these three, a word must be said. (See Col. 1:9; Ps. 25:9; Ps. 32:8; Isa. 58: 11; John 16:13; etc.).

The Word of God is an authoritative guide and rule of faith (II Tim. 3:16). It contains all that is needed for this life's journey. The Word of God is often painfully plain, and it gives guidance which believers ought to follow. Thus the Word teaches that God wants every believer to be holy (Eph. 1:4). God states that adequate giving should be the policy of each believer (I Cor. 16:2). Both of these examples show how the Bible is a definite and authoritative guide. Each example will prove a thorn in the side to some Christians who have never gotten this far with Him. And if they have not gone this far, little likelihood exists that they will go further.

The Bible also states that God wants men to be saved (I Tim. 2:14); that he that winneth souls is wise (Prov. 11:30); that the gospel *must* be proclaimed to every creature (Acts 1: 8); that only God's children are going to accomplish this task (certainly the children of the evil one are not going to do it— and to whom can we look for the fulfillment of the command if not to God's children?); that believers ought to be built up in the most holy faith (Eph. 4:11, 12) etc.

The foregoing examples are specific, concrete ones. They are not open to all kinds of interpretations. They have a definite quality about them, a radical aspect which shocks men by their demands. Men do not always like them, and they fear what they may mean for them, but they cannot change them. They are an integral part of the Lordship of Christ in the life of each Christian. This use of the Scriptures is a direct one.

The Word of God also serves to guide in an indirect manner. The Holy Spirit can take some portion of the Word of God and make it relevant to the problems men face or to the decisions they must make. The life of C. T. Studd is a case in point of indirect guidance through the Bible. Having decided to be a foreign missionary, he met with great family opposition. His mother had friends bring pressure to bear, and he was constantly informed of the great blow his departure might be to her. Deeply distraught he was standing on a railroad station platform one night, under a flickering light. In despair he asked God to give him a word. He opened his New Testament at random, and the verse which stood out was "And a man's foes shall be they of his own household." And his biographer states, "From that moment he never looked back."

Beyond the Word, God reveals His will in specific instances through circumstances. Our ways are ordered of the Lord, and what befalls us is not happenstance or accident. God can and does open and shut doors according to His gracious good pleasure. The surrendered Christian has the definite assurance that God is leading and guiding in all of the circumstances of life.

The call of Jonathan Goforth involved circumstances of one order. Dr. G. L. Mackay of Formosa was to speak in Knox Church, Ingersoll, Canada. A schoolmate pressed Goforth to attend the meeting. And it was at this meeting that his soul was touched by the message of the speaker, and his heart was turned to foreign missions. The vision came because a friend insisted on his going to a meeting. Surely this was no accident in the plan of God, and eternity will reveal the lasting value of that one circumstantial act on the part of a school chum.

Circumstances are both negative and positive. God shuts doors to prevent men from entering (Acts 16:7; Rev. 3:7, 8). This is the negative side. God also opens doors to permit them entry (I Cor. 16:8, 9). This is the positive side. Obviously there are dangers attached to circumstances in guidance. The danger does not come because of what God does, but because of the nature of even the regenerate man. Chief among the dangers in guidance here is that of trying to make the circumstances fit the will of the believer. Frequently there is a struggle to discover the proper pathway between an over-activism and an over-passivism with much doubt as to how active or how passive the believer ought to be.

An illustration of passivity or activity in connection with guidance will manifest this more clearly. Assuming that a man is in a pastorate and comes to believe that God wants him to make a change, he is faced with three choices. He can do nothing outwardly regarding the belief, except to communicate that belief to God and simply to wait on Him to open another door. Or he can begin an active campaign to open another door. This he can do by writing to churches which are pastorless, notifying "influential" friends of his wish, and seeking in every way to open a door. A third alternative would be to move somewhere between the two poles of extreme activity and passivity.

Complete passivity may be an excuse for inaction. Activity may only force circumstances and lead to forcing Providence. Both have their dangers. Believers should be careful to know themselves as they know these, so that they can come to the place where conscience is satisfied that Providence has not been thwarted either by over activity or under activity. Circumstances, to be circumstances, must be of the Lord and not the flesh or the will of the flesh.

The life of C. T. Studd affords a glimpse of negative and positive circumstances molding a life for God. Studd returned to England broken in health. Mrs. Studd was likewise broken, and it appeared as though God had cast them aside despite the years of additional service they might normally anticipate. However, the closed door of China became an open door in another direction. Studd got a greater vision for the continent of Africa and began a ministry of almost two decades. And this, after he was eliminated from the China field! But Africa could not contain him. In this latter period of his life the Worldwide Evangelization Crusade was born, having for its vision the completion of the missionary task. Just as Paul was turned from Asia that he might become the Apostle to the Gentiles in Europe, so Studd was turned from China to Africa that the world might have his leadership. From a human viewpoint, however, the circumstances in the lives of the Studd family were anything but propitious.

At this juncture a word must be dropped about circumstances as they relate to guidance for foreign missionary work. Every Christian who is honest with himself and with God should be able to answer this question: "Are the circumstances of my life preventing me (that is, are the doors shut) from becoming a foreign missionary for Jesus Christ? Are the doors shut to me or is it simply that I have never done anything to discover whether they are open or shut? Have I assumed that the doors are shut, and am I waiting for some circumstances which will demonstrate that they are flung wide open?"

The life of James Gilmour of Mongolia answers the questions just raised. He said, "This command (go ye into all the world) seems to me to be strictly a missionary injunction, and, as far as I can see, those to whom it was first delivered regarded it in that light, so that, apart altogether from choice and other lower reasons, my going forth is a matter of obedience to a plain command; and in place of seeking to assign a reason for going abroad, I would prefer to say that I have failed to discover any reason why I should stay at home." (Author's underlining.)

It is not without many human examples that the suspicion is generated that the average believer has given no thought to the question whether the circumstances of life act as a preventing force. There are far too many Christians for whom this excuse could not be given and whose lives are being frittered away in an existence which is not meaningful in terms of God's will for the world. The absence of special circumstances pointing to the foreign field cannot be construed to mean that the door is necessarily shut, any more than temporary unemployment can be considered an indication that God never wants you to work again.

The false use of the lack of circumstances and the misuse of circumstances to keep a Christian at home cannot be condoned. A man must be true to himself as well as to his God. But the man who is not true to himself cannot be true to his God, neither can he be true to himself if he is not true to His God. No man ought to hide behind any circumstance, positive or negative, which will prevent the fulfilling of the will of God for him.

Circumstances, to be correct, must operate in conformity to the revealed Word of God. When they do not square with the Word, care must be taken to obey the Word rather than the circumstances. Christians must remember that while circumstances occur according to the will of God, they must nevertheless be conscious that some circumstances fall within the shadow of the permissive rather than the directive will of God. Job's peculiar case illustrates this truth. Satan created circumstances in Job's life with the permission of God. The evil that came upon him was not thought up by God but by the enemy of God. Yet God was to use the evil for good and for the accomplishment of His own righteous purposes. Despite all of the misfortune which fell upon Job and the interpretation placed upon that misfortune by his "friends" Job refused to permit circumstances to shake his faith, alter his course, or deny his God. The same Evil One who had power in the life of Job has power on the earth today to deceive, as it were, the very elect. So, circumstances are always linked to the Word.

Beyond the Word and circumstances there is a third means whereby the Christian can come to the knowledge of God's will for his life. This is the work of the Holy Spirit in the heart of the true believer. The Paraclete was sent to lead him in the fullness of truth and to guide him on this earthly journey (John 16:17 ff.). He indwells his heart and speaks to him His sure word of light. Obviously, He always speaks in a context which is biblical and never in contradiction to or in defiance of the Word. The Spirit can guide only those whose minds are open to His imprint and whose hearts are in touch with Him. His voice is easily quenched by sin and the clamor of life often drowns out His Words (Eph. 5:18; I Thess. 5:19). One who does not have this gracious experience of the speaking of the Holy Spirit is missing a blessing which is his in Christ.

Assuming that the believer is rightly related to Christ and that sin is not hindering the work of the Spirit, then guidance comes to him in prayer, in Bible meditation, and in the use of sanctified common sense. God expects him to be familiar with His Word (Ps. 119:11; II Tim. 2:15), and to approach Him in prayer. All Christians know this; all Christians believe this to be true; some Christians actually practice it. But the use of sanctified common sense is different. The seeker ought to know from the Scriptures and from life that God does not ordinarily do miraculously what He can do naturally and normally. And what can be known and understood via his common sense God does not reveal to him in night visions, nor in supernatural ways. Common sense becomes sanctified when the child of God is walking in His light. Sanctified common sense does not need a supernatural revelation to demonstrate that debauchery by high living, late nights, and laziness is an offense to his God. And this same sanctified common sense can do much to direct his paths in foreign missionary work.

In those moments of life when decisions must be reached, where there is no knowledge to be derived from the Word or from apparent circumstances as to the choice, the Holy Spirit grants to the believer's heart a blessed certainty of what he ought to do. It may be, for example, that a believer has committed his life to God for missionary service but does not know in which field he ought to serve. And the circumstances of life have not given any indication either. Here it is not a matter of accepting or rejecting the will of God, but of finding where the further will of God will lead, having already made a committal for foreign service. The Holy Spirit, as one meditates and prays, will give to the heart of the believer some assurance or will some way make it plain what the choice ought to be. He may also check him when the circumstances of life appear to dictate a decision which is not the will of God, but which may be either a test to see whether he is walking closely with his God or a temptation from the Devil whose way he ought not follow. This need not be a choice between a lesser or a greater good, but can be a choice between two goods.

In the life of Paul the Holy Spirit gave him a vision of the man of Macedonia and in the words in Acts 16:10, "And after he had seen the vision, immediately we endeavoured to go into Macedonia, assuredly gathering that the Lord had called us for to preach the gospel unto them." In the life of Jeremiah one discovers the same principle. God gave him assurance while in prison that he was to buy the field in Anathoth. And it was only when his uncle's son came into the prison to sell it to him that these amazing words are recorded, ". . . Then, I knew that this was the word of the Lord" (Jeremiah 32:8). The Spirit of the living God had spoken to him with assurance, and the circumstances of life proved the validity of this inner revelation.

Guidance by the Holy Spirit does not come in one easy lesson, and there are no foolproof instruction sheets. Jesus promised that His people should have it, but practice and experience constitute a vital element of that guidance. The great saint whose sanatorium in Switzerland was a haven for sick people had so learned what it was to be guided by the Spirit that he could tell almost immediately whether God was going to heal the people who came to his house of rest. And this despite the physical malady harbored within his body which was to lead to his own death. His guidance was a consequence of many years of study in the school of the Spirit. This ought not discourage those who are younger saints, because God will not let them go astray immature as they may be, providing their hearts are right and in sincerity and honesty and with earnestness they seek that work of the Spirit in heart and life.

John G. Paton's life illustrates the impelling power of the Holy Spirit working in a life. A synod of the Reformed Presbyterian Church of Scotland was looking for a missionary to join the Rev. John Inglis in New Hebrides. They took a poll of the synod in the hope that the votes of the members would reveal one who should go. When the votes were counted, it was seen that the action was inconclusive. And as the biographer of Paton says, "a cloud of sadness appeared to fall over all the synod. The Lord kept saying within me, 'Since none better qualified can be got, rise and offer yourself!' Almost overpowering was the impulse to answer aloud, 'Here am I, send me.' But I was dreadfully afraid . . . and yet I felt a growing assurance that this was the call of God to His servant and . . . the voice within me sounded like the voice from God." Indeed the Holy Spirit was speaking to John G. Paton's heart, calling him, and at the same time granting to him heart assurance that this was the will of God for his life.

Already someone will be saying to himself, "What has all this got to do with the missionary call? Is not all this prelude just a little removed from the question which was posed in the beginning, "What constitutes a missionary call?" Emphatically the reply must be made that the foregoing is more important than one realizes. For if the circumstances of life are such that it is impossible for a Christian to become a foreign missionary, then he at least can know that the call has not come to him. There is a latent danger of using apparently unpropitious circumstances as a reason to remain at home. Unless, therefore, the circumstances are such that they actually do keep him at home, he had better be careful about interpreting circumstances. William Carey had a wife whose mind became unbalanced in India. Circumstances would have dictated that he return to England, but he did not. C. T. Studd was in very ill health, suffering from awful attacks of asthma in Africa. The circumstance of health should normally have forced his return to the homeland, but he remained in Africa unto death. The outbreak of the Boxer Rebellion in China should normally have convinced the missionaries that circumstances were demanding their complete retirement from China, but they remained to preach the gospel nonetheless.

Second, if the Spirit of God has spoken to a man's heart in such a way as to convince him without question or doubt that the mission field is not for him, then this mention of the guidance of the Holy Spirit is an answer to his question. But each must be sure that it is the voice of the Spirit of God and not the voice of self, or of ambition, or of avarice speaking.

At any rate the time has now come to consider those positive elements which constitute a call to the foreign field. The call here is used to include whatever means God uses to draw to the spiritual and intellectual attention of a man the job that needs to be done, the facing of which leads to a decision to go to the field. In the vast majority of cases, it is the presentation of the challenge to him whether mediated by books, sermons, missionary speakers, statistics, the Word of God, circumstances, or the impelling voice of the Holy Spirit. Whatever it is, behind all of these means certain elementary means stand out.

The Bible is the best means for learning the will of God. Through it a believer can discern the revealed mind of God for missions. This knowledge which comes to him from the Word, at least in some definitive sense, constitutes a call to the foreign fields of the world.

The Bible declares that Jesus came to redeem the world of men and that God's desire is for men to be saved. (I Tim. 2:4–6.) John says: ". . . he is a propitiation for our sins: and not for ours only, but for the sins of the whole world" (I John 2:2). Paul says: ". . . this is good and acceptable in the sight of God our Saviour; Who will have all men to be saved, and to come unto the knowledge of the truth" (I Tim. 2:3, 4). From this he can perceive that in Christ, via His substitutionary atonement, the disposition of God is for all men to be saved. And

Christians are commanded to be the messengers to bring to the lost and the dying the gospel of God's Son.

As if it were not enough for God to insist that His outlook for men embraces the possibility of their salvation through the ministry of the Word, God also reveals the purity and righteousness of Himself by the insistence that there is a place of eternal separation to which the unsaved must go if God is to remain God and justice is to have any significant meaning. Hell, however, does not exist as a place to which God sends men as a delighted fiend who enjoys the thought of suffering and separation. Hell in full measure represents the holiness of God and is so awful for that reason. (Rev. 20:14.) It represents the offense of sin in the sight of a righteous God, but nowhere does it say that God delights in what hell is or that men go there. (Ezek. 33:11; Matt. 18:8, 9; Matt. 25:41.) God does not *want* to send men there, but being what He is, even God could not alter the situation without losing the attributes which make him God.

The doctrine of hell in its stark reality stands as a warning beacon not only to the lost, but also the saved. For the true believer, hell is a cogent reason why he should become a bearer of the good news of the gospel that "Jesus Saves." The possibility, nay the certainty, that these men almost surely will not hear unless he puts "go" into his feet, ought to constitute some form of a call. "O son of man, I have set thee a watchman ... To declare, I say, at this time his righteousness: that he might be just and the justifier of him which believeth in Jesus" (Ezek. 33:7, Romans 3:26). Apart from any other reasons such as the disposition of God toward men and the others which shall be advanced, the knowledge of hell ought to constrain men to speak to those "other sheep" (John 10: 16) for whom Christ also died.

The thought of hell and the lostness of men without Christ have moved many to become missionaries of the cross. David Brainerd felt that inner constraint rising out of the knowledge that men without Christ are lost. Adoniram Judson was haunted during the daytime by visions of vast nations lying in the prison house of sin; and by night he went sleepless thinking of the teeming millions beyond the sea sinking into Christless graves. To him there came the constant challenge, "In the face of this situation what shall I do?" John Williams said that his heart was constantly with the poor heathen, and when he examined his motives he could not forget "the value of an immortal soul—the thousands that were passing daily from time to eternity." So also in the nineteenth century, missionary historians are frank to admit that the belief in hell occasioned tremendous activity to get to the heathen before they died for they were without hope because they were without Christ.

Jesus Christ has commissioned men to go. With this Commission He did not originate something new in His vision of the world. He simply reiterated, enlarged, and strengthened what was already disclosed to be in the will and plan of God. The incarnation and the death of Jesus bring to fruition what God had in mind from eternity. Before this earth existed, and before man had been created, Jesus was the Lamb of God slain for the sins of men. Human history has at its center this grand motive and theme. Always the view of God embraces the world. Nowhere can men find ground for the belief that God is interested in one race, or one people, or one nation. ". . . for the same Lord over all is rich unto all that call upon him. For whosoever shall call upon the name of the Lord shall be saved. And hath made of one blood all nations of men. . . . That they should seek the Lord, . . . For in him we live, and move, and have our being; . . ." (Romans 10:12, 13; Acts 17:26–28).

Believers may be ignorant of the plan of God for the world, and they may be disobedient to the claims of God, but no Christian with any appreciable knowledge of the Word can deny that the purpose of God is to have Christ brought to every creature. And if the Scriptures teach them any other lesson besides this, it is the lesson that God works through human instrumentalities. Thus the purpose of God for the world shall become a reality through men. And the men are the children of God who are subject to their Lord and who follow after Him in denial of self and in the assumption of the cross.

Had Jesus left no commandment to take the gospel to every creature, the purpose and plan of God has been sufficiently revealed in the Word to bind Christians nevertheless. From cover to cover the Bible reiterates that the children of God are stewards of His grace and to them has been given the responsibility for carrying out the work of the Master. Christians cannot sit by and naïvely believe that this does not constitute a call to positive action. God does not idly send supernatural revelations to men when He has already confirmed what He wants done in the Word. The call is connected, then, with the possession of the revealed mind of God in relation to missions. Believers should enjoy the heart certainty that they are where God wants them to be, but wherever that may be they are obligated to press the claim of God for world evangelization and to engage in it to the fullest possible extent.

The Word of God in itself has been sufficient through the ages to send men forth to the ends of the earth. James Gilmour, who was mentioned previously, had this to say: "But I go out as a missionary not that I may follow the dictates of common sense, but that I may obey the command of Christ, 'Go into all the world and preach.' He who said 'preach,' said also, 'Go ye into and preach,' and what Christ hath joined together let not man put asunder." The Great Commission had a singular hold on the heart of David Livingstone. True it is that the words of Moffat sent him to Africa. Moffat said, "I have sometimes seen, in the morning sun, the smoke of a thousand villages where no missionary has ever been." And this, linked with the Great Commission already burned on his heart, led Livingstone to Africa for Christ. It was John

Nevius who spoke of his call as one involving an "urgent conviction of duty." And this conviction sprang out of his intimate knowledge of the Word of God.

In the face of these facts it remains for men to answer the question, "Why *not* go?" rather than the question "Why go?" Any reasonable consideration of the missionary question ought to convince an objective and honest inquirer that it is time to accept the call which comes through the Word of God, unless circumstances or the inward voice of the Holy Spirit speak otherwise.

IV

Perhaps the reader is sincere and feels that there is something holding him back from making the decision to launch out for God as a missionary. Generally the reasons for hesitation follow a definite pattern and the problems have a sameness. So if you do feel that the foreign field is claiming you and yet you have been hesitating for one reason or another, perhaps the discussion of some of these problems will solve your dilemma.

Many reasons are given by believers why they do not think they ought to go to the foreign fields and, while some are legitimate, others are only excuses. And often these excuses are not recognized by the Christian as excuses. He likes to think of them as legitimate.

"I have never had a call" is a prominent reason for planning on work in the home field. And it is true that most people do not have a "call" in the sense that they anticipate it. The kind of call (usually connected with the supernatural or just the expectation that it will be "unusual" and will be recognized when it comes) many individuals hazily envision, does not exist and never has been known among the thousands of missionaries who have gone before. While one may never have had an unusual call, it cannot be denied that there is a command. When the command you have is balanced against the call you do not have, common sense and an appreciation of the Scriptures dictate that you obey the command without waiting for the call. Christians do not have to be enrolled in the king's army; they are automatically members of that army when they are regenerated. They exist to obey the divine Commander not to wait for a call to action. That call came when they were changed from sons of Adam to sons of God. The only valid manner in which the absence of a "call" exempts a man from obedience to the divine command is when he has knowledge of a definite "call" to something which will keep him from this other task. Even then, whatever the other work may be, he is still constrained by the command of God to place foreign missions at the center of his thinking.

For the man who really wants to know, the lives of hundreds of missionaries are available for investigation. Few missionaries have been motivated by some vision in the night. The majority, including most of the ones we call "great," have been constrained to go by the commandment in the Word, by the needs of the field, by their knowledge of the lostness of the heathen world, or by the inspiration mediated to them by some soul on fire for God and with a passion for lost men. God does not give night visions when through normal channels the missionary call can be effectively presented.

One aspect of requiring a special call for missionary service is the violence it does to the rest of Scripture. No man would think of interpreting his Bible in this way in other matters. Men accept the blessings which the Bible promises. They do not ask for any special indication that they fall under the blessing nor do they assume that the blessing is not for them unless they receive some additional extra-biblical revelation. Men ought not draw a line of distinction between the obligations of Christianity and the privileges of it. Nor should they claim only the privileges and leave the responsibilities for the conscience of the few.

"I must earn a living and provide for my family," is an argu-

ment commonly advanced against missionary service. One
earnest person solved this problem when he realized that he
could enter some form of full time Christian service in which
he could earn his living and at the same time serve the Lord
fully. Leaving the business world, he became a teacher in a
Christian school, eventually becoming the headmaster of the
school. It meant a decrease in salary and a walk by faith, but
the heart desire to serve the Lord was fulfilled. And he had
assurance that the will of God for him was in the teaching
field. Earning a living does not become a barrier against missionary work. How much of a living, on the other hand, is a
likely tension. No one can overlook the truth that Christian
workers generally are more poorly paid for what they do than
other workers in non-Christian occupations. But the amount
of money as the decisive factor reveals the worship of Mam-
mon rather than the worship of God.

"My health will not permit me to go to the foreign field."
Dr. Robert E. Speer once answered this argument by telling
a story he had heard from the lips of a friend. This friend
met and talked with a student in Iowa. This student gave as a
reason for his remaining at home the fact that he had suffered
a sunstroke. He said, "I had it here in this state." The friend
replied: "I have lived most of my life in India, and I have
never had a sunstroke, and you propose to spend your life
where you have already had one sunstroke and where for all
you know you may have another."

Health is sometimes a legitimate barrier, but the right to
make that decision lies beyond the individual. Medical doctors connected with mission boards know the hazards involved and will soon state whether it is dangerous in their
opinion. And again God has used ill people in the work of
spreading the gospel. Paul had an infirmity in the flesh. C. T.
Studd was able to begin a magnificent work in Africa after
years in China despite a serious physical handicap. God did
not remove the handicap in either case but gave grace to over-

come the handicap. Some people have been known to enjoy far better health on the foreign field than at home. And again conditions may prevail which dictate that the risk of bad health may be worthwhile because of a man's value to the progress of the gospel. "Calculated Hazard" is a term used in missionary advance as well as in military strategy. To avoid taking chances is the normal order of life, but Christians are not living "normal" lives any more than a state of war is a normal condition for nations. Be sure that reasons of health truly are an indication of the Lord that you ought to remain at home.

"I am too old to go" is another favorite. Suspicion sometimes arises that believers resist God until they are over age and then use that claim to excuse themselves from the thought of foreign service. Mission boards properly consider age as a factor in the appointment of candidates for the foreign field. But often age is not the barrier you think. For administrators, office workers, etc. age is not a decisive factor. Boards make exceptions to age limits, too. Perhaps you are one of the people for whom an exception may be made. But the age problem is not answered until every avenue has been explored and until every possible door has been closed in your face. Simply to use age as the excuse without having taken steps to verify the idea is neither sensible nor excusable. Age may not be a barrier!

"I have home responsibilities—my parents," is still another problem which faces some who would like to go. Perhaps conditions are not as bad as you make them out. The Bible, however, speaks as though the forsaking of loved ones may be required of those who take up their crosses to follow Jesus. A re-examination of the home circumstances may actually show that your parents can get along without you—even though it is more of a financial burden than you would like to see. Many missionaries have found that obedience to the divine command has cost others something as well as themselves. Surely the children of many missionaries are called upon to forego privileges which children at home take for granted, but this does not deter their parents from continuing in missionary service. And the very hardships men would like to avoid for the sake of parents or loved ones may be exactly what God would use to bring them to the place of complete surrender and faith in Him. Unless the case against going because of this reason is ironclad the Christian should re-examine his decision.

"I'm all set for life and God is blessing me in exactly the thing that I am doing. Why should I make a change now?" This excuse is not often a valid one. Abraham was well settled and was bountifully blessed before he left his home and kindred for the land of promise, but God disturbed his life. Luke was a fine physician, but Jesus made him a healer of the souls of men. Being set for life and seeing God bless what you are presently doing is not a final criterion. His will is the only consideration. God may in some measure bless even the disobedience of His children because it serves His purpose, but a greater blessing, a wider service, and a more potent ministry awaits the obedient one who sacrifices all and steps out in faith. Inertia which comes from being located in one place, and any attendant blessings, do not always mean that God will not shake a man loose and change the direction of his life to accomplish His eternal aim. Always the final decision must be His will regardless of the cost.

"I don't have a suitable background for missionary work." How often you hear this cry. Often it *is* too late to spend the years which formal study, including college and seminary, requires. God does work outside the normal course of events, however. And whatever background you may have will help in some phase of the work. God uses businessmen, dentists, technicians, teachers, nurses, and carpenters. Innumerable calls come today. Professional and non-professional missionaries are needed in our generation. A business man, or a doctor, or lawyer, or dentist can combine business in a foreign land with missionary work to the people of that land. A self-supporting missionary of the non-professional type can do much to spread the gospel. Jesus chose men who were ill-suited for missionary work so far as their backgrounds were concerned. One was a tax-gatherer, others were fishermen. John, Peter, and Matthew did well despite the lack of formal training.

"I was called to China, but the door to China was shut." How many times people turn back because one door is shut! In secular pursuits if a man finds a door shut to a particular job, he looks for another door. Livingstone at first looked toward China, but he was led to Africa. Judson started for India, but the closed door here became an open door to Burma. Studd went to China, but he finished his life in Africa. The field is vast, and one closed door does not end the possibilities. It is not always a question of one field or no field. Even the Apostle Paul was turned back from one field that he might become the Apostle to Europe. Before you quit, try some other fields. There may be a real opening, and the other field is white unto harvest too.

"I do not *feel* called." The call has nothing to do with feeling. Feeling comes from physical externals oftentimes and is not dependable. Never are men asked to obey God as a matter of feeling, but they are asked to obey whether they like it or not. Obviously the flesh may revolt against the thought of doing some things. Feeling may tell you that you would rather not go, when obedience and the Spirit of God are driving you forth. Will counts more than feeling. Heaven deliver the missionary cause which is based upon feeling! It does not last and brings ruin. Will can make you go where feeling cannot; will can make you persist when feeling would have you yield; will which subjects itself to feeling is not will delivered from the bondage of the old nature. Forget feeling and begin obeying is a good precept for all aspects of the Christian life, and primarily for missions!

"I was turned down by a mission board." Just as in the case

of finding the door shut to one land, you can search for another open door, so a second or third mission board may accept you. Different mission boards have different standards, different requirements, different openings. The decision of the board that they do not wish to use you does not mean that no other board can use you. Other boards may be anxiously waiting for one with the very qualifications and training that you possess.

"I can't seem to love the heathen," is a common cry among believers. And this lack of love for the heathen holds some back from foreign service. Our business is to love God and not to worry about the sheep. Surely men can expect that when they come to that place of supreme love of God, they will enjoy a corresponding love for the persons He loves. Even the absence of a great passion for doing a job need not keep them from doing the job. God will have regard for the honest Christian who goes to work for Him when there is no passion, when that individual is constrained to labor for God out of simple obedience to the divine command.

How silly will our excuses appear in eternity, and how ashamed will some of God's children be when they stand before the judgment seat of Christ to give account of their deeds in the flesh.

V

When a man has decided to become a missionary, he should make preparations for service abroad. These preparations include formal study which shall be discussed subsequent to the suggestions for private preparations which any interested person may pursue.

First and foremost, he should engage in the study of the Word of God. This may be twofold: either he may study the Bible by himself or through correspondence courses offered by any reputable institution. The study of the Bible pri-

vately is not to be despised and sufficient material is available
for anyone to obtain a good command of the Scriptures.

He should read missionary biographies for spiritual encour-
agement and edification. This reading will acquaint him with
mission fields and their problems, and will provide him with
a knowledge of the people and the countries. He will enter
into the sufferings, hardships, privileges, and rewards of the
missionaries as they serve God. And if this study does not
arouse within a Christian a greater passion for the work it will
be most unusual.

A prospective missionary should go where there is missionary zeal and sentiment. He should join with others of like
mind, and take an active part in their endeavors and discussions. This contact will encourage him in missionary interest,
and he will be able to help others also. Mutual sharing inevitably redounds to the general advancement of all.

Churches offer mission study classes from time to time. The
candidate should find such a program of study at the local
level and attend the classes. The church which offers such a
study class is likely to be a missionary-minded church, and
from this contact other openings for additional missionary development will come.

Preparation for the field should include a study of mission
fields. He should find out what the opportunities are, where
the needs are greatest, where his own church group operates
mission stations and what the requirements are for service.
God speaks to men out of the knowledge they possess, and the
future field of service may be disclosed to him following a
survey of the fields and when he has learned all he can about
them.

The individual should start being a missionary right where
he is. Five thousand miles of ocean will never make a man a
missionary. If he is not concerned for souls here and now, he
will not be concerned for souls when he gets overseas. All
around are people who need Jesus Christ. He ought to intro-

duce men to Him and make his mistakes in personal soul winning at home. He should learn the techniques of soul winning and become fairly expert in this field before he is ready for overseas service.

Early contact with the mission board under which he anticipates service is desirable. He ought to ask about their educational requirements, the opportunities they offer and the openings they have. He should learn about their financial policies and field regulations, inquire into their theological basis, and ask questions about their methods and techniques. Does the board engage in an evangelistic ministry or is it primarily interested in social service work? Is its leadership good and can the board be depended upon? Just as a board has the right to inquire into the qualifications of a candidate so a candidate has the right to ask the board searching questions before he makes formal application. If there is any doubt about a given mission board, he owes it to himself to look into more than one board and weigh one over against the other. If his interest lies in a faith mission board, he should remember that there are scores of them, and one or two are likely to commend themselves to him more highly than any others. To be careful and to take one's time is the path of wisdom.

A man who wishes to become a missionary should prepare himself formally for service. And he should be sure that what he gets will fit him for the particular work he will engage in. Speed or undue haste is not worthy of the servant of the Lord. No matter how great haste appears to be necessary he must take time to get the best training he can get. A year or two more training is not a waste of time, and the fruit of such training will, in the long run, justify the time he spends. A good education is cheapest in the long run, and the institutions in which he studies should be all he wishes them to be.

A candidate should be encouraged to possess many additional qualifications which he can make his own without too much trouble. Ability to drive and repair an automobile, keep books, play a musical instrument, oversee building operations, and a hundred other skills will make him more valuable to the mission agency. In a day when most men are asking their employers how much they will grant to them without seeking to discover how much they can bring to the employer, the Christian missionary candidate should remember that his service is one in which he seeks to bring himself and all that he has and can have to the service of the Master.

The foregoing suggestions are posited upon the assumption that the prospective missionary will also develop within him the other attributes without which he cannot become a good missionary or without which no man can live a decent Christian life. The cultivation of the spiritual life, the prayer life, and the life of secret devotion are among those suggested in addition to the concrete suggestions peculiar to formal preparation for possible missionary service.

CHAPTER IV

Choice and Selection of Missionary Personnel

~~~~~~

SOME PEOPLE VIEW THE MISSIONARY VOCATION AS SUITABLE FOR those who cannot succeed at home. If a Christian is a bit "queer" or not quite "normal," then perhaps he may be a good candidate for the mission field. While this may appear to be an exaggeration or a caricature, it is not so far removed from the truth, for too many people, including Christians, do look upon missionaries as a peculiar species of individual.

In the minds of many, the leading qualifications for a foreign missionary are piousness and "niceness," but this impression is far enough removed from reality so as not to be humorous. Other characteristics and qualifications govern the thinking of missionary administrators who are faced with the choice and selection of personnel.

Boards do make mistakes in the selection of candidates. No missionary statesman can say that his record is perfect. All boards, denominational or faith, face this problem and all of them err in judgment. Misfits do get to the field and are returned home permanently. Such errors are costly. They consume money which could well be used elsewhere. And laymen secretly feel that such mistakes are inexcusable. After all, does not the mission board have the guidance of the Holy Spirit, and since this is a spiritual work ought they not be preserved from error?

Missionary leadership is not completely different from other kinds of leadership. The men are human and prone to err. Despite their utmost sincerity, their best intentions, and constant recourse to prayer and the guidance of the Holy Spirit they do not always succeed when they choose new candidates. This illustrates the innate sinfulness in all men no matter how exalted their consecration, and it should create in all a sense of humility and dependence, together with the knowledge that the number of mistakes would be greater were it not for the superintending providence of the Lord of the church. When those executives charged with the final choice of sending out candidates have sought valiantly to know the will of God and have exercised to the fullest all of their God-given human faculties with discretion and care, they still must leave the final results with God. Always the imponderables and the intangibles stand in the background and no statistical evidence proves that missionaries are not subjected to the same frailties, disenablements, and "accidents" common to all men.

What administrator has such prescience that he is able to foresee what the future has in store for the missionaries he helps to commission? Who could know that a missionary after a few years of service would, in the act of repairing a well, fall into it, hit his head on a rock, die, and leave behind a wife and six children to be returned to the United States? Who could know in advance that Black Water fever would take the life of a physically strong man after five years of service and bring to an apparently untimely end the activity of a splendid servant of God? Who could foretell that political trouble in China would bring to an end the life of a physician at the hands of the Communists?

An administrator cannot always know in advance what psychological factors will render impotent some candidate in whom he had great hopes; not always is he able to discern what climatic conditions, stress and strain will do to the temperament of a missionary on the field nor how it will, like a little leaven, leaven the whole lump and bring disharmony, discordance and disruption to a mission station. The administrator does all he can; and having done all he makes mistakes; and having done well still other disasters overtake him. He must learn to leave all in the hands of God—Who knows, cares and understands.

Bystanders, and Christians too, make light of missionaries. They criticize their shortcomings, laugh at their provincialisms, and decry their limited outlooks. The now famous "Laymen's Missionary Report," which bears the name of Hocking of Harvard on its pages, intimates that missionaries are puny, sub-cultural, and far from representative of the best in American religious life. And if it were true, and if all the shortcomings attributed to missionaries actually existed, no administrator in selecting personnel would be anxious to appoint such creatures, but every administrator is limited as to the field from which to make his selections.

Perhaps if the lay people who made the survey, and who doubtless thought themselves to be fair examples of what good Christians ought to be, had offered themselves as candidates for the foreign field or if they had served as missionary administrators, they would have been far less critical. Who can obscure the vital and unfortunate truth that no candidates can be chosen as missionaries who do not apply? No administrator can accept men who do not offer themselves. Administrators work with what they have, not with what they would like to have. And those who criticize should first ask themselves why they are not among those who apply for overseas service.

In the United States during the past war, every man was liable to conscription. Those who were adjudged fit were drafted. The unfit were cast aside. The cream of American manhood can be skimmed off for national defense in any emergency, and the individual has no personal choice; men go whether they wish to go or not. Now the Christian is obligated to fulfill the Great Commission of Jesus Christ. All are called to go, but few offer themselves in answer to that call. And from among the few who do apply the boards must make their choices. To this hour the supply has never been equal to the demand; the number of candidates has never been greater than the number which could be used. Among the faith mission boards especially there is a permanent scarcity of male candidates for the mission fields. Thus in 1953 one of the largest faith boards reported that out of 1028 missionaries only 334 were men. The women were twice as numerous as the men.

Missionary work is difficult, exacting, and demanding of the best that men have to give. By what law of logic or by what revelation from God can it be said that God calls women to do the work of men? Not that the labors of women, diligent, patient, and faithful, are to be despised. Rather God is mercifully using consecrated women in places where men ought to be—not because God refuses men, but because men refuse to heed the call of God. Away with the idea that any pious, nice young man or woman can be a missionary! God wants red-blooded, talented, yielded, aggressive, persistent men and women. He desires men and women who could have made names and fortunes for themselves in America but who chose "rather to suffer affliction with the people of God, than to enjoy the pleasures of sin for a season; esteeming the reproach of Christ greater riches than the treasures of Egypt."

All boards want the best personnel they can attract, but missions is a minority cause, and somehow the best do not seem to sense the challenge and never recognize that the foreign field offers them more opportunity for the use of their talents with a harvest that outlasts the temporal. When such talented people present themselves to mission boards, they are not turned away without good reason, and from them shall inevitably come the future leadership of the missionary cause. But until they accept the challenge and present their lives for service the boards will have to choose the best from among those who apply.

Now what precisely does a mission board look for in a candidate who applies to go overseas? Whatever the ideal is, many candidates who do not meet this ideal may still be sent if they measure up sufficiently so that a board with some degree of assurance can forecast reasonable chances for a successful missionary career.

Health is a prime factor in deciding on missionary candidates. The robust do not always outlive the less robust, and the most magnificent specimen of physical health may go down under the impact of disease. But boards do want candidates who are reasonably healthy. A chronic condition such as recurring asthma, heart conditions, organic physical impediments, or a quiescent tuberculosis are good reasons for declining to send a candidate. However, no Christian should try to excuse himself on the ground that he has some physical condition which will rule him out for overseas service. Only qualified physicians with broad experience should make that decision. No individual should make a decision in the area of health by himself. What he considers an impediment may not be one to the examining board while other impediments which a man thinks inconsequential may be thought by the physical examiners to be positive reason for not accepting him.

Sometimes boards take a calculated risk with an individual whose health is precarious but whose gifts and accomplishments outweigh the factor of health and make it worth the extra hazard of sending him out. Then again, conditions which would keep a man from going to India may not keep the same man from going to certain parts of Africa or to South America. The mission boards know the problems of the areas in which they operate, and sound counsel from them will dispel the ignorance which either would keep a man from applying or applying when he ought to remain at home.

Health includes not only the physical but also the psychological. Most missionaries go to climates which are physically trying. Sanitary conditions generally are pitiable or totally absent. The nervous strain of continued absence from home, laboring in a strange environment, subjection to disease, filth, hatred, and a thousand minor distractions take their toll on the missionary. Each person has a "point of no return," and when that point has been reached the individual is apt to disintegrate and break down. Each man's breaking point varies, and while the Christian faith does, by sublimation, enable a man to heighten his breaking point yet all have one and all will break down if subjected to difficulties beyond their endurance. The boards must calculate this factor and make a subjective judgment about an elusive and intangible facet of one's life. Not a few missionaries break down under the weight of nervous strain induced by climate, sanitary conditions, and environmental factors.

We must remember that missionary life will do to people what would never happen to them were they to remain at home. Normal civilian life in the United States, bad as it may be and in spite of the increasing number of mental breakdowns, does not begin to approximate the severity of conditions on the average mission field. The best and the finest under extreme circumstances will break. Those whose breaking point is low are not good risks, and a board which discovers this factor in advance will reject the candidate. And rejection is no slur upon any individual.

Age is a qualification for missionary service. Rare cases crop up in which missionaries begin service late in life. This is the exception, not the rule. Over the years an age limit of thirty-two has been a rough dividing line which marks off the place beyond which a board will not ordinarily go in appointing a missionary. It used to be thought that language was a chief barrier after thirty-two years of age. That is no longer true. But after thirty-two men tend to be set in their ways; they have often lost aspects of pliability and adaptability. Adjustments usually come harder and the length of probable service shortens. Often family life for a man has reached a place where with three or four children the monetary cost of getting that missionary into active service is prohibitive. Boards do not like to send out as new missionaries a family consisting of more than four members, and even that number may be enough to prevent appointment. Family conditions would not militate against sending out a single missionary over thirty-two years of age, but the other factors which do must first be overcome.

3 Educational background is a governing factor in the choice and selection of missionary personnel. The average denominational board requires its male candidates to be graduates of collegiate institutions and to hold a divinity degree from a theological seminary. Seven years of college and seminary work is the norm. This norm does not apply for specialized work such as dentistry and medicine. For the latter the norm would be collegiate work, medical school graduation, internship and special work in tropical diseases if, for example, the missionary is going to Africa.

The American Baptist Foreign Missionary Society and the Conservative Baptist Foreign Mission Society appoint candidates with less training than college and seminary. Some of their related seminaries have a five-year course leading to the bachelor of theology degree, a course which high-school graduates pursue. In effect, the first two years embrace collegiate work and the remaining three seminary work. Baptist churches have the power to ordain, and since the churches are independent, many of the ministers within their framework have less than college and seminary training themselves. This operates against unvarying standards both for the home ministry and for the foreign mission field. Forces are now in operation which tend to standardize the training for the home and foreign ministries, and ultimately it can be anticipated that the move will succeed.

Faith boards do not demand the same amount or the same type of training for their candidates. Most of them will take as missionaries those who have had a minimum of three year's training beyond high school. Bible institutes offer the kind of training desired as preparation for the foreign field. The emphasis is on the English Bible, doctrine, missions, and allied subjects. In line with the increasing demand for more education for missionaries—a demand necessitated by government restrictions against missionaries not educated to suit their own standards—many Bible institutes now offer a four-year course with a major in Bible which leads to a bachelor of arts degree in Bible.

The non-denominational boards will take candidates who are graduates of collegiate institutions but insist upon adequate Bible training to supplement the liberal arts work. Seminary graduates receive a cordial welcome from these boards, but the unhappy fact is that far fewer seminary graduates apply than they can use. Should it not be recorded that seminaries are not noted for their missionary zeal, and enthusiasm for missions can be dulled and desire quenched? The slant of the average seminary is in the direction of preparation for the home ministry, and the work of the foreign field is supplemental rather than fundamental. This observation is made not for the sake of criticism but with the hope that future seminary leadership will steer a more missionary-minded course. All of these institutions work under pressures which, if not resisted, pull them away from original purposes and primary aims, or which lead to disbalance with overemphasis on the home ministries.

Non-denominational boards differ little in educational requirements for physicians, dentists, and nurses. They do not have on their staffs as many of these proportionately as do the denominational boards, but the general educational background is similar. Educational missionaries likewise tend to have more training, and training which is similar to that demanded by the denominations. Since faith boards rarely engage in educational work beyond the high-school level the type of educational background is similar, but the length of time spent and the degrees needed by the candidates will vary somewhat.

f Mission boards are looking for men and women who have executive ability bulwarked by <u>force of character</u>. A missionary is a leader and an organizer. He superintends operations and oversees the workers. As devolution becomes more common the work of the missionary will change, and he will assume duties and perform functions under the superintendency of the "younger church." But in many fields that time has not yet come, and the need for superintending skill is still marked. This executive ability implies initiative, self-reliance, and abounding energy. Missionaries have to rely upon themselves, to follow their own suggestions, to create and improvise as they go along. It is not common to have all the tools, the knowledge, and the skill which a situation may demand and the missionary must fill the gap, be able to substitute, invent, improvise, and create. Force of character should accompany executive skill. This trait is indispensable for it has in it the seeds by which a man can stimulate, inspire and arouse others to creative action.

Sanctified common sense or balance of judgment is looked for by mission boards. A man whose feet are on the ground even though his heart is inclined toward heavenly things is a pearl of great price. This kind of person is a practical being who knows the value of a dollar and who realistically understands that perfection is not to be found on this earth. The missionary spends money, oversees native workers, has charge of building operations oftentimes, and is forever settling disputes and controversies which are bound to arise. These call for common sense and balanced judgment.

Intestinal fortitude combined with a sense of goal is another sought-after trait. It means that the man has carry-

through and will bring to a conclusion what he has commenced. That type of persistence which believes it is always
too soon to quit is desirable. The man who does not know he
is beaten and who battles as strongly at the end as when he first
began is the man who eventually will win. Thus it could be
written from the mission field itself: "send us a despiser of
difficulties, who will not be discouraged under the most adverse circumstances, who will unite unflinching courage with
consummate tact, know how to do impossible things and
maintain a pertinacity that borders on stubbornness with a
suavity of manner that softens asperity." And while this description may be that which fits the ideal man, boards still
want those who measure up to this standard to some degree.
In sheltered fields as well as in pioneer fields insuperable difficulties always will insure the usefulness of this trait in a
missionary.

5 Boards are on the outlook for uneven temperament, and
this includes within its borders undue sensitivity. The one
who is offended easily; whose feelings are on the surface;
whose mind is filled with grievances and grudges; who
grouches when he cannot have his own way; who sulks and
whimpers in the corner—this man is a trial on any mission
field. To be able to work harmoniously is a fundamental qualification. If a man is quarrelsome, let him remain at home. The
happiness and efficiency of an entire station may be ruined by
one individual whose temperament is defective and whose life
brings blight rather than blessing. If a man exhibits churlish-
ness, unevenness of disposition, or a hypercritical spirit, he is
a poor risk.

Part of temperament has to do with one's outlook on life.
Is the man cheerful or despondent; is he optimistic or pessimistic? Does he incline toward the dark side rather than the
bright side of life? The candidate who can sing and mean
"There Is Sunshine in My Soul Today" will find a hearty welcome on any mission field. Every bad trait will be doubly ac-

centuated abroad, and three thousand miles of ocean does not thereby improve a man any more than it makes a missionary. Of course candidate secretaries must take this into account.

What provokes fellow-missionaries is the individual who thinks he has the only pipe-line to heaven. He believes that God has shown him, in answer to prayer, what ought to be done, and all the arguments adduced by his colleagues leave him unmoved. In his mind no thought seems ever to enter that his colleagues pray too and that God answers their prayers as well as his. His every pronouncement has the ring of a papal *ex cathedra* to it, and he naïvely persuades himself that the last word has been said. The discussion is over, and his ears are closed. This type of candidate is a poor risk, and when boards find they have one on their hands they will not appoint him. This kind does not often last more than one term on the field if he lasts that long.

Harmony in doctrinal viewpoints is essential for a missionary candidate. A missionary whose beliefs are conservative is not likely to be happy working alongside a missionary whose persuasions are liberal. For one missionary to teach converts that the Bible is inerrant while another missionary teaches the same converts that the Bible contains the word of God but is not wholly the word of God and has definite historical, geological, or other errors in it, cannot result in harmony. For one to reject the virgin birth and preach against it while another accepts it and preaches for it will produce controversy. This problem of doctrinal divergencies between liberalism and conservatism is not as yet a problem for faith boards. It is a much greater problem in denominational missions. The cases of Dryden Phelps and Dr. Seagrave tormented the American Baptist Convention for a period of time. Essentially these men were the objects of attack because of basic doctrinal differences which labeled them as theological liberals.

When stressing doctrinal differences, liberalism and conservatism are not the sole points of conflict. Within mission families where no liberalism exists and where candidates are screened with extreme care for doctrinal conformity, a secondary doctrinal problem persists. This centers around issues which are peripheral but which may cause devastating dissension anyhow. Certain faith boards carefully question candidates regarding their views on eternal security. Unless assured that those candidates who reject eternal security in favor of a possible loss of salvation subsequent to salvation are teachable and willing not to make their view a direct issue the boards will not hazard dissension by sending them out.

An intolerant hyper-dispensationalist or hyper-Calvinist (or even a fanatical Calvinist or Arminian) who is not humble and willing to endure teaching not in agreement with his own will inevitably cause trouble. More than one station has been torn by differing viewpoints derived from opposing Christian standards or ethical concepts too. At a station staffed by Americans and Englishmen high tension developed over the question whether the women should or should not have their hair curled. Harmony of doctrine, both major and peripheral, as well as harmony of personality, ethics, and moral concepts will do much to insure satisfactory work at any station. Every board is anxious to preserve harmony and every candidate himself should be just as careful to insure his own happiness and the well being of the missionary community. If the group with which a man wants to work does not reflect his views, he has little chance for a successful missionary career under those auspices.

Marriage is on the list of items that missionary appointment committees study. Prospective missionary candidates should be made to understand that boards do not appoint one member of the family. They do not wish to send wives to the foreign field because their husbands are missionaries. If the sole reason for a woman's becoming a missionary is her marriage to a man who is one or who is a candidate for the field, hardly any board will want that couple. In the end it is disastrous to send two people to the field when only one of them has been called to go. The wife is a missionary just as much as her husband. She is expected to carry on missionary work within the limits of her strength and family responsibilities. Men should be conscious of this hazard prior to marriage, and in the selection of a wife they should find out whether the prospective mates are in sympathy with their missionary call and themselves willing volunteers for missionary endeavor.

When Christians are considering matrimony, another factor enters into the picture. One of the individuals in the couple may be inadequately educated and may not be able to meet the standards set up by the board. If suitable arrangements cannot be made for that partner to obtain the requisite training, the question must be asked whether it is the will of God for the marriage to take place and both individuals be lost to the mission field. Since the husband and his wife must pass the scrutiny of the board, and if either one of them fails to pass that scrutiny both stay home, this means that no one who has a call to the mission field should marry thoughtlessly.

Children complicate the picture especially when there are more than two of them. Recent trends in American life following World War II have resulted in increasing numbers of married students. Seminaries which formerly never thought of providing married students' apartments now have them. The fact that so many people marry before completing their education is not the chief part of the problem. The problem arises with the additions to the family. Mission boards welcome married couples, but they prefer that they be without children if possible. But some boards will take couples with as many as two children. After that number has been passed, the financial factor, not to mention the problems of adjustment, language, and travel difficulties, multiplies the complications. Boards are not unwilling to care for children born while their parents are in service, but they are hesitant about large families who are starting out as novices.

In addition to the foregoing, prospective missionaries should be able to do many other kinds of work that are invaluable to the missionary vocation. Driving a car, repairing an automobile, carpentry, masonry, bricklaying, playing musical instruments, children's work, singing, typewriting, bookkeeping, teaching and a score of other skills helpful to the attainment of missionary objectives will be taken into consideration. No one can know too much or be able to do too much. And the more the candidate has to offer the better his chances of acceptance by the mission agency.

Throughout the listing of the factors considered by mission boards nothing has been said about the spiritual life and call of the prospective missionary. Perhaps these items have been kept until the end because we assume they are prerequisites without which no man should be accepted for missionary service, or because stressing them at the conclusion will leave a more powerful impression on the heart and mind. What constitutes a call is dealt with elsewhere and therefore does not enter into the picture here but, whatever a call is, each candidate for the mission field must have it.

Assuming the existence of a bona fide call to the foreign field, Christian character and spiritual life are vital, and deficiencies are fatal. A man may not measure up fully to the characteristics which might be entitled secular, but however high he may rate on the secular traits he is not likely to be appointed for service unless he measures up to the spiritual qualifications. What, then, comprises Christian character and spiritual life?

Christian character is the hallmark by which the genuineness and depth of Christian experience can be measured along with spiritual life. A truly redeemed man in whose life the Spirit of God has wrought changes is a man of integrity, honesty, and holiness. His word is his bond, and his commitments are faithfully fulfilled. What he says can be depended upon as being true. His vision is unobstructed in heavenly things, and the love of this world has long since been crucified, and in place thereof he has a consuming passion for the things of the world to come which is his real home. He has no foot in this world, but both feet are in heaven. He is marked by a simplicity, a humility, a teachableness, and a self-sacrificing nature that borders on the strange to those who have not caught his vision or known his God. He is frank and open, winsome, sincere, and above all—a man, in the truest sense of that word.

By spiritual life is meant the cultivation of the inner life through which the believer maintains his unbroken fellowship with God. The devotional life speaks for itself and is reflected in the outward demeanor. Does the candidate find time to read and study the Word of the living God? Does he enjoy this or is it rote for him? Does he know that Word of God and is he familiar with its contents so that he can use this tool effectively? Has the Word of God become a part of him and is his soul steeped in it?

What about the prayer life? Does he pray? What is the scope and burden of his praying? Does he know how to come to grips with God, and has previous experience demonstrated that he has learned dependence upon Him for the supply of needs and for the wisdom, power, results, and dynamic without which his ministry cannot reach its maximum height of effectiveness?

Thus do mission boards look at their candidates and make inquiry into their lives that they might know whom to send out and whom to reject. These characteristics which have been delineated are among the ones inquired about. On the basis of their evaluations the boards come to important decisions. The futures of missionaries depend on what they decide as well as the destinies of those to whom the missionaries shall minister. Boards have no intuitive process for guidance;

they have no other access to the knowledge of the will of God that is not equally available to all Christians. They pray sincerely that they may discern the will of God, and board members are at least as interested in knowing what God's will is as are the candidates.

God guides mission leaders through their common sense. He has given them experience by which they can detect those who are not good material. Mistakes made previously warn them what to look for in candidates. They can size up men, for they know that even good men may not be the men of God's choice for the mission field.

Whatever decision a board makes, the candidate can only suppose that these older brethren in the faith are to be trusted and that they have sincerely tried their best to discern God's will. If the answer is in the affirmative, he can rejoice and look toward a sailing date. If the reply is in the negative, he has several choices. He can seek service elsewhere under some other agency. One rejection does not necessarily mean that it is not the will of God for him to go. Mistakes of rejection do occur as do mistakes in accepting the unfit.

A second option the man who has been rejected has is to discern in his rejection the pattern of God's hand and finger and to assume that God has other plans for his life. He has done his best and offered himself for service. If contributing causes cannot be corrected and if the future does not hold further promise for possible overseas service, he can accept this as a token from God to stay home and at home be what God wants him to be. One eminent missionary leader early covenanted with God that he would never speak a word of rejection to a man without telling him frankly the reasons underlying that rejection. Undoubtedly most mission boards will happily explain to a man exactly why they have refused to accept his candidacy so that he may either give up his plans for the field or concentrate on the defects that possibly by remedial effort he may again become a candidate.

Sometimes boards neither accept nor reject candidates but continue them with concrete proposals about existing defects, recommending that when these defects have been corrected the board will look over the candidate once more with the view to approving him for service. One young man was rejected by a faith board despite collegiate training but due to an obvious deficiency in Bible training and background. The suggestion of additional work was well received, and at a later date his candidacy was approved. He was a better man for having had the additional work, and the mission field to which he was assigned was richer for having secured a man better-trained and equipped than he possibly could have been without the additional educational discipline.

Much has been learned by sad experience over a hundred or more years of North American foreign missionary activity. Every life and every dollar must be used with caution and care. And when all is said and done, missionary leaders must leave the product of their labors and their decisions in the hands of God—decisions both good and bad, but decisions which have been made by earnest, sincere, devout servants of God who have done the best they could do.

CHAPTER V

Mission Boards and Societies

~~~~~~

FOREIGN AND HOME MISSIONARY ACTIVITY OPERATES NORMALLY through two major media: denominational mission boards and faith mission boards. Denominational missions are represented by such agencies as the Board of Foreign Missions of the Presbyterian Church, U.S.A., and by American Baptist Foreign Mission Society of the American Baptist Convention. Faith boards are represented by agencies like the Sudan Interior Mission, the Africa Inland Mission and others. Besides these two major media for missionary endeavor others might be mentioned which, while not of great importance numerically or even financially, complete the structure of organized missionary work.

Among the lesser agencies engaged in missionary activity in other than denominational boards and societies and non-denominational or faith missions and societies are the following:

1. *Supporting and fund raising and transmitting agencies which cannot properly be called boards or societies since they are not sending agencies.* The Russian Missionary Service, the Dohnavur Fellowship, and the D. M. Stearns Missionary Fund, Inc. are in this category along with some others.

2. *The non-sending groups who perform specialized services.* Among these are the American Bible Society, the American Leprosy Missions, Inc., Agricultural Missions, Inc., Inter-Varsity Christian Fellowship, Gospel Recordings, Inc., and

the Laymen's Missionary Movement of North America, Inc. These agencies are not missionary boards or societies as such, although they are missionary in nature, and they are related to missionary enterprises. Thus the Gospel Recordings Incorporated makes gospel recordings in scores of languages and sends these "platters" on request to missionaries of all faiths and denominations all over the world. While it is not a missionary agency as such, it is an arm of missions and a missionary to the missionaries. The Inter-Varsity Christian Fellowship, like the Student Volunteer Movement for Christian Missions, Inc., is a recruiting agency for foreign and home missions. In the case of the Inter-Varsity Fellowship, the special department within the fellowship is known as the Foreign Missions Fellowship. It is not a missionary agency but recruits missionaries who eventually filter into denominational and faith boards and societies as missionaries.

3. *Boards for educational institutions in foreign lands.* In this group are agencies such as Yale-in-China Association, Inc., the American University at Cairo, the Vellore Christian Medical College Board, Inc., and the Japan International Christian University Foundation, Inc. Most, if not all, of the agencies dealing with educational institutions are related to the Department of Foreign Missions of the National Council of the Churches of Christ in the United States of America.

Still other agencies exist for missionary endeavor which are neither sending boards nor societies nor do they fit into the categories which have just been described. These other agencies are associations of missionary boards and societies which have banded together for mutual help and aid. By far the strongest numerically and financially is the Foreign Missions Division of the National Council of Churches. With a denominational constituency which includes most of the major Protestant and Greek Orthodox groups in America, this association represents sending boards and societies with a home backing of more than thirty millions of Americans and financial income in excess of sixty millions of dollars (1952).

A second agency is the Evangelical Foreign Missions Association which is related to the National Association of Evangelicals in much the same way that the Department of Foreign Missions is related to the National Council of Churches. Approximately half as many sending agencies are related to the Evangelical Foreign Missions Association as are in the National Council grouping (63–36). The income for 1952 was approximately ten millions of dollars.

A third agency is the Interdenominational Foreign Mission Association of North America. This group includes in its membership most of the well-known faith or non-denominational missionary boards and societies. It does not include in its membership any denomination nor does it number in its constituency any mission board that is related directly or indirectly to a particular denomination. Among the members of this group are the Africa Inland Mission, the Sudan Interior Mission, the Evangelical Alliance Mission, the Wycliffe Bible Translators and others. More than five thousand missionaries are related to the member boards although twenty to twenty-five per cent of these are from outside North America. For 1952 the various agencies collected more than ten millions of dollars.

A fourth association of missionary agencies is the Associated Missions of the International Council of Christian Churches which has an affiliate for North America under the name of the Foreign Missions Committee of the American Council of Christian Churches. Far and away the largest segment of the American Council group is the General Association of Regular Baptist Churches whose missionary giving and missionary personnel make up seventy-five per cent or more of the missionary activity of the entire association.

More than two score denominational and non-denominational missionary agencies are not represented by any of the

four associations just described. Among the largest non-denominational agencies not represented by any association nor
having membership in any association are the New Tribes
Mission and the International Child Evangelism Fellowship.
Among the denominations, the largest sending agencies include the Southern Baptist Convention with less than a thousand missionaries and an income of better than seven millions
of dollars in 1952, and the Christian and Missionary Alliance
with almost seven hundred missionaries and an income in
excess of two and one-half millions of dollars.

A vast proportion of all missionary work is handled by the
agencies and associations which have been listed this far, but
other forces and groups operate on foreign fields in a missionary context—groups we need not consider closely for these
purposes. Thus there are many missionary projects sponsored
and supported by churches on the field. They do not concern
this discussion. Non-professional missionaries abound. They
may be physicians, dentists, engineers, agriculturists, businessmen or they may labor in scores of other occupations. These
people do missionary work incidental to their professions, but
they seek to be physicians, lawyers, etc. on a foreign field so
that, while they are not professional missionaries, they are able
to do missionary work in places and under circumstances
where professional missionaries could not operate. Beyond
these are the independent missionaries—those who are unrelated to any definite sending agency and who are supported
financially by friends or by a local church or several churches.
Some indeed are really independent missionaries who labor
without any visible means of support and who depend upon
God for the supply of their material needs.

Inasmuch as the vast majority of missionaries are sent out
either by denominational or non-denominational boards and
societies, the discussion will be limited to the composition of
these boards and their general operating practices, and examples will be selected at random from both types. In passing,

mention should be made that American missionary practice is somewhat different from the European. In Europe most foreign missionary work is carried on through societies which are independent of the denominations. In America the greater proportion of missionary work is carried on through denominational boards rather than through non-denominationally controlled societies. The American practice has undoubtedly led to competition between denominations and resulted in the definite perpetuation of their distinctives which in turn has promoted division. The non-denominational societies in America have been interdenominational so far as their missionaries are concerned and consequently have been troubled less with division through the propagation of peculiar distinctives. In operating policies these boards have often tended to employ immersion as the only form of baptism and have not practiced pedo-baptism.

The American Baptist Convention provides a splendid example of how most of the denominational mission boards operate. Their missionaries, so far as their foreign missions program operates, do not represent a particular church or group of churches. They represent the whole denomination and through this have a constituency which embraces the membership of the churches affiliated with the Convention. They are not missionaries of this or that church whatever the source of their support, but they are American Baptist missionaries representing the entire group. It is a group enterprise having a theological viewpoint and those distinctives which mark it off from other denominations. The idea behind American Baptist missions is that in unity there is strength and that together a large number of people can do better what they might never be able to do through individual churches working alone or what they would do less satisfactorily and more expensively.

Among the American Baptists, many hold that their missionaries represent not only Baptists or the American Baptist

Convention but also the church of Christ as it embraces other denominational groups. Others would not so hold and indeed would vociferously deny that such is true or could be true. Increasingly, elements within the American Baptist Convention are less prone to emphasize their Baptist distinctives with many individuals and churches adhering to open communion, open membership, and with less interest in the specific mode of baptism. Some churches and ministers have affiliated themselves with other non-Baptist church groups as a demonstration of the rising ecumenical spirit and consciousness. All of this marks the trend away from Baptist endeavors exclusively and points the way toward unity, cooperation, comity, and closer relations with other Christian missionary groups.

Control of the foreign missionary program of the American Baptist Convention rests in the hands of the Convention itself through its elected delegates. Of the two sending agencies for foreign missions (The American Baptist Foreign Mission Society and the Women's American Baptist Foreign Mission Society), the general procedures for control are similar. The ABFMS is controlled by a Board of Managers which has twenty-seven members. A member may serve for a period not to exceed nine years, at the end of which time he must retire from membership on the Board for at least one year. The normal term of service is three years, most members of the Board being re-elected twice to fill out a nine-year term. The members are themselves elected at the annual meetings of the American Baptist Convention through the normal electoral channels and processes. The Convention which elects the members of the Board is theoretically democratic in the Swiss sense but is actually a representative democracy since affiliated churches may be represented according to their memberships and these delegates in turn cast their votes in a manner which actually, if not in theory, makes the process one of representative democracy.

The Board itself operates through administrative personnel

which it appoints and for which it is responsible. The Board itself is in turn responsible to the Convention. The corps of administrative secretaries are the agents of the Board and are responsible for carrying out the policies and directives of the Board. That the Board will listen to the recommendations and adopt the suggestions of the paid secretariat is, of course, to be expected inasmuch as the secretariat is supposed to be technically qualified and personally experienced in the methods, procedures, and operations of the missionary program. Among the administrative personnel will be found a general secretary, a number of foreign secretaries for specified geographical areas of the world, and a candidate secretary.

Financially, the Board of Managers is responsible for the expenditures of monies allotted to it, but it is not responsible for the raising of the money. In the earlier history of the Northern Baptists the individual societies operated independently of each other. Each society raised its own money and presented its own cause to the constituency. This was costly and at times meant that some areas of Baptist life received far more support than others. Whichever organization had the best propaganda department and was able to sell its cause to the members of the constituency got the money. Today the different societies do not compete with each other for the dollars of the membership. Through the Unified Budget, each dollar of benevolent giving is divided according to a pre-arranged plan. In this way the foreign missionary agencies may anticipate that a proportion of each dollar will belong to them as may the State Conventions, the Board of Education, the Home Mission Societies, and others. The mission boards are not permitted to make general or specific appeals for their own needs. The Council of Finance and Promotion now known as the Council on Missionary Cooperation makes all of the appeals for funds for the support of the program.

Each year the ABFMS submits its prospective budgetary needs to the Budget Research Committee of the Convention which works in close cooperation with the Finance Committee and which coordinates and consolidates the whole budget situation for the entire constituency. Through the General Council which holds *de jure* power for the Convention between sessions comes the annual request at the May meetings for adoption of the yearly budget for the total work of the Convention. When the Research Committee computes the budget needs of the boards, they take into account the endowments each board possesses and the income which can be anticipated from the endowments.

Some critics have attacked denominational missionary work charging that it is not really a faith work, because budgets are set up and programs agreed upon in advance. It should be remembered that when the annual budget of the Convention has been approved at the May meetings, the money has not been raised. To the extent that income from endowments do not meet the financial needs of the program, to that extent that denomination or any denomination must have faith to believe that its own constituency will back up the program and supply the required monies before the end of the financial year. If the money does not come in, the program must be curtailed to the extent that the money is not raised. Or they must go into debt. Rarely is the budget heavily oversubscribed during a given year, and oftentimes the actual giving is below the amount adopted by the Convention as its operating budget.

The raising of the budget each year is the business of the Convention executives. The State Conventions and the City Mission Societies have percentages assigned to them or what might be called quotas that they are expected to meet. In turn the executives of the State Conventions and City Mission Societies look to the local churches to help meet these quotas through the benevolent giving of the members of the local churches. From time to time, special pleas are sent out when the income does not keep pace with the commitments. In one sense the raising of this money differs from what later shall be

seen to be one of the peculiar tenets of a few non-denominational mission agencies. The American Baptist Convention
makes known its needs to the constituency and asks them to
help supply those needs. A few non-denominational boards refuse to make their needs known except in prayer to God, and
they never ask anyone to contribute to their work. All denominational boards and most of the faith or non-denominational boards in one way or another make their needs known
and invite people to participate in meeting them.

That portion of the Unified Budget which is assigned for
the ABFMS comes under the supervision and control of the
Board of Managers of the society. This Board approves expenditures, accepts candidates, and conducts the general business of this foreign missionary arm of the Convention. The
Board can issue directives to the paid secretaries, reverse their
decisions, or in any way conduct the business of the Board as
they feel led of God to do. The Board itself is responsible to
the Convention at large which is the final body through whom
the Board derives its existence and its right to function. The
Board is not independent and it is not self-perpetuating. The
Board cannot even be continuous in years of service since no
member serves more than nine years without interruption.
The secretaries may be and usually are permanent salaried
employees of the Board but they may be removed from their
offices at the discretion of the Board.

The Presbyterian Church, U.S.A. operates similarly to the
American Baptist Convention. This church has only one Foreign Mission Board that is a sending agency. All foreign missionary operations are carried on through this one board. It is
the creature of the General Assembly of the Presbyterian
Church to which it is responsible and through whose machinery the members of the Foreign Mission Board are selected.

The General Assembly of the Presbyterian Church, U.S.A.
is a representative body. Delegates from the various Presby-

teries are sent by their respective Presbyteries to the annual meetings of the General Assembly. Included among the delegates are both ministers and elders, but there are no lay delegates as in the case of the American Baptist Convention meetings at which there will be ministers, deacons, and laymen. The delegates to the General Assembly elect each year the new members of the Foreign Mission Board in place of those whose terms of office have expired on a rotating basis similar to the American Baptist Convention.

The members of the Board of Foreign Missions are the responsible agents for the control and operation of the missionary program during their terms of office. In turn they are responsible to the General Assembly from whom they derive their powers. A paid corps of secretaries serve the Foreign Mission Board in permanent capacities, although they may be removed when the occasion arises. These secretaries range in order much the same as those of the American Baptist Convention and have duties and responsibilities of a similar nature.

The relation of the membership of the Presbyterian Church to the Board of Foreign Missions is one step removed from that of the American Convention. Whereas a local church in the ABC sends its delegates directly from the church to the annual Convention meetings and there elects the mission board members directly, the same is not true of the Presbyterian Church. The individual Presbytery, whose membership is made up of ministers (who incidentally do not have membership in any local church but in the Presbytery of which the church is a part) and ordained elders (members of the church session), sends its elected delegates to the meetings of the General Assembly. Thus the General Assembly is constituted of members who are one step further removed from the membership of the local church and its elective powers.

The administrative expenses of the General Assembly are raised through a head tax imposed on the churches. Missionary monies on the other hand come under the heading of benevolences and as such are part of the budget adopted by the General Assembly at its annual meetings. Again the element of faith is distinctly present because the budget is voted on the assumption that the membership of the church will give sufficient funds to underwrite the budget. A prescribed portion of the budget is designated for foreign missions, and the General Assembly goes on record before receipt of the funds as to the amount they trust God will move the hearts of their people to provide. Then follows the raising of the monies voted, and this is carried on through the usual church channels and by means of the promotional aids at the command of the leadership. The Foreign Mission Board does not itself appeal to the churches nor promote its own program at the expense of other church agencies and boards.

Often the foreign missionary appeal for financial aid is the strategic appeal which carries the other segments of the average denominational budget. Across the years this means that the unifying of denominational budgets into a "package deal" has done harm to foreign missions. The fact that the average denominational mission board is not permitted to appeal directly to the constituency nor is it permitted to retain funds beyond the normal proportion of the budget allotted to it has slowed down the foreign missionary impact. Contrariwise it has helped projects and agencies which do not have the same intrinsic appeal to the affections of church members, but for which there is genuine need for financial support not likely to be secured on the basis of their own appeal. The Department of Foreign Missions of the National Council of Churches has taken cognizance of this, and its reporting committee has boldly voiced strong opposition to and has been highly critical of this type of policy long in effect in the denominations. This committee has spoken openly in anticipation of the day when the mission boards will be unshackled and permitted once again to go directly to the man in the pew with their own appeals and reap whatever benefits may accrue to them on the basis of the intrinsic worth of their appeals.

Each situation has its own strong and weak points. It is true that the foreign mission appeal may well carry the financial program of the whole denomination. It is surely true that to some extent denominational missions suffer from that involved relationship. This weakness does not inhere in the structure of non-denominational missions. These boards have no other agencies requiring part of their total support. They operate no home mission boards, no Christian institutions, and they have no publication societies for the home churches. Their appeals are slanted directly toward foreign missions, and they can assure every donor that every penny contributed will go for that one purpose. It is also true that while non-denominational boards do not suffer from the same difficulty to which the average denominational board is subjected, yet the denominational boards have distinct advantages not possessed by non-denominational boards. The denominational boards have a defined constituency; fixed, not fluid bodies of followers. The non-denominational boards do not have as cohesive a constituency, and their appeals cannot be made as directly to a given body of people. But they do not suffer from the limitations imposed by a total denominational budget of which the foreign missions budget is but a segment.

The non-denominational boards differ from denominational ones in important details which will become obvious as the structure of these boards is now outlined. First and foremost among the differences is the control of the agency itself. Being unrelated to a denomination its control is vested in a few individuals whose selection and election are not the result of representative government. The faith boards are controlled by a board of trustees or one which has identical functions although called by some other name. This governing board is self-perpetuating and is responsible only to itself, not to any larger constituency which has power to govern it. When members of the board need to be replaced, the board itself chooses those members who shall serve on it. In this sense the faith boards resemble the unrelated educational institutions in American life whose governing boards are again self-perpetuating and responsible only to themselves in a direct way. By no means should it be assumed that a self-perpetuating trustee board means complete absence of control by outside forces. In the educational institutions the alumni exercise considerable control in an indirect fashion. The student body and those who are expected to become students bear weight and exercise an influence. In the faith mission boards the people who support those boards carry real weight, the chief expression of which is financial. Ordinarily these boards attract a constituency which is extremely sensitive and which thinks in a highly conservative theological framework. Not held together by the binding ties of a church (it is not meant that they have no church affiliations) and not susceptible to the influences of a pastor whose interest lies in his denomination, it takes much less to cause them to withhold their support as an expression of disapproval. Purported theological vagaries, whispered innuendoes, and talk of "compromise" all make it essential for the faith boards to be aware of their constituencies and to walk carefully in order that they might not alienate those from whom their support comes.

From the histories of non-denominational faith mission boards, one can deduce the obvious conclusion that most of them were founded by an individual with a vision for the lost and unreached. The impelling nature of the vision captivated the imagination of others, and gradually the number of missionaries increased and in proportion the financial income. Thus the China Inland Mission was the result of the vision of Hudson Taylor; the Sudan Interior Mission with more than a thousand missionaries was the result of the vision of Bingham; the Latin American Mission was the result of the vision of Strachan; the Worldwide Evangelization Crusade was the result of the vision of Studd. Begun as small movements, they have grown to sizable proportions until today the faith boards in North America send out around four missionaries for every six or seven sent out by all of the denominations affiliated with the Department of Foreign Missions of the National Council of Churches with their vastly superior constituency numerically and their far greater financial resources.

A second major difference which characterizes the faith from the denominational boards lies in the differences of their missionary personnel. They welcome candidates from all of the evangelical denominations without prejudice. Thus Presbyterians, Methodists, Baptists, Congregationalists and scores of other denominations are represented among the overseas forces of these mission boards. The barriers which have traditionally separated denominations have not been barriers for the faith boards. Their major barrier has always been their strict adherence to a rigidly conservative theological position in which they have emphasized the virgin birth, the vicarious atonement of Christ, the physical resurrection from the dead, the reality of hell as well as of heaven, the real deity of Jesus Christ and the inerrancy of the Scriptures.

Administratively, faith boards operate under a plan whereby they have a home director who is the chief administrator at the home base and whose labors include the raising of money, the choice and selection of personnel, and other activities pertinent to the base. In addition they usually employ a field director who has full authority and responsibility for operations on the field. Since many of these boards operate in one general geographical area, they ordinarily have but one field director. Where they operate in geographically separated areas, there would be a corresponding division of labor and administration for different areas. The administrators are responsible to the board of directors and most frequently are members of the self-perpetuating boards.

A third major difference lies in the realm of financial policies and the raising of money. Three varying philosophies underlie the operations of the faith missions and in each instance those who put into practice these philosophies believe them to be biblically founded and in accordance with the divine plan of God.

The first of the financial philosophies is that practiced by agencies like the Overseas Missionary Fellowship (formerly the China Inland Mission), and the Worldwide Evangelization Crusade. These agencies have consistently made it a practice not to ask for funds from anyone. They do not even make their financial needs known to people outside the family. They speak to God about their needs and look to Him for the supply of them. This approach has been called "faith missions" to distinguish the approach from those who make requests of men for support. The people who practice this faith policy do not imply by their practice that those who do not follow their example are less spiritual or that they are not on biblical ground. In this form of endeavor the missionaries share and share alike. Times of testing come, and the financial side of their missionary work is often one of great sacrifice as compared to missionaries under denominational boards.

A second type of faith board is that one which will make its needs known to men asking them to pray but not asking them for money. If people know of the need and are moved to give on the basis of that knowledge, the board is satisfied that God has worked providentially in the hearts of men to supply the need. But no one is solicited nor is anyone asked directly for funds. Whether or not the request to pray for the supply of financial need is not in itself a request for financial aid is a moot question. Some Christians conclude that people cannot pray without doing what they are able to do by way of giving at the same time.

The third type of faith board varies hardly at all from the typical denominational board. This type makes its needs known and invites people to participate in meeting the need.

Missionaries are not sent out to the field without their support being guaranteed or underwritten one way or another. Individuals or churches may take over the support of a missionary, but the missionary does not sail for the field unless and until his passage, equipment, and monthly stipend is in hand. The element of faith enters into the picture when a candidate is accepted by the board. His acceptance is conditioned by the conviction that God will supply the need, and when the need is supplied the board deems it conclusive evidence that the finger of God has moved in approval of the sending forth of the candidate. Both the candidate and the board pray to this end. The boards which use this third policy do not hold rigidly to it. The funds which are received are dispersed on a share and share alike basis.

The Bible does not seem to specify any one type as the only biblical method for the support of missionaries. The Holy Spirit does lead different people in different ways, and since none of these methods is condemned and each finds some rationale for its use from the Scriptures themselves, care should be exercised that spiritual pride does not cause anyone to look down on methods used by equally spiritual and Holy Spirit led children of God. Christians should be reminded constantly that God works in a thousand ways to accomplish His purposes. In a spirit of penitence, humility, and with the knowledge that they are sinful creatures whose best intentions are marred by the marks of corrupt natures, they should give to others the benefit of the doubt. They may not be as wrong as some people would like to think.

Financially the faith boards suffer from a chronic problem that does not trouble denominational boards. Donors can be obtained more readily for missionaries who go to the field. But few people understand the complexity of missionary administration, and they fail to realize that it costs money to operate a board on the home front. Often the workers are better provided for on the foreign field than are the workers on the home field. Overhead for missionary operations may run from ten to fifteen per cent of the total budget and contrary to uninformed opinion it is not wasted money, and it is absolutely essential to the orderly progress of missionary endeavor. Donors who perceive this dilemma and who direct their contributions for publicity, office operations, etc. are scarce. Denominational missions through their budgetary methods are able to control what faith boards can do little about.

In the three types of faith board a common policy of sharing characterizes them. Thus month by month as the monies come in, the missionaries share proportionately so that some do not have more than others or some suffer severe hardships while their colleagues are living off the fat of the land in comparison to those who have little. A recurring tragedy is the cessation of support for a missionary or a family due to death, disruption in a local church, or for some other reason. This tends to leave a missionary stranded until other sources of income become available. In denominational missions this is not apt to happen for special appeals to a large constituency can easily overcome the defection of a small section of the membership.

All mission boards, non-denominational and denominational, screen their candidates carefully according to their own standards. They do not wish to appoint any individual who might prove to be an unsatisfactory missionary or who might have to be returned to the homeland. Naturally mistakes are made and some prove unfit. But the cost is high and no one is able to compute the psychological consequences in the lives of the unfortunate. By the same token prospective missionaries should screen mission boards in order to find that board or agency which will guarantee to them the maximum opportunity for successful service in terms of their convictions, backgrounds, associates, and general satisfaction with the policies of the board.

For those who are geared into the life of a denomination this is not nearly so difficult. Normally they filter into the missionary agencies of their own groups and find a happy outlet for their energies and endeavors. It is even possible for candidates to cross over the line from one denomination to another without too much difficulty. Usually the individual does this for a good reason, and he finds fulfillment for his missionary ambitions in the new denominational attachment.

For those who are not geared to a denomination, or whose interests lie in a field in which their own denomination has no opportunities for service, the question becomes a live one. Any one of six or seven agencies might be available, and the candidate should investigate the possible mission boards carefully. He will probably find that he is not in agreement with the policies of some of them, and he should seek out that board under which he thinks he will be able to work most cooperatively and render the most effective service for the cause of Christ. Boards do differ, and just because a board is making Christ known to those who know Him not does not mean the board is perfect or that any and all candidates would be happy in service under that board.

Every reliable board will be happy to explain fully its principles and practices for it too wants only those candidates who will be satisfied with conditions and be able to do their best for Christ. Check before you go, and avoid in advance tragedies that do happen occasionally even where the best intentions are involved on the side of the board and the individual.

CHAPTER VI

Missionary Administration

~~~~~~

IT COSTS MONEY TO ADMINISTER A MISSIONARY ORGANIZATION. The cost varies from board to board, but ten to fifteen per cent of the annual expenditures can be estimated as the cost of administration. The job of the administrator and his colleagues is not so thrilling or exotic as that of the intrepid pioneer, the Bible translator, the itinerant evangelist. It does not command the same respect of the supporters of missions who somehow feel they want their own missionary on the foreign field. Thus the question is always asked: "Is administration necessary? Why not send one hundred cents out of every dollar to the foreign field?"

Thoughtful reflection will soon prove how necessary administration is, and it will demonstrate that the cost of it is in line with the realities of the total structure of the foreign missionary enterprise. Cheap administration, financially speaking, is not always cheap. Sometimes it can be most expensive. The person who is paid the least salary may produce the least work. But missionary administrators are not overpaid, and since the worth of any individual agency is often a reflection of what the administration is like, there is no substitute for a good one. But that does not answer the question whether administration is necessary in the first place.

In foreign missionary work there are two bases for the endeavor. One is the home base and the other the field base. The one without the other is impotent. A home base without field

116

operations is a delusion; it is a racket, not a mission board. This, of course, would not apply to those agencies whose chief business is to support missionaries and whose operations are legitimate although they do not act as sending agencies themselves. To engage in field operations in which a number of missionaries are deployed is also impossible without a home base of some kind. No extensive missionary work is being carried on today on any mission field or fields which does not have a home base as well as field operations.

The New Testament warrants the conclusion that missionary administration is biblical and that it is not just a manmade scheme introduced as a superfluous appendage to foreign missionary work. The precept of the Scriptures, "Let all things be done decently and in order" (I Cor. 14:40), pertains to missions as well as to all other phases of the Christian life and witness. Those who oppose organization do so, not on a biblical basis, but on the basis of a false exegesis which will not stand the test of scholarship. It may be true that too much organization may exist in some cases and that the existence of organization may lead to excess, centralization, hierarchy, and a monolithic totalitarianism if it goes unchecked. The abuse of a principle does not invalidate the principle, and to carry organization beyond the limits of biblical warrant does not mean that there should be no organization at all.

Those who believe that a church should have no formal organization or officers are on shaky biblical ground. In the Old Testament, Jethro, the father-in-law of Moses, gave that leader sound advice about the division of labor for an overworked servant of God. In the sixth chapter of Acts there is the charter for the office of Deacon. The leaders of the young but expanding church desperately needed help, and the office of Deacon was a divine creation to give the church form and structure for its needful operations. Acts 8 records how the Apostles sent Peter and John to Samaria when the work of Philip was so successful that reinforcements were needed. Surely this implies administration, division of labor, and a sending power.

When Paul and Barnabus began their first missionary journey sent by the Holy Spirit, they were also sent by the church. Prayer was made, hands were laid on them, and the two missionaries were sent away. The church was the sending agency, and authority as well as organization can be seen incipiently in the process. The church was led by the Holy Spirit, and this principle should never be overlooked either. All missionary administration should be Spirit-led and directed. Despite this, at a later date, Paul and Barnabus disagreed, and their quarrel led to separation, each one going his own way. While one cannot conclude that a mistake was made in sending them forth to work as co-laborers, yet the circumstances clearly show that conflicts, frictions, and personality clashes beset missionary labors from the apostolic age onward.

Acts 15 discusses the first apostolic missionary council. A field problem of great import arose. The matter was so vital theologically that no decision was made on the field. It was referred to the home base for clarification. From this we learn that some problems are not susceptible to solution on the field —they must be referred to the highest echelons of the leadership for mature consideration, discussion, and finally for a policy making decision which will govern all fields and all work. No one can question either the ability or the decision of Paul with reference to the matter at hand. Both he and Barnabus were correct in their thinking, but the final decision came at the highest levels. Had there been no high levels to appeal to, no administration at the home base, Paul and Barnabus might conceivably have lost the struggle, and the early church might have been corrupted and polluted in its bloodstream from the very beginning. Law might have triumphed over grace, and men might have been brought into the same bondage from which they hoped to be delivered. Who can gainsay the fact that the same Paul who brought the matter of circumcision to the brethren at the home base in Jerusalem later wrote to churches he himself had founded and argued triumphantly and gloriously again and again against the same error which was settled at the Jerusalem Council.

The decision of the Council was no unilateral papal decree. It was the concensus of the brethren arrived at after mature thought, and under the guidance of the Holy Spirit. This missionary council alone is adequate New Testament warrant for missionary administration.

Missionary recruits should not hesitate to inquire into the management and operation of the mission board under which they hope to serve. They are entitled to know whether it is properly organized and rightly administered. Just because a board professes to be doing Christian work does not mean that sinful practices and mean deceits cannot predominate. Boards can make promises they never intend to keep and, once a candidate is on foreign shores, advantage can be taken of him in ways that are sub-Christian if not actually dishonest. One of the best assurances for a long and fruitful ministry is appointment by a board that is absolutely honest.

Arguing *ad hominem* a good case can be made out for organization and administration from the practical side. The alternative to missionary operations with organization and administration is independent missions. The weaknesses of independent missions are so numerous and the disadvantages so grave that it is difficult to understand why people might wish to go out as independent missionaries.

On the home end the independent missionary is expensive and inefficient. Somewhere he must have a constituency which will support his work. Unless he is sending his own prayer letters directly to his supporters from the field, he will lose touch with those on whom he counts for help. If he keeps in contact with them, he will be taking out valuable time that should be spent in missionary work on the field. If he gets someone at home to handle this work for him, then he is already falling into the pit of administrative devices which he condemns. He must come home to promote his cause, and this in itself is prone to increase his expenses and decrease his efficiency. His backers are ordinarily men and women of inexperience. They do not know what to do or how to do it. Passport problems, the transfer of currency, travel arrangements, and relations with foreign governments are perplexing administrative problems which require skill, patience, and exhaustive knowledge and know-how.

The independent missionary must come home on furlough. His work is left to itself. Illnesses take their toll, and he has no one to replace him or to fill in for him in that event. When he leaves the field permanently, rarely does anyone else take over his work. It is not perpetuated and loses ground or is snuffed out. The independent missionary has a difficult time learning the language. He has no school for language which he can attend unless he tries to insinuate himself into the language school which the administration of some board has set up. If no language school is open to him, he goes among the people, picks up the language haphazardly and many times fails to pick it up well enough to enjoy a truly profitable ministry among the nationals.

The mission station which has more than two people in its membership can expect some friction because of temperament and personality differences. But the independent missionary who has no colleagues and who is a station unto himself experiences the opposite reaction. He needs fellowship for it is better to face things with others than to face them alone. His own personal welfare is jeopardized and the possibilities for breakdown increased. He has no schools for his children unless he resorts to mission schools operated by boards which have administration or if he trains them at home. In the former case he again admits the need for cooperative effort; in the latter valuable time is taken from his work of evangelizing the nationals.

Independent work adds to the multiplication of sects. This

in turn is disastrous because of the consequences in the minds of the people being reached. They observe the lack of unity, and they see competing individuals and groups. They are at a loss to understand the ramifications or to know the historical background out of which these things come. The testimony before the heathen hurts rather than helps the cause, and on an over-all basis one must ask the question whether the work of Christ has truly been advanced by most independent work. Rarely if ever is there any real understanding or cooperative effort between the independent missionary and the boards which labor in the same geographical area.

When the record is examined, two major reasons stand out why people become independent missionaries. One reason is that they have been rejected by organized mission boards and refuse to take this as an indication of the will of God. Consequently, they persist in their determination to go in spite of the setbacks. A second major reason is a constitutional independency which expresses itself in solitary action. Independents may be termed the "lone wolves" of missionary endeavor. Since the Christian faith knows nothing of solitary Christianity it may be supposed that in most cases the independent missionary represents a deviation from the norm.

We have seen that independent missionary effort is costly, not nearly so efficient, and generally rejected by the great majority of sincere Bible believers who have equal facility for understanding the Word and the will of God. It becomes apparent that some form of cooperative effort, properly organized and some boards rightly administered are actually the normal means for the evangelization of the world at least for the present. Having established this from a consideration of the Bible basis for administration and by an evaluation of the independent versus the organizational missionary, it remains to discuss the aspects of administration and the involvements and difficulties. Few lay people comprehend how vast is the operation of a far flung mission board and how intricate and detailed the planning and the execution of the task by any board.

Missions is big business financially. Huge sums of money are spent each year in the propagation of the gospel. The spending of huge sums of money does not indicate that enough is being done or that the place has been reached where additional funds and missionaries are no longer needed. Large as the sums of money are the amount will have to be doubled and tripled before the surface of the total task has been scratched. It was estimated that in 1952 more than eighty million dollars were spent on foreign missions. The American Board of Commissioners for Foreign Missions had an income of almost a million and three quarters. The Methodist Church had nine and a half million dollars income. The Presbyterian Church, U.S.A. had an income of almost six million dollars. The Southern Presbyterian Church enjoyed an income of better than a million and a half dollars. The American Bible Society had an income of one and a quarter million dollars. The mission boards affiliated with the Evangelical Foreign Missions Association had an income in 1951 of almost ten million dollars. The Interdenominational Foreign Missions Association of North America reported an income of almost eleven million dollars for 1953.

Any mission board which has on its rolls two hundred or more missionaries and has an income sufficient to care for that number of missionaries is engaged in big business. The accounting for those funds is a large task. Disbursing these funds to the field, with the need for field offices and treasurers as well as home offices and financial agents, is a big job. In addition to the current operating funds of a mission board there are numerous properties which have value. These properties are frequently widely distributed. Thus, for example, the Southern Baptist Foreign Mission Board has properties in South America, India, Africa, Hawaii, Japan, and other places geographically separated by distance. Their investments in plants and properties, schools, and hospitals, must be watched over and protected. Wars, revolutions, disasters by natural causes, depreciation, riots, fire and theft can wipe out years of work and financial investments not to mention the toll of life among the members of the national churches. Then too boards across the years receive endowment funds which produce income quarterly, semi-annually or annually. These invested endowments often run into millions of dollars. They must be watched over and the portfolios pruned and adjusted according to the exigencies of the moment.

The ownership of properties overseas involves more than their purchase and upkeep. Most frequently the properties have to be constructed from the ground up. The mission board becomes an employer. For this construction work the board must employ native labor. In turn this involves labor relations, architectural problems, construction supervision, salary payments and a host of incidental details. More and more the erection of properties is being subjected to governmental restrictions. The very act of buying land is now a difficult thing in many countries. Securing building sites is not as simple as it used to be. Where foreign lands are under the aegis of the white man in the guise of colonial possessions, restrictions sometimes are more severe and the purchase of property more difficult. Not all European powers welcome missionary endeavor among their colonial peoples. A hundred years of experience has shown that missionary work causes unrest and eventuates in tensions and struggles. Being a revolutionary faith with vast implications in the religious, social, economic, and political life of a people, such consequences are inevitable. The white missionary brings a gospel which promotes equality and tears down barriers of separation. He brings, inadvertently or not, western culture with its democratic ideology, and its modern machinery. The native beholds and desires the "things" that the white man has and when he reaches out for them a cultural, social, economic, and political revolution is bound to come.

The missionary is bound to his property once he has it. Taxes, repairs, fire, war, and the thousand other dangers must be faced and overcome. The investment increases and as the cost of construction rises with changing economic standards the replacement costs rise and boards are faced with new problems and difficulties. When speaking of mission property, nothing has been said of the investments spent on colleges, hospitals, and orphanages which call for larger sums of money and create grave problems in times of revolution when governments are unfriendly and expropriation of these properties take place.

The ownership of property and the financial operation of mission boards are complicated facets of the total picture. But these are problems which may be termed secular in nature. They exist before missionaries begin their labors and still exist when missionaries are no longer in the country. Prior to evangelism, time, wisdom and energy must be spent on them even though they may appear to be superfluous and time consuming and wasteful. They are the sinews of war and without them missionaries cannot do their work. Administrative workers get no glory, face no physical dangers, and can tell no thrilling stories of conversions and transformed lives. They fight no battles, but without their work no battles could be fought. Therefore, let no man despise those whose lives have been dedicated to the task of making possible the work of the field missionaries themselves. The coach on the football team never plays himself and to his heroes goes the glory. But there has never been a good team without a good coach. And a good mission board will have a good administration.

Missionary administration deals with personnel. And personnel management constitutes one of the largest duties of a board. Its ramifications reach into unexpected areas and touch on human lives in every phase and department.

The board deals with personnel before they get to a foreign field. Denominational boards not infrequently are in direct or indirect contact with prospective missionary candidates through college and seminary days. Candidates must be selected from among the applicants and the unfit weeded out. Missionary administrators must inquire into each life, searching for the hidden as well as for the easily seen segments of a life. They must weigh and evaluate the individual and make that crucial decision either to accept or to reject him. The administrators must work with missionaries, read their reports, counsel them in their problems, provide for their health, vacations, furloughs, children, compounds, travel, passports, and even the arrangements for the birth of their children.

When a candidate is appointed, the hard work for the administrator begins. Now the field for service must be determined and the candidate prepared for departure to the field. He must be oriented somewhat to the field before leaving. His equipment must be gathered. Here the board knows from past experience what a man ought to take with him. He must be prepared for a four-, five-, or six-year period and must take with him enough equipment for that length of time. The board provides the money for the purchases, probably has its own purchasing agency or one through which, by cooperation, it can secure items for export. Everything must be crated, and delivered to the boat. Licenses for export must be obtained, bills of lading cleared, etc. The board knows that trans-shipments may have to be made two, three, or four times before the consignments reach their ultimate destination. Often they do reach their destination on the backs of sweating nationals who file through the underbrush to an outstation.

It is easier to ship goods than to ship men. Every board must secure passports for human personnel, and these are harder to get than licenses to export material goods. Rarely does an individual mission board maintain its own Washington office for the securing of passports. Cooperative agencies usually represent a number of boards, and because of their experience they are able to do a better job than individual mission boards could hope to do. Perhaps one example will suffice to illustrate the point. The National Association of Evangelicals has a missionary arm known as the Evangelical Foreign Missions Association. In the interests of its constituency the N.A.E. maintains an office in Washington, D.C. This office facilitates the issuance of passports and handles the foreign affairs and foreign relations problems of the member boards in the nation's capitol. In addition the N.A.E. operates a purchasing agency in the City of New York out of which office the boards are able to secure supplies and equipment for departing missionaries. The member boards could not individually provide equal facilities nor could they perform these functions as effectively as the N.A.E. The prohibitive cost would deter individual agencies from maintaining an office which a group project makes worthwhile.

Missionary administrators must concern themselves continuously with changing governments, politics, and interruptions of missionaries seeking to get to the field. The State Department of the United States is sometimes a bottleneck when it comes to securing passports. To obtain visas from foreign governments is also exceedingly difficult if not impossible in some cases. Of late, missionaries to India have had trouble getting back into that country, and new missionaries rarely are able to secure visas. A few of the South American countries dominated by the Roman Church have kept out Protestant missionaries consistently. In some instances missionaries have been able to secure passports only because they have gone to do linguistic and translation work rather than direct missionary work. But all of this is a major problem for the missionary administrator.

The conduct of overseas work brings administrative problems in relation to missionaries and their families. The first of these problems deals with the missionaries and their health.

In order to protect them, vacations have to be arranged for part of each year and regular furloughs must be scheduled. This is complicated by the need to replace furloughed missionaries and to provide coverage during vacation periods. Health itself enters the picture because the missionaries fall heir to the ills that beset the nationals of the countries in which they labor. Malaria, dysentery, black water fever, and scores of endemic and epidemic diseases which plague the Oriental and African world also plague the missionaries. Excessive humidity and heat which are dangerous for the white man help to render impotent missionaries who seek to bring Christ to the nations.

Children are another problem in personnel relations once the candidate gets to the field. Each child means an increase in the amount of money needed to support the family. This includes the annual cost of living plus travel, furlough costs, health protection, and education. In certain places children actually are a handicap to the work; in others they are an asset and advantage—but in either situation they create problems which must be handled. Boards do provide educational facilities overseas when this is feasible. The educational facilities may possibly reach through high school although they often do not go this far. For collegiate work the missionaries' children come home to the United States. Cooperative high school work often is located away from the homes of the missionaries and many children are gathered in them from various localities. This works a hardship on the children and on the missionaries who are forced to separate themselves from their children at a relatively early age.

When any mission board tries to provide educational facilities abroad, those facilities cost money both directly and indirectly. Buildings must be erected and personnel selected and sent out as missionaries—missionaries who teach the children of missionaries but still missionaries who may or may not do much actual missionary work among the nationals of the country where the school is located. Boards do not go into educational work because they want to do so, but sheer necessity forces them to provide this ancillary activity which arises because married couples engage in missionary endeavor. New mission boards which spring up with a passion for reaching the unreached and for getting the gospel out in order to complete the Great Commission usually start by declaiming against anything except evangelistic missionary work. Experience quickly changes that attitude for the harsh realities of life force even mission boards to do things which they did not expect to do when first they commenced their labors.

If it be true that the children of missionaries require educational opportunities, it is true that the children of the native Christians must also be trained to read, write, and have the gospel brought to them. As soon as men are won to Christ a Christian community comes into being, and this community of necessity includes the children of the converts. Many mission boards never expect to engage in educational work outside of that for their own missionaries' children. But again stern necessity has overruled good impulses, and sooner or later boards find themselves in a position where they must educate their nationals' children. The younger the board the less need there is for this, but the older the boards become the greater is their Christian community and the more they are forced into supplying educational facilities with all that it implies. Obviously the boards can hope for the day when they will no longer be needed, when the national church will take over the responsibility for providing educational training for their own children and will do it under national auspices with national teachers, national money, and national direction.

Children cannot be divorced from the problems which arise in relationship to their own mothers. The wife of the missionary is herself a missionary. The increase of her family is bound to cut into her missionary life. Assuming the existence and use of national help in the upbringing so that the mother need not wash, iron, or cook, the very fact that there is a child does place limitations on the missionary usefulness of the mother. On the other hand when missionary couples do not have children the nationals think it strange, and they are prone to misunderstand, believing that there is something wrong with the missionaries. Children often provide a springboard into the hearts of people and so have a definite place in the total scheme of missions even though their presence complicates life.

After long years of useful service—if they live to a retirement age—missionaries are superannuated. Provision for superannuated missionaries is a responsibility which devolves on every mission board and thus on its administration. How this is handled depends on the board itself. Denominational mission boards generally work through their own denominational pension system. Thus the Presbyterian church has a pension system in which missionaries are participants by the payment of retirement monies into that system across the years. The American Baptist Convention has its ministers and missionaries retirement plan. The new Conservative Baptist Foreign Mission Society has a pension plan in which they employ the services of the Presbyterian Ministers Fund, the oldest ministerial life insurance and annuity company in the United States. The non-denominational or faith boards operate in one of two categories. Either they secure pension policies through insurance channels or they continue their retired missionaries on the regular missionary stipend until death discharges their responsibility. This, of course, means that the support of retired missionaries comes out of current funds. Whether it is more profitable to do it this way or through the setting aside of yearly amounts for retirement goals is a moot question. If the missionaries survive retirement for a few short years, it would undoubtedly be profitable; if not then it might be more expensive. But statistical data has not been gathered from which any reliable conclusion can be drawn.

Missionary administration must include international banking operations. Since eighty-five per cent or more of the collected funds of the average sending agency is disbursed abroad and since millions of dollars are sent overseas each year the banking operations connected with the transfer of these funds is a large job. In the days when China was an open door for missionary activity, many of the denominational boards cooperated by having a central treasury in Shanghai to which funds from the United States were shipped for exchange and for distribution to the missionaries all over that great land. This was advantageous when the various boards were widely separated and when not too many of their missionaries were sent to China. The China Inland Mission which concentrated all of its missionary activity on that field maintained its own office and distributing agency in China.

Today, the boards which concentrate in a given geographical field like Africa generally transfer their funds from the United States to one or more of their major field offices in Africa from whence it is distributed to the individual missionaries.

The shipment of money is by cable, and the amounts are drawn on banks which do business on an international level or with banks which have connections with foreign banks. The sending of money is not the sole factor involved in this operation. The money from the United States must be exchanged for foreign currency common to the field where it is to be spent. But currency values fluctuate and in times of inflation, they fluctuate widely enough to make the exchange problem one which has in it some risk. Missionaries may gain or lose in the exchange of currency depending on the rise or fall of the international money market. How missionaries may lose purchasing power through raging inflation is illustrated in China after World War II and following the downfall of

General Chiang Kai Shek. A pound of rice may be used as a typical commodity which has value. One day a pound of rice would sell for a certain rate in Chinese money. The next day the same pound of rice would sell for twice as much money as the day before. A missionary who had exchanged his American money for Chinese money on Monday might find that the actual purchasing power of his money was cut in half within twenty-four hours after he had received the foreign currency and before he had been able to buy commodities which would retain their value. As the inflation progressed, more and more money was required to purchase a pound of rice for the money had less and less real value.

The American who remains in the United States deals in the currency of his own country. Fluctuations do occur and the changes in price for food and other commodities between 1939 and 1954 do reflect the inflationary trend in our own country. But the missionary deals with the hazards of inflation in the currency of his own country and also in the currency of the country in which he serves as a missionary. As the value of American money itself changes from day to day, the missionary may benefit or lose in foreign currency even when the foreign currency remains stable. Thus the mundane elements of life touch missions and boards and while Christ's kingdom is not of this world, yet the things of this world press closely upon God's servants, who, while they are not of the world, yet are in the world.

The administration of a mission board has a two-fold relation—the first is the relationship to the missionaries themselves and the second is the board's relationship to the constituency which supports the missionaries. These might be distinguished by saying that there are field problems and there are home problems. One of the chief home problems is the relationship of the missionary administration to the home churches.

Inasmuch as missionaries are supported by home churches

they are essential to the preservation and extension of the enterprise. One missionary on the field needs the support of many people at home. It takes about three thousand American Baptists to keep each missionary out under the ABFMS and the WABFMS. It takes about seven thousand Southern Baptists to keep one of their foreign missionaries overseas. It takes about twenty-five hundred Presbyterian U.S.A. members to keep abroad one of their missionaries. It takes less than one hundred Christian and Missionary Alliance members to keep one of their missionaries overseas. Granted that the discrepancies are wide as to the number of members needed to keep one missionary overseas, the indisputable fact does not change that it requires more people at home to hold the ropes than the number who are on foreign shores. Since the support for the missionaries comes from the homeland, the administrator must keep in close contact with the churches which underwrite the mission program.

The churches at home are strategic to missionary advance from three vantage points. From them must come the sinews of war—money. From them must also come the future missionaries. They must be recruited from among the membership of the supporting churches be it a denominational program or a faith board with independent churches behind it. From the churches must come the prayer support which sustains missions, a support of which more shall be said in another connection.

Financial support for missions does not come in by itself. The one or two notable exceptions of faith mission boards which never ask for financial help and which never make their needs known does not account for more than a fraction of the total missionary work of the churches. The vast majority of the churches use the human means at their disposal to secure, year by year, the support for their programs. Known principles, which when employed will bring results, underlie the financial aspect of the enterprise.

Boards realize that information and knowledge help to raise money. People do not ordinarily give to enterprises and projects of which they know nothing. The Spirit of God may lead men occasionally to give large sums of money to projects with which they are not acquainted, but for every gift like this there are ten thousand gifts which come because men were first acquainted with the need and the Spirit of God led them to do something concrete about that need. Keeping the constituency informed is basic to the financial underwriting of the program. Both denominational and faith boards realistically approach the problem and use modern methods to educate people regarding their activities. By regular publications of a magazine type, they lay their cases before Christians. The American Baptists have *Missions* magazine, the Presbyterians employ as a channel *Presbyterian Life* and *Outreach,* the China Inland Mission for years published *China's Millions,* now called *The Millions,* the West Indies Mission publishes *Whitened Harvest,* and the Sudan Interior Mission publishes the *Sudan Witness.*

The list of publications printed by the numerous boards goes beyond the possibility of listing, but the Missionary Research Library has published a check list of the foreign missionary agencies in the United States which it will undoubtedly recheck and revise from time to time. This invaluable work (1953) replaces and supplements earlier listings of foreign missionary agencies.

Many boards send out news sheets at regular intervals. These give up-to-date information on mission matters. Requests for prayer and for praise are included in many of them. Trends, sailing dates, new candidates, and items of general interest may be in these letters. Prayer letters from missionaries are a favorite means for keeping in touch with the constituency. These are more limited in scope for the individual missionary will supply his board with the names of friends and acquaintances who might be interested in his work. To these friends the prayer letters of individual missionaries are sent.

Another means of keeping a constituency informed and alive to missionary endeavor is to "farm out" missionaries to individual churches. By this method one or two or three churches can know that a particular missionary "belongs" to them, and for him and his family they have a financial responsibility and obligation. By "personalizing" the missionary to a given group, latent interest is stirred up and tangible results are derived. Indirectly the whole missionary cause is helped by this type of approach. The ladies in many churches enjoy preparing bandages, old clothing, Christmas boxes, and "white gifts" for their missionaries, and this is above and beyond the formal support. Churches within denominations often like to designate their money for a specific individual. This is especially true where theological differences may exist and local groups want to be sure that their money is used for causes and individuals whose work and ministry they personally approve.

Other propaganda material is designed, printed, and distributed to the churches. Posters, brochures, tracts, books, biographies, appeals, and prayer calendars are employed by the boards. Some faith boards send out calendars each year with the field in the background and a monthly calendar appended. In this fashion the board and its work is kept before the constituency 365 days in the year.

Missions is a spiritual work and yet God works through means. Most boards have a lot to learn about methods and means of informing their peoples and securing from them the support missions so richly deserve but which they do not command generally from those who belong to the churches. They will never begin to pour out of their treasure until they catch a vision of what needs to be done and of what their part is in doing it. Through education and by the visual and oral presentation of the challenge of the work, the demonstration of the needs, and also by a statement of the results which flow from mission work people will be moved to action. It is in this vital area that boards lately have begun to employ more modern means of communication. Visual aids have done more to impress people and to acquaint them with missions than all the written material put together. By black and white and colored film, board after board has brought graphically to its people the story of missionary endeavor. Most of the larger denominations now have film libraries in several centers, and their local churches may secure whatever is available from these libraries. Faith boards are using films more and more, and their representatives gladly bring them in person to local churches for showing. In this case an offering is taken for the work of the board, and from these films the sinews of war have partly come. In spite of all this the boards are behind the world which spends huge sums of money to advertise its products and to keep its names before the public. This is not to recommend that the missionary administrators copy all of the world's practices, but the Lord of the church does command His servants to be as wise as serpents, and in the parable of the unjust steward He indicates that those who serve Him are not to be asleep or careless in their labors for the Master.

Ministers of the church are another key to missionary success, and every administrator understands that the success or failure of the missionary program of the local church depends on the minister of the church. He can be a strong advocate for missions, and by the stress he places on it and the methods he employs he can do more than any administrator can do himself. Perhaps this is why the denominations at their annual meetings devote some part of the program to missions. The service for the commissioning of missionaries can be a strong weapon for developing enthusiasm among the delegates who are both ministers and laymen. Pageants, films, missionary messages, reports from the boards and societies all are designed to inform, encourage and enthuse. The faith boards do not have the same opportunity since their constituencies are not held together by denominational ties. But more and more the faith boards are holding summer missionary conferences to which their constituencies are invited.

It is not without reason that administrators look to the local ministers for they get financial support from them and from their churches. If they did not need to be concerned about them, half of their problems would be eliminated. Again missionary administration is defective by not doing more to help local ministers conduct missionary programs which would be productive. Although the cost might appear high at first glance, the returns eventually would more than offset the original cost. Every church should have a yearly missionary conference at the end of which pledges should be gathered for the coming year. Mission boards could set up such a missionary conference for any church and conduct it for an experimental period until the minister and his people learned the details of the program and became skilled in planning and carrying out one for themselves. By using missionaries on furlough and speakers with a missionary interest and passion, any church could rejuvenate missionary interest within a few years, and commence a forward movement which would enlist the sympathies and support of most of the church members. Since the churches, on the whole, have not gotten a vision of what missionary conferences can do, it is up to the mission boards to spearhead the attack and in their relationship to the home churches start fires which will burn vigorously for years to come.

Finances are but one of the facets in the relation of mission boards to their churches. Boards must keep in close contact with these same churches for another reason. They must have missionaries, and these missionaries must come from the churches which support them. Denominational boards in particular are apt to limit themselves to the selection and choice of missionary personnel who come from within their own special fellowship. The Southern Baptist Convention would not appoint for service anyone who is not a Baptist. They might conceivably accept a Baptist from some other like group, but the chances are not as great as if the individual came from Southern Baptist sources. Lutherans are not apt to appoint Baptists, nor Episcopalians Nazarenes. Despite an increasing trend toward ecumenicity it does not seem to be reflected in the policies of the denominational mission boards by the appointment of candidates who come from a different fellowship. The faith boards normally are willing to accept as potential missionaries any candidates who stand theologically in the tradition of the historic faith regardless of the denominational affiliation. Thus faith boards can go farther afield in recruitment and can encourage candidates from both denominational and independent churches whereas most denominations would still look askance at any denominational group seeking to recruit candidates from among their constituency.

Denominational administration cooperates in a larger framework to attract missionary personnel. They do this through the Student Volunteer Movement for Christian Missions, Incorporated. In the neighborhood of fifty thousand dollars a year is spent by this agency for the recruitment of personnel. Names like Robert Speer and John R. Mott have been intimately associated with this movement in days gone by. In recent years it has been more active, and conferences similar to those conducted by the missionary arm of the Inter-Varsity Christian Fellowship (Foreign Missions Fellowship) have been convened. The Foreign Missions Fellowship of the Inter-Varsity Christian Fellowship has been a non-denominational agency whose promotional program for missionary recruitment has been remarkably successful. Originally begun as a separate agency, the Foreign Missions Fellowship had behind it the vision and daring of men like Robert C. McQuilkin, one-time president of Columbia Bible

College, an institution with unusual missionary passion. The fellowship later was coordinated within the larger activities of the Inter-Varsity Christian Fellowship. In its operations on the secular college campuses of North America, this group ministers to denominational and non-denominational students. Some of the larger denominations have numbered among their applicants for overseas service numerous men and women whose lives were touched and their vision stimulated through this agency. It has been said that some candidates applying to denominational boards having come from this background are inclined to be suspicious of these boards because of the charges of "modernism" which are being hurled back and forth. The Inter-Varsity Christian Fellowship itself does not condemn denominations nor does it try to wean the students from their church connections whether independent or denominational.

Summer conference grounds have grown in popularity in the last two decades. Again, they can be found in two spheres, denominational and non-denominational. These conference grounds have brought together young people whose lives have been challenged for missions. The Southern Presbyterians have Montreat in North Carolina, the Southern Baptists have Ridgecrest in North Carolina, the American Baptists have Green Lake in Wisconsin, and Thousand Pines in California, and the Methodists have Ocean Grove in New Jersey. Non-denominational conferences include Mount Hermon in California, Winona Lake in Indiana, Keswick in New Jersey, and literally scores of others in the United States and Canada. At these conferences mission executives present the challenge of the foreign field, and they attempt to enlist young people to that consecration of life and talents for the service of the Master overseas.

Mission leaders desire to attract candidates who are spiritual, intelligent, and outstanding. But again their hands are tied and to a large extent they have to depend upon the leadership of the local churches. Innumerable churches cannot point to a single young person who has gone forth from those churches into any form of Christian service in fifty years. On the other hand certain churches seem to send forth great numbers of their young people into various forms of Christian service. When an investigation is made, one is not surprised to discover that the minister of the church or someone in a key position is responsible for the dedication of young lives to Christian service. Further investigation shows that the ministers who have a successful response in one parish will also be successful in other churches to which they minister. And when a minister who has been successful in enlisting his young people for service moves to another charge, the people of the church he leaves have caught his vision and generally insist on replacing their former minister with a man of like passion.

Once again the responsibility of those who engage in missionary leadership is to stir up the ministers who in turn will stir up their churches. Efficient missionary administrators see to it that missionaries with ability who are on furlough visit strategic churches to present the claims of Christ on young lives for foreign missionary service. Any mission board which lacks candidates for its stations overseas lacks those candidates because the missionary leadership itself is ineffectual and has failed to do its part on the home front in the raising up of suitable candidates. Bemoaning the lack of candidates does not bring them into the fold. Young people will respond, but they must be informed and challenged before responding. And any missionary leadership which will not go out and raise up recruits is not good leadership.

The denominational and the faith boards have difficulties with recruitment. The denominations often lack numbers; the faith boards lack men, not women. Leader after leader in the faith boards bemoans the lack of suitable male candidates for the fields. They are always asking, "Where are the men?"

This has unfortunately given rise to erroneous statements about the proportion of women to men. Widely-quoted figures have included the assertion that there are seven women for every man on the foreign field. Fortunately, this is untrue. The ratio of women to men may be as high as sixteen or eighteen to eleven, and in some boards it may be as high as two to one. But when all Protestant missionary work for North America is taken into consideration, it is not two to one.

Men seem inclined toward work under denominational boards. No evidence is available as to the reasons underlying this preference. It would be easy to assume that the financial factor is the leading cause since the denominational salary stipends for their missionaries are higher. However, no concrete evidence has been brought forth to substantiate this theory. To the leadership of the faith boards the challenge must be given that if they do not secure men in sufficient numbers it is part of their business as administrators to go out and get the men they need. If they have failed so far, they are not to conclude that it is not the will of God for them to have additional men nor are they to suppose that it is an impossible task to obtain them. New methods and approaches may be needed. There are Christian men in abundance, and the obligation to enlist them for service is part of the missionary administrator's task. He ought not shirk that task. He should do something about it. He may pray earnestly for male candidates—but faith without works is dead, and having prayed he should work as though he had never prayed.

Missionary administration has still another duty in its relationship to the home churches. This is the enlistment of their people to pray. More clichés have been written about prayer than possibly any other biblical theme. Everywhere people profess to believe in the efficacy of prayer. In fact people talk about prayer, but they do not pray. Further consideration will be given to prayer in another section but here a few observations will suffice.

God has ordained that His people shall approach Him and secure from Him His aid and His blessings, spiritual and material, through prayer. Prayer is both simple and profound; it is easy yet hard; it is often quickly answered, yet sometimes it is delayed. Prayer has its own rules and is subject to no abuses, for abuses render prayer valueless. And all missionary work in all aspects must be undergirded by prayer. The failure of missionary endeavor, if men had the insight to see into the invisible world, would most often be due to the failures in prayer. Christians who look at any given situation can be deceived into concluding that failures come from other causes when actually the real reason for the failures has been lack of prayer. Things are not always as they seem, and the breakdown in health of a missionary and consequent failure of his endeavors may have been due to a lack of prayer which would have kept him healthy. Disagreements and personality clashes might have been prevented if somebody had prayed more and talked less. Church dissensions might never have come to pass if more prayer had been offered to God. Doors which have closed to missionary activity may not have been the consequence of revolution but rather the failure to pray which would have prevented the outward circumstances leading to the closing of the doors. Financial hardships due to decreases in giving might well be caused by lack of prayer which would have opened the hearts of Christians to sacrificial giving even in times of depression and personal distress. So Christians ought to ask themselves the question: "Although this is the apparent reason for that which happened, what is the *real* reason?" The apparent and the real are in direct apposition more frequently than we like to think. One should not conclude from this that the obvious is never the real reason, but only that such is true when all other factors are equal and unremitting prayer has been one of those factors.

In enlisting Christians to pray no ready formula can be applied. In formal meetings, prayer for missions should never be forgotten. Thus a minister should pray for missions publicly and unitedly with his people at the Sunday worship services. The Wednesday evening prayer service should allow for some time to be devoted to the subject of missions and missionaries. All of this is assumed as transpiring already. But here the problem is to generate that private prayer by individuals on a daily basis which will literally shake the doors of heaven by the number of petitions and the passion and zeal with which they are offered—even strong tears and crying which reveal to God the inner heart and deepest desires of His people. The results of this kind of praying are dramatic. First, it will stir up those who pray to greater consecration in giving. One cannot pray for the supply of financial needs without himself becoming aware of those needs and being led of the Holy Spirit to give as he is able himself in response to his own prayers. Boards who send out prayer letters without asking for money realize that when an individual prays for the financial need, the Spirit of God will first lay that need on the heart of the very one who prays. Second, praying will open the door so that the Lord of the harvest will speak to hearts about missionary service. If the people who are praying are young enough to go themselves, the Spirit will speak first to their hearts and show them their opportunity for dedication of life and talents to the foreign field. If they are too old to go, the Spirit will speak to their hearts about their own children, and He will lead them to dedicate those children to the cause of God and to promote missions before them so that the Spirit in turn may deal with the children. And if they have no children, they can challenge other lives through their consecration and efforts and by prayer move other mothers, fathers, and young people to a place of similar consecration.

The Moravian example of unbroken intercession twenty-four hours a day leaves no doubt as to the success of such an undertaking. Out of less than every hundred believers one would become a foreign missionary. And to this hour few groups have been able to approach the record set by people whose hearts were aflame with a prayer passion for the lost and dying.

Mission boards and their administration are able to guide their constituencies better in the direction of effective prayer than an individual missionary can do. They can list the larger as well as the smaller needs and look to the total impact rather than to the isolated situation. Larger numbers of people can be solicited to join in asking for the same answers to prayer with dramatic results. No missionary administration is good administration which does not capitalize on prayer and seek consciously to encourage as many people as possible to practice holy intercession for missions. Creative solutions to difficult problems will come more quickly and with clarity and dispatch to those who use prayer as a God-given means for furthering missions. Every administrator should accept this responsibility for obtaining prayer support as a cardinal function connected with his position and spend the time and money incidental to making this prayer support a living reality. This is simply good sense and pays off rich dividends. It is profitable.

Missionary leadership is like military leadership when thought of as planning the overall strategy of missionary labor and when plotting the battles not on a single front but on a vast series of fronts covering the planet men call earth. A mission board which works a number of fields widely divorced by oceans and continents must employ a leadership which sees the work as a coordinated whole. The operations of one field are not unrelated to the other fields. All of them are parts of a total picture. Perhaps the chief failure of missionary leadership in the broadest sense has been the inability of that leadership to think and act in terms of the total structure of missionary endeavor. Each board tends to think about its interests, its constituency, its financial needs, its candidates, its peculiar battle. Of late there has been a narrowing process evolving which has shaken this parochialism. Most mission boards may be found working and operating together in larger segments. Thus the Division of Foreign Missions brings the larger old line denominations together. The Interdenominational Foreign Mission Association of North America brings together the faith missions. The Evangelical Foreign Missions Association brings together the adherents of the National Association of Evangelicals, and the Associated Missions of the International Council of Christian Churches brings together the constituent membership of that group. Undoubtedly, up to this point, the members of the Division of Foreign Missions have worked more in cooperative ways than the others. But the future is hopeful for all of them if they band together for strategic consultations and long range planning with division of labor, comity understandings, and genuine interest and concern in sister organizations which are part of the total structure of missionary labor today.

Leadership constantly faces questions which cannot be settled by one individual and never by solitary endeavor. The questions asked include the following: Where shall our work be done? How shall we get there, stay there, and "dig in"? By what methods and means will we be best able to get the job done? To what classes and segments of the population shall we minister? What is the strategy which in this age gives us the greatest hope for finishing our job? Now no individual missionary can hope to see the field as a world-wide whole. He cannot see the forest because of the trees of his local situation. In dealing with strategy the leadership of missionary forces has been lacking in that integration which this day demands. This is no plea for the unification of all missionary operations under one standard. To adopt an attitude like that would be unrealistic and removed from the actual conditions which prevail today. But it is not unrealistic to seek a common ground with any and all agencies which are in substantial agreement about the nature of the task and the theological basis of the task, and for them to act in concert at least to the extent that the witness will not be duplicated extensively unless and until the unreached regions have been given the gospel partially. No board today can witness effectively everywhere, and there is unoccupied territory for any group wishing to expand its testimony or enlarge its field of operations.

A tragic lack of understanding of the work being done by agencies other than the one with which an administrator has connections accounts for the refusal of many to cooperate with or even learn from those he knows nothing about. In part this may be accounted for by the busy schedules of administrators which allow them little time for what may appear at first glance to be unfruitful and a waste of precious time. The value of a speaking acquaintance with the practices, policies, and turn of mind of other administrators is great. When one is not in agreement with policies of another board, those policies may be rejected, but the knowledge of what others do will in itself project the thinking of an administrator along lines which will confirm his own opinions or bring him to a place where a modification or change of his board's policies ensues. No board is so perfect that it cannot profit from the experience of another board or in some fashion discover approaches to problems new to itself and usable in its own work. Boards which have lost their evangelistic passion will be influenced by their contacts with boards which are aflame with the desire to see men regenerated and whose fiery evangelism is producing concrete results. Likewise a board with a tremendous evangelistic outreach may learn from other boards how vital is the application of the gospel principles to economic and social life. Since no single board is the true yardstick of *all* that a biblical board ought to be and since all are deficient in one way or another, it behooves them to be alive to the currents and aware of defective areas in which changes ought to be made.

The foregoing discloses some of the areas in which missionary administration works and affords an opportunity for an intelligent appraisal of the elemental or skeletal structure of its operations. Again it should be asked whether or not the extensive operations of the missionary effort could be expedited better by individuals and individual churches without the benefit of specialized missionary administration. Can a world-wide enterprise involving almost twenty thousand missionaries and spending more than four score millions of dollars each year be carried on with greater dispatch and less cost by corps of experts or by amateurs working separately? The answer to this query is patent. Missionary work does not differ too much from a military force. Centralization of the high command is not an evil. Cooperative effort for the waging of an all out war on every battle front is the only manner in which victory can be won. Individual effort is costly, parochial, and less rewarding in totality. Spasmodic, sporadic effort cannot replace long-term, well-planned, economically-arranged operations. The day of individualism in missions is gone forever. The church must become the church, and Christians in common one with another must work together to finish the job which lies before them.

Additional mission boards are no longer needed unless the present channels dry up or get clogged up so that God must turn to new agencies and find new channels for the outpouring of His blessings in evangelization. Today enough agencies exist so that the people of God could, through the existent agencies, complete the task of world evangelization. For churches not related to any particular denomination, there are enough faith mission boards through whom to work so that they need no new ones. For the denominations, mission boards now are operating in sufficient quantity so that new ones are not needed.

The answer, then, is plain. God is working through organized efforts in missions. Missionary administration is needed and needed as never before because of the gigantic all-front conflict which Christians face as they war against the devil and entrenched evil, be it spiritual, economic, political or social. While individuals may still arise to chart new paths and create new forces and employ new methods, it would be unwise to forget that all of the great pioneers themselves created agencies and administrations of a vast and cooperative nature to fulfill the individual vision. Thus the pioneer leaders were not uncooperative, solitary men who worked and died alone. They saw the need and labored in harmonious, close-knit and cooperative patterns to do together work which could not be done better alone.

CHAPTER VII

Missionaries and Money

MISSIONARIES HAVE TO EAT—AN OBSERVATION WHICH IS APPARent and trite. They also must buy clothes, give to the work of the Lord, pay medical bills, and do what other people normally do. Although the missionary is not engaged in his occupation for monetary considerations, that truth does not obscure the necessity for his having a source of income for his needs. And it is the financial considerations of missionary life to which attention is directed.

Missionaries are almost in a class by themselves when it comes to salaries. Practically all other kinds of work have standards different from those applied to missionaries. This inheres for the ministry at home, for denominational executives, and for business at large. Much of American life financially is governed by the relations between labor and capital. Hosts of people have their incomes determined annually by negotiations between leaders of businesses and leaders of labor unions. Missionaries have no labor unions, and their standards of pay vary unbelievably from any other known standard.

In general, the first principle which operates for the missionary is the principle that the financial return for his labor is not to be computed on the basis of his intrinsic worth, but it is to be based upon the idea of support. It is not compensation either for hours spent or skill involved or years of service.

Never is the question asked, "What is he worth?," but rather "How much is the bare necessity for himself, his wife and his children?" A minister is paid his salary without regard to his family relationships. So also in secular occupations. A single man will receive a salary equal to that of a married man with five children. The rate of pay is determined by the job and not by the family numbers. But for the missionary such is not the case. Therefore, a missionary with a family could not survive on the stipend normally allotted to a single man, because that stipend is not compensation but a cost of living proposition for the one person. Consequently, missionary pay by and large is proportionate. There is a base rate for a single person, a base rate for a married person, and additional increases for each child in the family. And when it is all added together it still is not compensation. It really covers the cost of living, each according to his need.

Missionary work knows no differences for diversities of occupation. The medical missionary receives no more than the evangelistic missionary; the teacher receives no more than either of the others. All are missionaries, and they share and share alike. In the homeland the opposite is true. The teacher receives less than the physician; the pastor of a small church receives less than the pastor of a large one even though the former may have a large family and the latter a small one. Financial distinctions abroad are wiped out, and all stand on an equal footing.

On the mission field there is no opportunity for advancement financially. At the home base and in secular occupations there are innumerable chances for financial betterment. Here, periodic increases for length of service and increases for greater work efficiency are common. The more competent physician can charge higher fees. The better preacher can secure a more remunerative pastorate. The more highly-skilled teacher or research scholar can reach a full professorship more quickly and with financial implications. But the missionary receives no periodic advances, and the level of efficiency has no bearing on salary stipend. After forty years of service, he is no better off than when he first began. The novice, just commencing to serve, begins where the veteran of forty years still is.

With all of this, acute differences exist within this very pattern. Thus the denominational boards for the most part pay a higher base salary than do the faith boards. The faith boards support a greater number of missionaries with the same amount of money proportionately because their financial payments are lower. This immediately discloses the varying viewpoints which exist among and within different missionary groups as to what constitutes a fair basis of support. Some do work under better financial conditions than others. Each looks at the problem from his vantage point and arrives at somewhat differing concepts of what constitutes adequate support.

Mission board policies discriminate finely even beyond what has just been described. Thus some boards operate on a "faith" basis in which the monies received are divided among the home and staff members and families on a proportionate basis. Here a maximum standard exists, and the division idea operates when the amount normally allotted does not come in for the support of the missionary family. Thus it is not unusual to read a report of a board that has paid only eighty-five per cent of its estimated costs for salaries even when those salaries have been computed at the barest minimum. The missionary whose salary has been fixed on a minimum standard now falls below that standard. In cases like this the normal policy for the mission board is not to go into debt, and generally when the financial year comes to a close, all indebtedness to missionaries is wiped out and a new beginning inaugurated.

Some mission boards send missionaries to many fields. A denominational board like that of the American Baptist Convention or the Conservative Baptist Foreign Mission Society will have missionaries in Africa, India, Burma, South America, and Europe. Conditions are never the same in all of these countries and will vary greatly within a particular geographic section. Thus African economic conditions depend upon what section of Africa the missionary is in. In South America conditions vary between Argentina and Brazil. For this reason mission boards who have laborers in different countries have another general policy which reflects a genuine understanding of these conditions. The base rate for the salaries will be the same all over the world, but to this base rate will be added cost of living bonuses to offset the actual differences as reflected by field costs. Five hundred American dollars in one country will buy more bread and butter than in another. And since the rate of pay is based not on compensation for services rendered but on support, the conditions on each field must be taken into account and adjustments made to reflect these differences lest it work undue hardship on certain missionaries whose fields of service are economically inflated over against some other field. But that is not all.

People think that the missionary is isolated, and they suppose that his income is immune from the inroads to which income in the homeland is subjected. At home appeals for the Red Cross, Community Chest, March of Dimes and a thousand others are constantly before all. The missionary is immune to many of these, but he is not immune to all of them, and he has calls and demands made upon him which cost money. The little that he has is subjected to rigorous and often compelling demands.

Most missionaries tithe as do consecrated Christians at home. Having given their lives to God for vocational service does not excuse them from giving of their substance to God. Only a small number of missionaries would argue against tithing. The greater number of them are generous and sacrificial in a proportionate sense depending on what they have to begin with. Missionaries have learned that they cannot encourage national Christians to do with their little what they themselves are not willing to do with what they have. This difficulty shines through and renders the national Christian incapable of understanding the missionary because of hard realities. On the average mission field, the economic condition of the national Christian compared to that of the denominational or faith missionary is striking. In some places, indeed in many places, the possession of an automobile automatically places the possessor in the category of a wealthy man. When the national Christian takes note of the automobile, he cannot reconcile that with any claim that the missionary is incapable of tithing; particularly when the missionary is encouraging the national Christian to tithe on an income and with material possessions far less in number and value than those of the missionary. According to the standards prevailing in the homeland, the missionary is poor, but according to the standards of the national Christians he is quite wealthy. So pressing can this problem become that in some fields the missionary who owns a tablecloth is regarded by the national of that country as being extremely wealthy. The national cannot comprehend why anyone would use such a wonderful luxury upon a table when the best use he can conceive of for such a cloth is to cover the body of his wife. The missionary by precept and practice must tithe however hard his condition as compared with home life.

Missionaries face constant calls for help of a financial nature. The sick and the starving, the needy everywhere, look upon the missionary as having wealth and as coming from a country of great wealth. He is the logical one to whom they turn in the expectation of getting something from him. And nationals are not without cunning and skill in the way they make their appeals. They may well ask for three times what they hope to get; and getting what they originally hoped for with the missionary giving less than what was asked, still leaves the missionary in the position where he has given what he cannot afford but with the dubious comfort that it was less than he might have given if he had fulfilled the actual and original request.

When all of the unfair requests have been denied, all fields have a residue of needy people whose claims no missionary could succor in a hundred years. These legitimate needs which arise out of the economic, and social conditions of a country no missionary can begin to alleviate, and one of the first lessons he must learn is to steel his heart against a recurring pattern of human need which he cannot possibly take care of.

But missionaries have demands made upon them which they cannot refuse. Guests do drop in and the missionary is forced to entertain them. These guests may be government officials, and the remotest station is not without its supply of unexpected guests. Naturally the missionary puts out the best he has and leaves an impression of economic ability which he does not truly have. He is abroad as at home the creature of his social instinct, and he is polite enough to do for visitors what he would not dream of doing were he alone with his immediate family. And all of this costs money and drains the pocketbook of the one who does not have much in the first place.

When money discussions arise, someone is bound to inquire why missionaries employ servants. Inasmuch as money for missionaries is not abundant and they are ill paid, why do they generally have nationals working for them? The inquirer asks this question honestly and without malice. He is genuinely puzzled because he is not able to afford servants for his own wife, and he somehow feels intuitively that what his wife does not have no missionary should have either—especially because the missionary is economically poor as he knows so well. Americans find it hard to understand this complication which appears out of place in the scheme of things, and they will never understand it without being grounded in the reasons underlying this apparently inconsistent policy.

Missionaries employ nationals for work women at home do themselves for a variety of reasons. When a husband and wife go to the mission field, the wife is justly and logically considered to be a missionary in her own right. She must pass the same rigid examinations physically, educationally, and psychologically. She is expected to make a contribution to the work in which they are engaged. The wife at home in no sense enters into the calling of her husband. Her work is most often that of homemaker. In this occupation she engages exclusively. Should she wish to engage in a career of her own then the pattern of her life differs, and her husband either must contribute his share to the normal work around the home or else they must employ someone to do it. On the mission field, the wife of the missionary is a homemaker to be sure. But she is also a missionary and is supposed to engage in that activity. To do so means she must have help around the home to care for those necessary functions which require attention under any circumstances. She cannot cook, clean house, wash the clothes, tend the babies, and do the thousand other household chores in addition to missionary work. She was not sent to the mission field to wash dishes and cook meals. She was sent to be a missionary.

On most mission fields, it is cheaper for one to engage the services of a national to do household and other work than it is to do the work oneself. The cost of labor is so small when compared to the benefits reaped that it is not good business sense to be without this help. Furthermore, the benefits accruing to the missionary through the employment of national help derives from the lack of municipal arrangements in many portions of the world. Where there is no public transportation, no mail delivery, no policemen, no telephones, and no washing machines life can be complicated. The missionary cannot personally convey every message nor is it convenient for him to travel to the place where the mail does come. In many places it is foolhardy and economically too expensive for the missionary to do his own shopping. The nationals can do it, paying their own way and saving the missionary money in the long run.

Despite the latent and often ill-concealed judgment that missionaries live like kings and enjoy life with the help of servants this indictment is far from true and fails to take into account the factors mentioned here. Servants have proved to be a necessity, not a luxury, and missionaries do not live like kings nor enjoy an easy life because they employ servants.

At least one other suggestion crops up in missionary discussions about the cost of keeping missionaries in the field. This suggestion makes it evident that some people expect missionaries to "go native." By this they mean that the missionaries should so identify themselves with the people that they will eat their kinds of food, wear their kinds of clothing, and live in their kind of homes. After all, why not let missionaries live like the natives? Of course those who ask the question normally would not think of applying the rule either to themselves or to their own children were they remotely tempted to become missionaries. Again, good and convenient reasons exist for declining this helpful and well meant advice.

Missionary statesmen today encourage identification of the missionary with the nationals. They believe that the day has passed when the missionary compound will stand alone and aloof from the squalid homes of the nationals. Gone forever, no doubt, is the forbidding wall of the compound designed to keep out all but those admitted by the gatekeeper. Gone forever are the investments in large homes and seemingly eternal places or centers of operations. The church has become mobile, and statesmen know that missionaries must get to the people and be identified with the people. But they know too that there are limits to which this can be accomplished successfully, and that however good it may seem in theory, it is attended by many grave and compelling disadvantages.

Living like the nationals is frequently death dealing to the missionary. And in the missionary the sending agency has a substantial investment. His passage, equipment, language learning expenses for several years, etc., represent an investment from which there is small return for the first few years. And if the missionary dies the investment is lost. To eat like a national, forgetting the basic facts of hygiene, and to consume food that is foreign to taste and digestion, and without enjoying the immunity which comes from generations of resistance to the germs and diseases is fatal. The exceptional missionary may be able so to live, but the run of the mill missionary simply cannot take it. If living like the national is death dealing, it is bound to be expensive too.

In many areas of the world the missionary loses face by the adoption of practices similar to those of the nationals. While some missionaries have no doubt leaned over backwards to prevent mingling with the nationals and have caused confusion and dissension, yet in most cases the nationals have some comprehension of the problem and do not expect the missionary to be identical with them. No unvarying rule can be laid down for situations and circumstances differ, and the missionary must adapt himself to the particular field. The principles underlying one's decisions should be appreciated and the choices made within an intelligent framework. These principles include that of protecting both the health of the missionary and the investment in his life. It also must cover the cost of doing it, the results prestige-wise which will be derived from it and any other factors pertinent to a given area where the decision has to be made.

A candidate for the mission field owes it to himself to explore fully the financial implications of missionary endeavor. He should investigate the financial arrangements of the board under which he hopes to serve. His acquaintanceship with financial policies should cover the major principles underlying his relationship to the board, and he should know precisely and exactly what the board will or will not do. No responsible board will fail to supply such information, and when the reply is not specific but intangible and non-material, the candidate would do well to canvass again his call to serve under that particular board.

Money can be the source of friction and can result in intense dissatisfaction with the board one serves. Therefore, each missionary should know in advance what his arrangements will be, and having made a mature decision on the basis of the facts, at no later date will he be able to charge the agency with ethical dishonesty. Once having decided that the monetary arrangements are satisfactory, the candidate is less than an integrated and well-balanced personality if it then becomes the basis for gross disharmony and an attenuated ministry. In other words it is sinful to complain of being ill used if you knew and understood the conditions and assented to them at the time of appointment. Only if an agency deliberately and wilfully misrepresents is there occasion for protest. The great majority of boards, denominational or faith, are honest.

Missionaries must understand in advance of their service abroad that their financial situation is an unchangeable one. Other stations in life afford chances for advancement dependent upon performance, experience, and length of service. Missionary service does not. What a missionary receives when he enters service will not increase. His earning powers stay static regardless of his production, zeal, and ability. There is no financial future for him so that money cannot be a major consideration. The acquisition of money is one of the sacrifices which the missionary makes.

Along with money, the missionary foregoes the privilege of changing jobs and employers. This is so closely allied to money that it deserves mention here. At home a man usually associates himself with a clearly-defined denomination or group and serves within that body all his life. But he will make a number of pastoral changes during the period of service, and these changes are often associated with increased opportunities as he gains experience and also increased stipend. But the missionary rarely has this opportunity. He ordinarily stays with the same board all the days of his service although there have been cases in which missionaries have ceased serving one board to take up work with another. But this is rare. The missionary learns a language and that fact limits his service to the area in which the language is used. He has no possibility of increased stipend as a missionary for all jobs are paid for on what is a cost of living basis. The missionary, therefore, can expect to remain in approximately the same place, at the same salary, and under the same board all of his working life. And candidates should appreciate this situation.

Missionary service does not open other doors by which additional income may be secured. At home a pastor expects to increase his income with funerals and weddings. Speaking engagements will come his way which will enlarge his income. Evangelistic services in other churches and the publication of books present ways of adding to the salary provided by his church. But missionaries do not profit by weddings and funerals. They have little time to write books. Evangelistic services produce no income for them. On furlough they need time to recover from the effects of their services overseas. They are sent on deputation journeys for the mission board, and the income received incidentally in this operation does not belong to them. On every hand the missionary is circumscribed financially.

Missionaries do sacrifice financially for the kingdom of God's sake. This is one place at which all missionaries must sacrifice, and it is a condition to which they must accustom themselves from the outset. They deserve more than they get, but the constraining love of Christ is more important to them than financial considerations. Let no one hurl a charge of "mercenary" at any missionary, and let everyone endeavor to improve the financial situation of these men and women of God.

CHAPTER VIII

The Objectives of Missionary Effort

~~~~~~

MISSIONARIES EXIST FOR A PURPOSE. THEY HAVE A WORK TO DO, a job to perform. With this in mind, valid questions must be answered, and a reply must be given which will be understood by reasonable and intelligent people. These questions include, "What is the objective or purpose of missionary work, i.e., what are you really trying to accomplish?" The answer to this question is properly the antecedent to another and equally important question but one which hinges upon the answer to the first one. The second question is "How will you accomplish the purposes you have in mind?" These two questions are the "what" and the "how" of missionary strategy, and they demand an analysis.

The history of Christian missions is replete with examples of men and women who wanted to do something for God. Some of them who have wanted to do something for God have not known clearly what they were trying to do; others who knew what they wanted to do have not known how to do it. As a consequence, missionary work has been impeded and hindered because the workers and the senders did not always possess a clear appreciation of the answers to these two questions.

Still other missionaries have been only moderately successful because they have entertained a faulty and defective understanding of the "what" and "how" of their missionary calling. Distorted, lopsided, and partial concepts of the full-orbed nature of the task have prevented some missionaries from securing maximum results for the effort they have exerted. This is not said in a critical manner for frequently such missionaries have done the best they knew how and, despite their limitations, they have done a great work for God. The church of Jesus Christ has profited from their mistakes, and it should build a better program as it learns from them what they did not see clearly at the time.

Men are all creatures of the day in which they live and are bound by the perspective of their age and enjoy along with it both its special insights and its color-blindness. Each age sees facets which previous ages did not see, and each age has its own blindness of understanding which a future age will uncover. In this sense they go from knowledge to knowledge and plane to plane. But the failures and shortcomings of a previous age do not excuse them for perpetuating those faults when further light has manifested to them the need for an enlargement of their understanding and for a revision of their thoughts and methodology.

The answers to the "what" and the "how" now deserve consideration. First the answer to the "what" will be given and succeeding chapters will embrace the discussion of the problem of the "how." Both are mentioned together in the discussion because they are inter-related, and failure at either pole will invalidate the other. To know what the church ought to do but not to do it because it does not know how, invalidates the first. To know how to do it is virtually impossible without first knowing what it is to do. And in the case of this latter problem, missionary endeavor has fallen into a slough of despond because some medical, educational and other missionary work has been engaged in without first making certain that those engaged in the work knew specifically and categorically what they were trying to do. They became healers of the body and educators of the mind without ever being missionaries. So the problem demanding an answer preeminently is "What are the legitimate objectives of missionary effort?"

Some objectives are philanthropic, some social, and some political in nature. But the missionary enterprise does not direct itself primarily to these areas of life. Negatively, then, the missionary does not come to the national to clothe him or to alter his dress. He is not there to reform industrial conditions or to check social abuses. Politics are not matters for his primary consideration. He is there neither to change the politics of the national nor to reform him according to his western concepts. Even morality is not a first consideration. The morals of any non-Christian group of people are in need of changes, but it is not the first business of the missionary nor is it a stated objective in his program as a servant of Jesus Christ.

Immediately when one makes a sweeping generalization like this, he is charged either with being an obscurantist or with being a "fundamentalist" without an awareness of the social implications of the gospel. And all generalizations are subject to qualifications of one kind or another. The generalization that missionaries are not sent abroad to heal the sick, reform politics, etc., arises from the basic assumption that the business of the missionary is a religious or spiritual business. Being religious or spiritual, it has in view an end and at no point should means be confused with the end. Thus medicine is a means to an end but never an end in itself. It is true that the Laymen's Missionary inquiry in the early 1930's as evidenced in *Rethinking Missions* did pronounce against the use of medicine as a means to an end and campaigned for medicine as an end in itself, but responsible missionary leadership then and now has never agreed with this pronouncement.

By no means should the negative statement be interpreted to imply that the missionary or the Christian church has no interest in bettering the conditions of the people to whom they minister. Such is not the case for the Christian faith is relevant to every area of life and cannot be divorced from any area of life without emasculating that faith to some extent. Rather, the missionary should relate these problems to the Christian faith in their proper perspective and see them in the light of their correct position. Politics, social service, etc., should not be thought of as legitimate ends in themselves. One cannot justify the expenditure of time and money on them unless there is a dynamic religious or spiritual attachment.

A goodly portion of the world is illiterate, but no missionary strategy is able to justify the expenditure of money and manpower to teach the illiterate to read unless it is a means to a better end. As good as it may be for the whole world to become literate, it is not now nor has it ever been the business of the church to make the world literate. Who would not like to see the whole world well clothed and well fed, but at no time in the past has it been nor is it now correct to suppose that the church has for itself a commission to clothe and feed the world. No statement of the Great Commission remotely begins to suggest that this is the spiritual business of Christ's followers. Nowhere is there a command nor is there a basic principle which would justify the Christian attempting to improve industrial conditions, reform morals and alter political structures.

The observation that the missionary does not concern himself directly with other than religious or spiritual ends finds its force and reconciliation in two facts. The first one is the trite and obvious one that at any given moment in the history of the Christian church there has never been enough time, money, or manpower to accomplish what is the primary objective of the Great Commission. The second one is equally obvious. Missionaries now cannot do what they would like to do and ought to do when devoting themselves exclusively to spiritual tasks. To spend effort and time for subsidiary and secondary things is to hamper and hinder the supreme aim and to slow down the progress of spiritual objectives.

Interest in and concern for the physical condition of the nationals is imperative. The improvement of industrial conditions, morals, and of agricultural production is legitimate. But these all flow out of a prior existing condition and are the results of or fruits of the gospel in the lives of men. They occur subsequent to and are neither antecedent to nor the concomitant of the spiritual objectives and labors of missionaries. When they fall into the category of means, the problem is entirely different, and they may then be concomitants justly related to spiritual or religious goals and objectives. But even here they must be kept within the boundaries of means and not confused with ends or objectives.

William Carey's life exemplifies what is meant here. It also presents problems revealing how varied may be one's approach to these difficult situations. Carey engaged in the production of indigo. In so doing, the attitude of his supporters at home was that "they earnestly caution and intreat them not to engage too deeply in the affairs of this life, lest it should damp their ardour, if not divert them from their work." But Carey himself engaged in this business enterprise for reasons that satisfied him. He wanted a place of employment for those who might lose caste by embracing the gospel. He also wanted to become self-supporting on the field, feeling that this was good missionary policy. Carey's position at the College of Fort William could hardly spare him from the criticism that he was engaging in non-missionary endeavor. But in his day and with his situation in view Carey used his connections with the college to further missionary endeavor. He came into close fellowship with Bengal's most learned Europeans and with many of the ablest Indian pundits of the diverse vernaculars of that land. His vision was to employ this array of multilingual Indian scholars to aid him in his language control for the express purpose of translating the Word of God into all the chief tongues of the land. Ward was only a printer, but printing was never an end in itself but only a means to promote the main objective. All the work that Carey did in translating the Bible would have counted for nought without a printing press.

For those who would argue that the correction of moral and social abuses are legitimate objectives for the missionary to seek, the life of Carey presents still another example to defend this approach. For many years he waged unceasing warfare against the Indian practice of Sati. In 1828 Lord Cavendish Bentinck outlawed Sati and the Privy Council upheld him. Did not Carey's part in this represent a deviation from primary missionary responsibilities and was not this peripheral? He was constrained to fight this evil because of the biblical injunction, "If thou forbear to deliver them that are drawn unto death, and those that are ready to be slain; if thou sayest, 'Behold, we knew it not'; doth not he that pondereth the heart consider it? and he that keepeth thy soul, doth not he know it? and shall not he render every man according to his works?" It can be argued that Carey, on the other hand, had not come to India to abolish Sati, and that while he was largely responsible for its abolition, his efforts did not impair nor hamper his major objectives and that his excursions into moral and political problems were in the main confined only to major ones. His campaign against Sati was secondary to his major work for he never went to India to engage in social amelioration but to preach the gospel. His enlightened social conscience caused him to speak out against pressing ills which he felt were condemned by the Word of God.

No missionary is sent out as a social agent or a political reformer and these activities do not commend themselves to a missionary as being fundamental. But he will speak out against evil wherever he finds it, and seek for the redress of grievances within the pattern and framework of his major task. And if he must make a choice between one or the other in an unpleasant alternative, however much he regrets the necessity, his choice must always be to deny himself the pleasure of the peripheral and secondary, his undying preference being given to the primary. The others eventually will flow forth like streams of living water as consequences of the living power of the gospel permeating the culture and bringing through an evolving process those changes which the missionary might hope for all the days of his life and not live to see himself.

The New Testament does not speak one word against the institution of slavery as such. Paul carefully refrains from offering any indictment, not because he has no consciousness of its wrongness and not because he favors the institution. Expediency governed his action, and he kept silent about slavery at that time undoubtedly because to speak then would have hurt the major end he had in view. But the principle was inherent in the structure of his thought, and with the passage of the years Christian consciousness saw the inconsistency of the institution, and it was ultimately doomed when the Holy Spirit was able to work in and through the hearts of men to accomplish that end.

If the missionary does not have for his basic objective the social, political and economic goals, what does he have in mind and how is he oriented to his work? Missions is a religious or spiritual business which governs the whole man. Missions is the product of the conviction that Christianity is the divine life in man and it is designed to bring men that life. Despite accusations of proselyting, and fanaticism, the aim of missions is to bring men divine life. While it is pleasant to feed the hungry, heal the sick, and bind up the wounds of the fallen, these are not in themselves the aim of missions. Methods cannot be confused with the aim nor shall methods be allowed to become the aim or to usurp the aim the missionary has in mind. By that is meant that philanthropy, however good it may be, ought not to supplant the real reason for being there. Nor ought the church to retain outworn methods which have demonstrated their own ineffectiveness in doing what it thinks to be its primary work.

The confusion of the last forty years in missions has been due to the circumstance that boards and agencies have not always been clear or in agreement as to their aims nor have they stuck closely to the attainment of the aims which they have sometimes defined. And it is here that a clear statement of the aim of missions should be given. Briefly, but not in its completeness, the aim of missions is to make Jesus Christ known to the whole world. This is to preach the gospel to every creature. This is the evangelization of the world. What this means and all that it embraces must now be developed so that there is a clear understanding of its meaning and ramifications.

Missionaries should first seek to preach the gospel to every creature or to evangelize the world. This does not mean to Christianize the world. This does not mean to make Christians of all men. Both are impossible and neither one of them has been suggested in the Bible. The Great Commission remains to be completed, and so long as people live who have not heard the Word of Life Christians are obligated to keep working. To some extent the goal of evangelizing the world is indefinite and depending upon one's eschatology that difference will continue. The pre-millennialist who believes in a thousand-year millennial reign of Jesus Christ on earth also believes that history will come to its fruition and end, not by normal processes but by divine intervention in and through the literal appearing of Jesus Christ in a physical body at the second coming or advent. This second advent to set up His earthly kingdom will signify that the Great Commission has been completed. And the church must be aware that so long as the second advent has not come there remains a missionary task for Christians. They must be busy about their Father's business. The a-millennialist and the post-millennialist take a different view. Particularly there are those who expect the slow but sure permeation of the gospel among men until the knowledge of God covers the earth as the water covers the seas. They see the fulfillment of human history within history, and while they look, eschatologically, for a future life above and beyond this world, they anticipate the establishment of righteousness and Christianity throughout the world before the end of time.

In any event two questions about the Great Commission are not answered in the Bible itself. Granted that the church has been commissioned to preach the gospel to every creature. Granted that it is to evangelize the world. The answer to the question when this task has been fulfilled is still unknown for men do not know the answer to the other questions, "How extensive and how intensive must this be?" Does the commission mean that missionaries must reach every creature in a literal fashion? Must each and every person be reached with the gospel? Furthermore, when has a man heard the gospel? Has he heard when we have given him John 3:16? Has he heard when a missionary has spoken to him once or twice or three times? And how can he tell that he has honestly given him the gospel? Perhaps he has communicated it to him as best he knows how, but even when he thinks he has preached the gospel, he may actually not have preached it to that individual or that group of people.

The commission is explicit in that missionaries are not simply to preach the gospel. This could be accomplished theoretically without bringing men into a saving relationship to Jesus Christ. The preaching of the gospel has for its aim not only the fulfillment of the commission but also the winning of individuals to a personal attachment to Jesus Christ. They are to make disciples. This changes the commission from just an academic projection in a detached framework and it makes it a live and vital and dynamic thing. The preaching or taking of the gospel has for its real objective the making of disciples.

One hundred years ago the missionary literature was filled with notions about snatching men as brands from the burning. Everywhere the emphasis lay upon winning individuals to Jesus Christ. This emphasis was not incorrect, but it was not properly related to other compelling aims which make up the objective of missionary effort. Winning an individual to Jesus Christ is not enough. The reasons for this are becoming more and more clear today. The Ecumenical movement has emphasized a neglected truth, and this truth cannot be obscured whatever may be one's appraisal of the movement itself. The truth is that men who profess Christ as Saviour and Lord are incorporated into two new relationships. The first is membership in the Body of Christ. This membership in the Body includes within its scope the saints in Christ who are already dead as well as those who are living, and it will include those in the future who come to know God in Christ. Calvin makes this nice distinction by indicating that they are members of the mystical body or what is often called the invisible church. It is invisible not in the sense that it cannot be seen empirically, although that is partially true, but it is invisible in the sense that only God knows with certainty who are true members of this body. Visible churches may number among their constituency many members who are not incorporated into the mystical body but who have been permitted to enter the visible organization for one reason or another.

The second truth is the one which the Ecumenical movement has stressed largely. This allows that Christianity by its nature can never be a solitary religion and that the faith is never to be observed in solitary form. If a man is born into the kingdom of God by faith and is a member of the mystical body, it cannot help but be true that he is also connected with and attached to all others who have been incorporated into the mystical body. To some extent, however imperfect, the mystical body has empirical manifestations and is visible before the world of men. There does exist a worldwide community of redeemed people who are the people of God. This *koinonia* or fellowship exists irrespective of differences which may separate or divide God's people on peripheral items. Archbishop William Temple was wrong in saying that this concept is "the great new fact of our time." He should have said that "the rediscovery of this old truth is the great new fact of our time." The negro of the Sudan as well as the Chinese Christian from Tibet and the Indian from Delhi are members of the same body both mystically and empirically. Each has a wider fellowship than that which is comprehended within his own locality or group. They are inextricably bound together in a loyalty to Christ and to one another which makes for stronger ties than those of nationalism, class, or culture. Every Christian is a Christian before he is an Anglican, a Presbyterian, a Baptist or whatever the group with which he happens to be affiliated. Consequently, every Christian should have a depth knowledge of his oneness in Christ with all other Christians who truly profess Him regardless of the differences which separate them.

Missions are designed to save men as brands from the burning, but the second pivotal truth is that when they are so saved from the burning they are automatically members of the body and from this membership are derived relationships which are a part of such membership. Consequently, it is not sufficient to preach the gospel and win men to Christ. They are to be incorporated into visible churches. They are to be made a part of the wider fellowship. Christianity cannot be solitary so long as there are two Christians side by side.* They must be related one to the other. These are reasons why God has ordained that men shall be not only incorporated into the mystical, invisible body but why they shall also be incorporated into a visible aggregation of the people of God. The problem of organizational form is not important at this point for differences do exist whether that form happens to be congregational, presbyterian, or episcopal. The important and not to be overlooked

* Lamott, *op. cit.*, pp. 5, 6, 20.

truth is that the people of God shall be a "gathered people," and the church is the institution into which they shall be gathered. The church is both an organism and an organization; it has both its mystical and its visible aspects. But it is concrete and empirical for the world to observe.

The church or the churches are the creation of God Himself. They are not creations of men and never have been. Men have distorted God's creation, and they have abused and mismanaged it. Evils like ecclesiasticism, heresy, politics, and sin have crept in. Purification has often been required; schism has rent it; reformation has overtaken it; and in some cases it has in part ceased to be a true church. Whatever may be the problems and however much apostasy there may be, the truth remains undimmed and the vision clear that God wills that there shall be a visible church or churches and in them shall be gathered the people of God who are the *koinonia*.

Missions exist to operate along the principle of cell division in the biological sphere. New cells shall grow out of older ones, and these in turn shall reproduce themselves. And all the cells in the whole wide world together form that visible body of Christ so far as it can be known. The business of the missionary is to win converts who shall be gathered into churches, for church planting is the business of missions. Let no one hide this truth, and God forbid, that in the creation of a single cell, division should be promoted to cancel out the biblical truth that every cell is linked to every other cell for all of the cells together form the visible body.

Missionaries are to plant churches, and these churches should be indigenous. The form of the organization will vary depending upon the connections of those who form the church, but indigenization is more of a cultural matter than an organizational one. When a church is indigenous, it has been adapted to the cultural environment and becomes homelike to an extent that non-Christians will note that it belongs to their own people. Such a church will be self-governing, self-supporting, and self-propagating. The discussion of this at greater length is reserved for another section of this work.

The terms of the Great Commission have not been exhausted when men have come to Christ and a church has been formed. The Christians are to be built up in the most holy faith or as Christ commanded, "Teaching them to observe all things whatsoever I have commanded you: . . ." This surely comprehends baptism, the Lord's table, and instruction, over, above, and beyond the minimal teaching necessary for salvation. It is essential for sustaining, deepening and broadening the lives of those who have entered into this new relationship and without which teaching they cannot hope to be conformed to the image of Christ or grow in grace and the knowledge of the Lord.

The teaching of the Christians will be performed by the missionaries in the beginning, but the existence of an indigenous church presupposes that a national ministry for preaching and teaching will be developed as soon as possible, and then this work will be turned over to the nationals. How to train national workers is dealt with in the discussion on the indigenous church.

The missionary aims finally to make himself superfluous. His job is to do away with his job as fast as he can. He is to make himself unessential and the sooner the better. Contrary to the expectations of the nineteenth century when missionaries dug in to stay forever, current missionary strategy recommends that missionaries think of their calling as temporary for a given location, living as it were with their suitcases in their hands, leaving as soon as it appears safe to do so. They are not to engage in activities which nationals are able to perform albeit less ably. And they are to train nationals to replace them from the beginning of their ministry. And when their labors are completed, they move to the next place to begin again the same cycle and go through the same process of cell division until at last the job of evangelization has been completed in fulfillment of the divine commission.

Thus the question "What is the church to do?" has been answered. This in turn leads to a consideration of the question, "How shall the church do it?" and answers to this perplexing and baffling question will be given in later chapters.

Lamott - Chapter 2
Brown - Chapter 1 & 2
Glover - Chapter 2
...issions at the - page 179
...cssroads"
Soltau

CHAPTER IX

Adjustments on the Field

‹‹

AN OCEAN VOYAGE WILL NOT MAKE A MISSIONARY. BUT AN ocean voyage will make a difference in the life and outlook of the missionary. Mission fields are not exotic, and the pictures one can find in the *National Geographic* and *Life* magazines in no way will reflect truly what the missionary will find when he arrives at the place of his service. Beginning with his departure from the home base, the missionary will need to make adjustments. But when he arrives finally on the field, he is faced with the immediate problem of making a series of adjustments so profound that his ways of life will be altered beyond the imagination of the uninitiated.

People are people, but all people are not the same. The similarities identify them with the human race and demonstrate that they are the creation of the same God but with that the similarities cease. Things may look alike on the surface. But they are not really alike. The nationals eat food, live in houses of one kind or another, wear clothes for the most part, and pass through the same life processes of infancy, puberty, adolescence, marriage, parenthood, old age, and death. The missionary is thrown into contact with this new culture, and he must make a series of radical adjustments to the culture and to the people and his environment. The period of adjustment lasts during the first term of missionary service. And this makes the first term of the missionary the most difficult.

Exhaustive studies have not been made recently about the length of service of missionaries, but a study which is now twenty years old does reveal the pitfalls which face the first term missionary, and it elaborates to some extent the departments of life which require the most adjustment. In this study (encompassing a number of mission boards), the records of six thousand missionaries were examined at random, one-half of the missionaries being men and one-half women. These missionaries had either died in service or had withdrawn from service at a time when six or seven years was the average length of service before the first furlough. It would be expected that the loss of personnel would occur mostly after the first furlough. But the facts were somewhat different. The largest number, nine per cent, withdrew in the third year of service. The percentage of withdrawal was less with the passing of the next three years. Thirty-four per cent of all losses occurred between the third and the end of the fifth years. Those who returned to the field for a second term tended to resign less frequently, and when a missionary had served eleven years, the rate of resignations was between one and one and one-half per cent annually.*

In surveying the reasons for missionary withdrawals from the field, interesting information came to light. About one-third of all withdrawals were due to poor health on the part of the missionary or his family. In two-thirds of these cases withdrawal was due to ill health on the part of the missionary himself. Fifteen per cent of the withdrawals were due to death of which only three per cent was death in the family, the major cause being the death of the male missionary. Fifteen per cent of all withdrawals in this study were due to misfits, five per cent to personal claims at home, five per cent to marriage, four per cent to dissatisfaction with conditions of the work, four per cent due to war. Under the major item of fifteen per cent

* William G. Lennox, *The Health and Turnover of Missionaries* (New York, The Foreign Missions Conference, 1933), pp. 66–7.

withdrawals for misfits, the breakdown is important. Of the fifteen per cent, six per cent was difficulty in temperament, four and four-tenths per cent unsatisfactory work, two per cent personal conduct, one and four-tenths per cent for faith or interest reasons, and the balance either not stated or for other than listed reasons.* All of this gives some clue to the importance of the adjustments which must be made in the first term of service to prevent this serious leakage which is expensive in personnel and money for the average mission board.

Health obviously is one of the key factors in adjustment. What a man is, often is a result of his physical condition. Consequently, the new missionary must adjust to the physical environment in which he works and take whatever steps are necessary to protect his health. Again statistics show that health problems depend largely on the field of service with Africa being the least desirable for missionaries on the whole. South America is one of the most desirable geographical areas. Whatever the geographical area and whatever the peculiarities of that area the missionary must be cognizant of his responsibilities and carefully follow all rules and regulations laid down by the mission board. These rules will be based upon practical experience over a long period of trial and error by missionaries.

No effort will be made to present a detailed study of all the rules which a missionary ought to follow for the sake of his health, but a few observations will suffice to show the importance of the matter. Whereas in America one rarely boils water, water must be boiled on most mission fields. The failure to be careful in this regard is death dealing in many instances. Hands must be washed before eating. In Africa only the most irresponsible and foolish missionary will refuse to wear a sun helmet. Even exercise is a matter for careful consideration. In some places it is dangerous to exercise too much.

* Lennox, *ibid.*, 79.

In the tropics the loss of salt through perspiration requires the use of additional salt to replace that which is lost due to climatic conditions. Rest, recreation, vacations, and relaxation involve adjustments from the life which the ordinary missionary has been accustomed to living in the United States, and unless he makes these essential adjustments he is likely to break down physically.

Food is another adjustment problem. Both the food itself and the eating habits of the missionary are at stake. The purchase, cooking, and care of food varies from the accustomed and involve adjustments of considerable moment. Some missionaries feel constrained to live and eat like nationals, discovering too late that they are not able to do so. When this discovery invalids the missionary home permanently or kills him, little can be done. In conversation with missionaries, many have traced grave physical handicaps to failures involving food either through carelessness or in the press of necessity which they felt to be justified. In far too many cultures vegetables are grown with the aid of human excrement as fertilizer, and this is one of the best instruments for making well people ill or for killing them. Though the missionary may yearn to live like the nationals and to identify himself perfectly with them, he should remember that he represents a sizable investment financially and otherwise, and that this investment should be protected sacredly and his life and health cared for. The good of the work, and the progress of the propagation of gospel for which he is willing to make sacrifices, demand this care.

The servant problem adds to the adjustment complications. In some countries, it is true, the missionary may be able to get along without the use of servants. In many others servants are both useful and necessary. Before any missionary determines that he shall get along without the use of servants, he should be sure that he is fully aware of the implications and is not acting out of a dogmatic misunderstanding of the true condition of life. In some areas of the world the kitchen is a crude structure away from the main house. No water is available except from the well which may be some distance away. The cooking facilities themselves would baffle an Eagle Scout, but the constant battle with the facilities and the physical conditions would render the missionary unfit for the other work which he has come to perform. If he must also go to the market to shop in competition with his neighbor's cooks, get cheated on his purchases, and lose face to such an extent that his main ministry is impaired, it would seem that the use of servants is profitable and desirable.

In India today the servant problem is acutely difficult where the caste system has a continued hold on large segments of the population. A servant who washes clothes will not cook, and one who carries water will not perform scavenger work. Local customs prevail with which the missionary must become familiar and about which adjustments must be made if he is to succeed. This can be trying and exasperating to a degree not appreciated by any except those who have experienced it.

The servant relationship is more than just a decision whether one shall employ them and how many one shall have. Once the decision to use servants is made further adjustments are essential. Servants can be servants or members of the family. In either case they become more intimate with the missionary and his home life than others. Servants talk, and what they say about the missionary and how they regard him may help or hurt his ministry among the people. He must adjust to these servants and watch with care his words and actions before them. And when more than one servant is employed, as frequently is necessary, there are problems within the servant group which must be attended to by the missionary and settled peacefully.

Children of the missionary complicate his adjustment period with an inevitability that is dismaying. In years gone by mission boards preferred to send out missionaries to the field who did not have children. Today the situation is working in reverse, and missionaries are being appointed with regularity who have one or more children. This is not said to pass judgment upon the wisdom of appointing missionaries with children or to suggest that missionaries ought to practice birth control until the period of initial adjustment has been passed. It is only written to meet the realities of an historical situation —that the advent of children for the first term missionary constitutes a serious adjustment problem. Perhaps the arrival of a letter from the wife of a former student now laboring in Indonesia will open a corner into the problem possibilities of children. In that part of the world babies suffer constantly from heat rash. And this will make any baby irritable and fretful. The mother spoke of taking the baby down to the river for a bath three or four times during the night. Now when a missionary couple have two babies and are beginning their careers and these careers are interrupted not once but a thousand times by problems inevitably concomitant with the advent of babies, one can appreciate the adjustments which must be made. When all of the comforts of modern America for the raising of babies are missing, and when medical help is far distant and feeding, washing, health, and disease have to be battled unceasingly, the missionaries are going to be hit and hit hard.

The missionaries' home life and conditions undergo radical changes during the period of adjustment. Coming from one environment to another, they set up a home, a home that will be different from that which they enjoyed in America. The field home cannot be the same as the home in America, but good sense dictates that it be as much of a home as it can be made under the circumstances and that it reflect to some extent that which the missionary has known in his native land. Taking along the little things that help to make a house a home aids in the period of adjustment. On the home level missionaries feel the drag of life and easily slide into a careless attitude that after all it does not matter. It does matter and for the missionary to neglect the small niceties of life is not good strategy. Dressing for an evening meal and using a tablecloth can do more to bolster flagging spirits than we suppose. If the little externals count, the home is the place where the missionary has got to be loving and Christian in every regard. He is watched constantly by his fellow workers and by the nationals. Every move that he makes is under scrutiny and a single false step can be fatal for his influence as a servant of God. Since in many climates missionaries must take drugs for malaria, drugs which react on the physical body of the missionary and cause him to be nervous, and dragged out, he must adjust to this perennial problem and be loving, considerate, tender, and Christian when he does not feel like being that way due to physical difficulties.

A missionary must adjust to the people he has come to serve. As will be suggested later, this adjustment cannot be accomplished without an extensive knowledge of the people and their customs. In the later connection the discussion will concern evangelism, but now it concerns the missionary as he gets used to the people. It will make a difference in the missionary's attitude when he discovers that it costs a national a month's wages to buy his wife a dress. The missionary must adjust to the economic conditions of the field and enter fully into an understanding of the financial problems, money standards, social customs, and general mores of the people.

Trying to understand people of a different culture is perplexing and confusing. People from other cultures do not do things the way we do, and they often do things that we consider to be "wrong." The word "wrong" is used in quotation marks because it cannot be naïvely assumed that everything with which western culture is in agreement is automatically right and that all others are wrong. Among some cultures, levirate marriage is still customary. This practice is found in the Old Testament where the brothers of the deceased who left no issue were expected to continue the line by generating offspring via the widow of the dead brother. Such action was not thought to be adulterous even though it involved sexual relations outside normal wedlock. Elsewhere it is not thought sinful for a man to engage in sexual relations with the younger sister of his wife. This latter example is adultery in western thinking and undoubtedly is adultery biblically speaking (and it is wrong), but the point is not the adultery but the perplexities and difficulties which beset the novice on the field who is in need of adjustment. Some actions he will find to be wrong, and some he will discover are rooted and grounded in different thought patterns which in other cultures may actually not be wrong. He must sift these out of the maze of conflicting viewpoints and make peace with his own soul as he tries to understand the nationals and their ways of life.

But the missionary discovers to his chagrin that if he has standards which he thinks are valid, there are missionaries who do not agree with him. And he must adjust to the radical displacement occurring within missions and among colleagues. Thus in some fields differing opinions may prevail about one problem. Some missionaries would admit a polygamist to full fellowship within the national church. Others would give him a status of a mediating sort in a semi-membership category. Still others would keep such a person only from holding official positions within the church. And here even a fourth category might spring up among those who would feel that a polygamist who does not put away all of his wives except one should have no place and no part in the life of the church officially or unofficially unless and until he were to put away all of his wives except one. The new missionary coming into a field where fellow missionaries are not in agreement will find himself truly perplexed especially if he begins as one would normally expect with the supposition that there are ironclad standards and agreements of right and wrong about which everyone is in total agreement. Then when he

finds this is not so, he is forced to adjust not only to the problem at the level of the native custom but also at the level of his
colleagues and the differences which exist among them.

Race with all that this word entails confronts the beginner.
In Africa he will live among negroes. The regenerated ones
are "brothers" in Christ. The unregenerated nationals are no
different from unregenerated white men in America except
in the pigment of the skin. But the difference in the color of
the skin may be the controlling factor. No missionary can afford the luxury of race antipathy whether that antipathy be
submerged beneath the outer crust of Christian doctrinal concepts which forbid it (for it will soon come out of its hiding
and plague the one who enjoys the antipathy) or whether it is
openly acknowledged. In either case the effectiveness of the
missionary is lost, and he might just as well stay at home. However, even where no real antagonism of a racial sort controls,
the missionary is nevertheless forced to radical adjustments at
this level also. Who can gainsay the existence of feelings of
superiority or the thought that other peoples are culturally
inferior or unequal even where antipathy does not exist? Let
it be said that this problem is not the peculiar possession of the
white man in his relationships to other races, but it is also the
problem of other races in their relationship and attitudes towards the white man. In the nineteenth century the white
man was looked upon by the Chinese as a rough, crude bar-
barian. And from their vantage point he was. Thus the new
missionary is face to face with the necessity for great adjustments first in his race attitude and then in cultural and dynamic structures of interrelational adaptation between men
of diverse colors.

Religion immediately forces the missionary into a reappraisal of his own convictions and inevitably into a comparison of his beliefs with those of the people he has come to convert. He faces a confusing array of outward facts, practices and
mechanical paraphernalia. Their significances he hardly can

appreciate. Their evils are frequently of a surface nature which to him are revolting. His initial reaction will probably be one of disgust accompanied by a strong desire to eradicate the pagan religion in its entirety. At first glance he will not be able to see that the religion of the nationals is bound together in a social and societal pattern which will defy his most strenuous efforts to detach it objectively. To throw out everything blindly will do no good. To accept "good elements" with equal blindness and to relate them to the Christian faith or to assume that they are integral parts of a common revelation (apart from their inter-relation to the total structure of the religion) is dangerous. But into the welter of this confusion the missionary is thrown and decisions must be arrived at as part of the adjustment to the new life. While it may not be amiss to use good elements of pagan religions as points of contact in making an approach to the Christian gospel, one must carefully warn the new missionary to be watchful and to refrain assiduously from hasty conclusions which may require rapid changes in a short interval of time.

A thorny question for the new missionary is the language. He comes to the field without the benefit of knowing the language. He may have studied linguistics, phonetics and phonemics. He may even have engaged in the study of the actual language before sailing (although this is infrequent). But once he gets to the field he is faced with what may be his hardest assignment—to learn the language of the people to whom he comes with the gospel. The success which the new missionary attains in the language will determine whether he will remain a "foreigner" to the people or become one of them. For some unknown psychological reason missionaries do not always have a compelling inner urge to excel in the language. So long as they are able to make themselves understood they are satisfied. But the same missionary who so easily satisfies himself at this point would be the first one at home to refuse the continued ministry of a Swede or a German who had come to

America but who could speak only broken English. It is an insult to a man's intelligence be he a national of Africa, China or India to neglect his language when you have professedly come to serve him without reservation.

Naturally languages differ greatly in the ease or difficulty with which they may be spoken. Tonal languages are among the hardest to grasp. The Chinese tongue is a tonal one, and the same phonetic sound may have four or five inflectional variations each one of which changes the meaning of the word. Without doubt thousands of missionaries have committed innumerable sins against the Chinese language because of this problem. But the difficulty of the language should in no way become a standing excuse for the missionary to neglect his command of it. His philosophy of missionary work should include the idea that language control is a *sina qua non* for him and that he will employ all of his zeal, energy, and enthusiasm to learn that language.

Language schools of one kind or another are provided by missionary agencies. Where the field is small and the number of missionaries numerically inconsequential, a national teacher may be provided. Where a large number of missionaries are involved, a special school in a given area may be set up. In still other situations a group of agencies may cooperate in the operation of a language school. Mission boards usually require their novices to pass a first and a second year language examination. Modern methods have enabled missionaries to learn languages faster and better than ever before. In the United States and Canada summer institutes of linguistics have brought immeasurable gain to prospective missionaries. Under the leadership of gifted men like Drs. Pike and Nida (the latter now Versions Secretary of the American Bible Society) dramatic changes have come in this field over the past decade.

Although this is not a technical study of linguistics and does not propose to cover the field, one or two concrete suggestions for the missionary during his period of adjustment may be of help. The new missionary should endeavor to prepare himself in advance of his going by taking as many courses as possible in the linguistic field. He should add to this any knowledge of semantics (which is the science of meanings as over against phonetics which is the science of sounds) which he can obtain. On the field the new missionary should listen to and talk the language all the time. The more he is able to expose himself to the language, and the more he is able to use the language and reproduce it in concrete situations the easier will be his task. He should compare the English Bible with the Bible in the language of the people. The Bible of the national tongue should become his Bible, and the development of familiarity with it will be of inestimable value.

The period of the first term of missionary work must unfortunately include language adjustment, and what has been said will permit the novice to glimpse in a small way a few of the problems attending this period of adjustment. The chief danger which the novice faces is the sense of frustration derived from the seemingly overwhelming barriers which confront him when first he commences. He should be encouraged to remember that thousands of other people have faced and overcome the same handicaps and that the task is not as difficult as it appears in the beginning.

As if it were not enough for the first termer to face the odds and troubles of the field itself, he must also face adjustments in relation to his own colleagues who are people of the same background and color. Queer people do get to the mission fields. The new missionary himself may be one of them. If he is not, there will be others who are. And with them he must get along from day to day. Modern industry has discovered that changes in personnel and dismissals from jobs do not occur for reasons one would logically assume. Men are not dismissed for inability to do the work assigned. The greatest single reason is inability to get along with people. And on the mission field the same problem exists.

The novice must remember that he comes without benefit of previous experience. He is faced with a new set of circumstances which he does not understand. He will see gaps and defects in the pattern from the moment he commences his work. He will see places where he thinks immediate changes should be effected. He will fail to understand why certain things are done the way they are. He will be gripped by the disappointment of the slowness with which things move. He wants to see results. Through all of this he must recall that usually there are good and sufficient reasons based on long and painful experience why missionaries do things the way they do. Second, he must remember that silence will be his best ally for the first year or two. He is there as a learner, and while in theory he has equality with senior or older missionaries and has the privilege of expressing opinions he had better learn the lessons of silence at first. He must give the older missionaries the benefit of the doubt. Some day he himself will be an older missionary and would like to enjoy from his younger colleagues the same patience and forbearance his older colleagues would like from him now. He should endeavor to understand the outlook and viewpoint both of the mission station and the individuals who are in the leadership. This will help him in the period of adjustment.

The most insidious temptation the novice faces is that of finding fault with his colleagues. In a mission station the workers are in constant personal contact. As a microcosm within a macrocosm abnormal enlargement of minutia is common. Matters which would be overlooked as of no consequence at home loom large on the horizon, and they assume dimensions greater than the actual facts warrant. Minor faults which at home would be laughed off become serious problems in this microcosm. And the new missionary needs a large stock of common grace to overcome these gross temptations to entertain a critical spirit of his colleagues and to find fault with their personal lives, mission decisions and work loads. Consequently, the man who can truly love his fellow workers and believe in them and in their sincerity will have gone a long way toward making an adjustment which will in turn help himself.

Peculiar problems for the new missionary issue out of sex and proprieties attendant thereto. Better than fifty per cent of all missionaries today are women. And the position of a single woman on the field presents difficulties. A single woman must exercise caution and be certain never to overstep the bounds. Her sex is in itself a handicap on the mission field because of the attitudes of the nationals toward women. Whatever the Christian faith has done for women across the centuries progress has not been made in the same fashion or to the same degree in other cultures. For this reason there are some "taboos" which women on the field must follow if they are to avoid complications.

A single woman cannot touch a man, and, of course, there is equal reason to assert positively that no man, and particularly no married man, should touch a single woman. Faced with never-ending situations involving sex in the national churches the foreign missionaries cannot exercise too much care and caution in this regard. No single woman should ever be alone with either an unmarried or a married man, and at all times the social amenities must be observed. The change for the single woman is more difficult than for a married couple, and she must develop a rich insight into the customs of the people she wishes to serve. There will be many activities and actions she will be forced to forego because of the sensitivities of the nationals to them. In America it would be different, but the place of her service forces upon her a framework of reference which is unique and she becomes as it were a slave to conventions in a variant culture.

The key word for the new missionary is "change." Faced

with the new environment nothing appears stable; all seems to be in flux; change is the order of the day. There is great reason, then, to emphasize one well-known truth. In the midst of the changing there is the unchanging. And when everything seems to have crumbled to dust, the missionary can still rest upon certain principles which remain constant and which do not vary from age to age. Man in his basic nature and needs does not change. He is a sinner who needs a Saviour. The gospel does not change. It was, it is, and it always will be the power of God unto salvation. Jesus Christ does not change. Change and decay all around the missionary need not cause him to take his eyes off the unchangeable. These certitudes he proclaims and to them he calls the attention of the new missionary with the recommendation that he ground himself in them so that whatever changes befall him he will enjoy a true perspective and be able to keep himself afloat in the seas of the changeable, because he is rooted and grounded in the unchangeable.

CHAPTER X

The Means by Which the Task Is Accomplished

~~~~~~

I. EVANGELISM

IN A PREVIOUS CHAPTER THE DISCUSSION CENTERED IN THE answer to the question, "What is the task of the church?" Now the question for which an answer is sought is "By what means shall the task be accomplished?" An objective clearly stated will assist a missionary in keeping his sights fixed and his goal unchanging. But a clearly stated objective must be linked indissolubly to the means by which the objective may be attained. It is insufficient, therefore, to define objectives without discovering and putting into operation methods designed to produce the results desired.

The Bible does give insight into methods which were used in Jesus' and Paul's day. It does not, however, limit the church to those methods exclusively nor does it pretend to be a textbook on the science of missions as such. Valid, determining, and ever true principles are laid down to undergird the work, and within the boundaries of those principles there is room for creative impulses for every age. The Bible certainly does not give any clues about the use of radio, television, flannelgraphs, motion pictures, or modes of transportation like the airplane. But within the principles laid down, the use of these media for the spread of the gospel is legitimate and acceptable.

One of the guiding principles underlying all missionary work is that the means must be in harmony with the end. At no time can men justify the concept that the end justifies the means. Never can the church assent to the proposition that missionaries may employ wrong means to accomplish good ends. Through the centuries some who hold, in theory, to Christian ethical principles have upheld the view that the end does justify the means. A wrong act used for a good end may then be employed. Unfortunately, a limited perspective and distorted vision which is impaired by man's innate sinfulness does not permit him to see with clarity that a wrong means will never produce a right end, or that a sinful act performed to attain a good end will automatically invalidate the objective and pervert even the end he has in view. Therefore, it may be said in missionary endeavor that whatever means commend themselves to missionaries as appropriate in themselves and consonant with good biblical ethics and morality may be employed.

A second principle undergirding means in missionary work is that the means must show themselves to be valid ones pragmatically. They must work. The empirical test must show that they actually accomplish what is the announced objective. This test will rule out many courses of action which in themselves are neither wrong nor unbiblical. Tested in the fires of missionary usefulness on the field they are found to be defective, and they must be scrapped. Furthermore, what may work in one situation may not work in another. So that in addition to the concept of the principle involved missionaries must remember that expediency also governs their actions and that some means may be inexpedient albeit not immoral.

Today's missionary has before him the history of the Christian church for two thousand years. This includes the Bible which is a record of missionary endeavor. From the experience of two thousand years, the missionary has much to learn about the means of spreading the gospel of Jesus Christ. Church history demonstrates that some methods which have been tried are not workable, and on them neither time nor money should be spent. But the same history shows other methods which have been tried and found satisfactory. These are known to work from experience, and one can normally hope for them to work again in this hour and in the days ahead.

One tried and proved method for spreading the gospel is evangelism. It is at the heart of all methods and indeed must be kept central in any of them. Medical missions is a means of getting out the gospel, but medical missions must be evangelistic. Education is a means of getting the gospel out to men, but education must be evangelistic. In other words, all forms or methods of missionary endeavor must be evangelistic. But having said this, evangelism rates a special place for itself and involves special considerations as a separate and distinct means for making the gospel known among men.

Well-meaning, sincere people have evolved some strange ideas of what evangelism really is. The story is told of one such individual who went to an unreached tribe numbering some twenty thousand people. He learned to repeat John 3: 16 in their language (or at least so he thought). Then he made the rounds of the tribe repeating John 3:16 to all. And when he had completed this task, he claimed that the tribe had been evangelized. One cannot hope that this constituted real evangelism, however good the motive, nor can one ignore the fact that this is a rare and exceptional incident. It should bring to all the realization that evangelism like all other forms of missionary endeavor presupposes the existence of certain qualifications and conditions. And evangelism is apt to be successful to the extent these prerequisites are met. Just as the successful practice of medicine presupposes adequate medical training and clinical experience so evangelism presupposes some things.

Evangelism will be most effective when those who engage in it have, first of all, a knowledge of the people to whom they minister. This knowledge includes the history of the people, the customs of the people, the mind of the people, and the religion of the people. No one could possibly understand America and its democratic system without understanding the background out of which this tradition has sprung. What America is today can be understood and explained by a knowledge of its past history and the roots out of which has come the America of this hour. No one can hope to make an impact on America who does not enjoy this historical knowledge. And so it is with the most primitive peoples to whom the gospel is taken. Ill-formed and unwritten as their history may be, by word of mouth and for generations, father will have passed to son and mother to daughter the substance of their history.

Anthropologically, groups of people develop customs peculiar to their culture, and no missionary can work effectively without knowing something both of these customs and the mores of the people. These customs usually cut across the customs he holds so dear and often distress the missionary and perplex him. In the western world white is used for weddings and black for funerals. In China the reverse is true. In some cultures a woman whose breasts are covered is a harlot or a street walker. In some places concubinage is a normal custom and in others sexual intercourse with the younger sister of one's wife is regarded as perfectly moral and legitimate. In every culture these customs are fixed by time and hallowed by tradition. They are passed from generation to generation without interruption. The customs are rooted in a philosophy of life, and oftentimes make good sense when understood in the light of the total pattern. Customs, utterly foreign to the missionary and seemingly without any consistency, when interpreted correctly make missionaries blush with shame as they learn from the nationals they have come to teach. But it is safe to say that no missionary can be a good evangelist who does not comprehend the customs of the people. The failure to do so results in embarrassments and dislocations which make ineffectual the endeavors of the most zealous missionary.

The mind of a people differs from the mind of all other peoples. No two races or groups of people think exactly alike. An understanding of the mind is another prerequisite to effective evangelism. By the mind of a people is meant their thought patterns, the way they themselves reason and react to life in its multiform relationships. Outward actions may be identical, but the mind behind the thought may differ greatly. Thus two people coming from different backgrounds may do the same thing but to each the act may have connotations which vary and may arise from a mind set that bears no relationship one to the other. This mind set of people may be seen among oriental peoples who are intensely concerned with "face." They must preserve "face" at all costs and for the blunt Anglo-Saxon temperament which is basically opposed to "face" and which is pragmatic and cold in its approach, the mind of the oriental is something of an enigma. But so long as the oriental mind is an enigma to the missionary he is deficient in his effort to present the gospel. The business, then, of the missionary is to bridge this gap by an understanding of the oriental mind (or the mind of the people to whom he goes) for without that understanding his work will be in vain to some degree.

Since no people are without some form of religion, and since all men are incurably religious, the missionary must be acquainted with the religious life and convictions of the people. All of life is incalculably influenced by religious convictions and for the missionary to dismiss lightly what is apt to be as precious as life itself is palpably absurd. Christianity itself cannot be mediated properly without a fair knowledge of the religion it is supposed to replace. For a missionary to conceive of an adequate outreach without a willingness to understand the competing religion is senseless. While all religions stand under the judgment of God and all are declared to be in error, by no means does this imply that the total revelation of God is completely obscured or effaced. However defaced the primitive revelation may be, all religion bears the marks of an original revelation which cannot be annihilated *en toto*. All religions will have points of contact and when used sparingly and wisely, they may simplify the task of the missionary in making an approach with the gospel he brings. He cannot help becoming a more efficient missionary when he possesses knowledge and understanding of the competing religion.

A second major prerequisite for evangelism is knowledge of the Scriptures. This is not listed in order of priority, for knowledge of the Word of God is second to none. Evangelism is sparked by the use of a message, and the only message the missionary has is to be found in the Bible. The Bible is the missionary's textbook, and a successful missionary has a command of that book. Conservative Christians adhere to the belief that the Bible *is* the Word of God, and that the Word of God has power. As a tool or instrument in the hands of the Holy Spirit, this Word quickens and gives life to men. The skillful use of the Bible in concrete situations can do more to produce results than a thousand well-chosen words about the Bible but which do not actually use the Bible itself. The Word of God deals with realistic situations in life and life does not change radically. The Bible has in it solutions in principle to life's problems. This storehouse of knowledge is theoretically available to the missionary, but it does not become his in actuality unless he is able to command that knowledge through his mastery of the Word of God. Reading books about the Bible and studying higher and lower criticism is no substitute for knowledge of the Bible itself. Ancillary studies related to the use of the Bible are not condemned for they serve a useful purpose, but unequivocally it must be stated that they are no substitutes for the first responsibility of the missionary which is a thorough knowledge of the Word of God.

The third basic prerequisite for evangelism is an experimental knowledge of Jesus Christ. Christ must be known by those who would make Him known. This is trite, no doubt, but true. Perhaps nationals may be converted through the instrumentality of an unconverted missionary. But this will not take place because of the unconverted missionary but in spite of him. The missionary who himself has never enjoyed an experimental knowledge of Jesus Christ may bring the Bible with him to the mission field. He may distribute this book to the people. And through the ministry of Bible distribution, people may be converted. It is even possible for a missionary to preach a true message which he never experienced himself. And through this preaching men may come to know God in Christ. But it will be the exception, not the rule.

In the field of salesmanship one principle is that a man must be "sold" on the product he sells. He must believe in that product and show a genuine enthusiasm for it. The gospel, when it has pierced the hearts of men, produces in men a genuine enthusiasm which they can communicate through personality to others. This enthusiasm is itself derived from the experience. While one may exhibit a buoyant spirit in other areas of life, one cannot exhibit that spirit about Christianity without a real experience. The subterfuge is bound to shine through and the veneer wear off in the tough battles of missionary life. For a lasting quality of endeavor, there is no substitute for that experimental knowledge of Jesus Christ.

The control of the language of the people is a fourth prerequisite. A missionary may speak through an interpreter and often is forced to do so in his early years of service. This is not the ideal and is a stop-gap method at best. Ultimately a command of the language is essential for first-rate missionary work. The nationals of many countries could probably describe eloquently the frustration and hurt they feel when missionaries who know their language choose to converse among themselves in the English tongue leaving their fellow-believers and co-workers with a feeling of great shame. How much more is it true that nationals will resent the inconsiderateness of a foreign missionary who professes to love them much, but who cares so little that he will not master their own tongue.

The language problem is more than simply learning a few words and the general grammatical construction of the language. A missionary must seek to acquire a fluency and a control of the language which will keep him from appearing foolish in the sight of the people he is desperately trying to reach. Anyone who has had experience trying to understand foreigners in America will appreciate the gravity of this difficulty. "How shall they hear without a preacher" speaks volumes to the one who is supposed to communicate divine truth to the people in a language they (the people) can understand. The missionary must learn the language and he does well to pay as much attention to it as possible so as to become fluent, understandable, grammatical, and normal to his hearers.

In addition to the prerequisites mentioned a missionary should enjoy no caste or race prejudices. These are fatal to evangelism and reveal the failure of the missionary to control the myths of race superiority or the biblical truth that all men are the created children of God who are equal in the sight of God and precious. God makes no distinctions among those who are in Christ Jesus His Son. There is neither black nor white, bond nor free, male nor female, but all one in Him.

Evangelism's chief methods are preaching and teaching and also the incarnating of the life of Christ in and through the individual missionary. The latter should characterize the life of the missionary whether he is engaged in evangelism or medical work or education. The former—preaching and teaching—are the proper elements of true evangelism. The duty of the missionary has not been discharged when he has told men about Jesus Christ. He has not fully preached the gospel unless he has also urged upon his hearers the need for repentance and for the acceptance of Jesus Christ. The declaration of the gospel in terms of the theological content without a compulsive suggestion for concrete action in response to the invitation does not fulfill the requirements of gospel preaching. Neither does preaching by itself fulfill the commission with which the church has been entrusted. Men are to be brought into touch and vital union with Jesus Christ, and then they are to be taught the truths of the Scriptures until they have been built up in the holy faith and conformed to the image of God's Son. Men are not to be brought and dumped after they have been brought. The work of conservation is as important as the work of bringing and the commission includes "Teaching them to observe all things whatsoever I have commanded you: . . ." Preaching and teaching may be performed by the spoken word, by radio, by books and tracts, by personal witnessing and conversations, or in a hundred other ways.

Evangelism may be individual or mass evangelism, reaching the few or the many, but evangelism must begin somewhere and positive suggestions can be made how to go about this task. The mission station should be in a trade center and in an area where there is good communication. The station should be in an educational center if this is possible and above all it should be designed, location-wise, to be the future center for the conservation and spread of the Christian faith. The missionary cannot think in terms of small geographic areas but rather in terms of provinces and countries, every station being located strategically for the propagation of the faith by the nationals throughout their entire area. From such strategic locations the missionary begins to reach the few and the many.

The plan for evangelism is twofold. First it must be comprehensive and then systematic. Comprehensive evangelism suggests an ultimate outreach which will touch all men. No plan for evangelism can do less than this and be consonant with the dictate of the Great Commission. Systematic evangelism means that method and skill are brought to bear with the aim of utilizing money and manpower to the greatest advantage.

Getting the most out of what is available is systematic and in accord with the principle that all things should be done decently and in order. Systematized evangelism will prevent overlapping and duplication. It will keep some fields from being overmanned while others are undermanned. Cooperative in outlook, time, money, and manpower will be saved. It will include the strategic and careful use of the local church and national leaders on the field. Instead of assigning to nationals menial labor and positions on the fringe, they will be incorporated into the main structure of the work and their efforts coordinated to make the best and greatest use of national leadership. Systematic evangelism is not quiescent evangelism. It is fluid and dynamic in its outreach stretching outward and going forward both through the work of the nationals and of the missionary himself. It will also take steps to conserve missionary fruit by placing responsibility on national leaders to hold regular meetings to shepherd and to strengthen converts, and to seek out the lethargic, the cold, and the weak in a positive program of conservation to prevent the loss of disciples through parental neglect.

The leading form of evangelism is itineration. This is the proper work of an evangelist. The work cannot be done by sitting at home, by writing, by praying, or by studying. These may accompany the effort but not replace it. A man may be taught through the medium of a letter or an interpreter, but the most lasting impression upon him will be made by a personal effort to reach him. This being true, itineration is a "must" for the evangelistic missionary who should go out into the hedges, the highways and byways to get in touch with the lost and the dying. Travel is the norm for evangelism, and the person so engaged should employ whatever convenient means lie at his hand—walking, train, plane, wheelbarrow, ass or horse. The sacrifices and the hardships are many and varied. The discomforts of travel, the dangers from accident and from the hands of men cannot be removed. The problems con-

nected with food, bugs, disease, and sickness are endemic. But
they are part of the work of evangelism.

Any evangelism which does not contribute directly to the
establishment of the kingdom of God is questionable and
ought not to enjoy the support of the church. Evangelism is,
as has been stated, the proclamation of the gospel of God's
grace through personality to personality; it is the setting forth
of God's message of love to men, the declaring of the truth
concerning the Lord Jesus Christ, that men may see in Him
the revelation of God, and believing, repent and follow Him.

In dealing with evangelism, the vivid example of the New
Testament stands before men. From this example, they may
garner nuggets of truth and helpful lessons as they endeavor
to complete the task in this age. One of the first facts which
cuts across the centuries and leaves them amazed and surprised
is the extent of the ground covered by the early church. Following Pentecost, hundreds of converts went back to their
own provinces with the news of the gospel. Persecution scat-
tered many abroad throughout the Roman Empire, but even
when this is taken into account the territory covered by the
early church is astounding. This coverage was not wasted effort. Christians in the early church secured results, lasting results. On one occasion three thousand converts were made; on
another five thousand converts. Everywhere they went they
attracted crowds, and they won multitudes to saving faith in
Christ.

Long ago church historians produced evidence to show that
the converts made by the early Christians came from all walks
of life. The Book of Acts discloses that "a great company of
the priests were obedient to the faith." Again it says, "And
some of them believed, and consorted with Paul and Silas; and
of the devout Greeks a great multitude, and of the chief
women not a few." Again "Therefore many of them believed;
also of honourable women which were Greeks, and of men,
not a few." The Christian faith cut across social lines, eco-

nomic lines and all other lines including race. The gospel attracted men and women from all walks of life. Free men, slaves, wealthy people, Jews and Gentiles alike were touched and transformed by the power of this gospel.

The increasing persecutions suffered by the ancient church clearly reveals the widening spread of that church and the menace it posed to existing institutions. Dynamically vital and politically offensive it awakened the hatred of its opponents and produced recurring waves of violent oppression and persecution. Particularly relevant is the spread of Christianity in the light of the sufferings the average convert faced when he became a follower of Christ. The social obloquy alone was a terrific obstacle. Everywhere the Christian was faced with the loss of social prestige and the privileges of his social status. It also meant giving up his relatives, his employment and other relationships. And in the face of gross superstition, false teachers, seducing spirits, and innumerable difficulties the church continued to spread. The progress of the gospel may have been hindered by these obstacles but the glory of the gospel was its incessant forward progress in the face of these difficulties.

The church must seriously ask itself this question, "What are the secrets of this pervasive and successful evangelism in the early church?" The answer to this question may help it to understand what it must do in this day to insure the rapid progress of the faith in a manner similar to that in which it spread in those early days. Any research will reveal what the factors were which enabled the early Christians to attain the great success they did. The leadership of the church was moved by an impelling desire to preach the gospel as widely as possible in their day. Not satisfied with a local approach they envisioned taking their message to as many people as they could. A second factor was the sense of responsibility which rested upon the hearts of all believers. Each recognized his own personal responsibility to spread the message; each was

THE MEANS BY WHICH THE TASK IS ACCOMPLISHED

an incipient evangelist; each had a personal testimony to give to his fellowmen. But more important still, each one did something about it. A third governing factor was the manner in which early Christians laid hold of their opportunities to witness to the saving power of the gospel. They were not inhibited nor were they apologetic. A forthright frankness characterized their approach, and before kings and princes they did not retreat an inch, but with life and fortune at stake willingly committed all for the sake of the Christ they loved. A fifth factor explaining the great success of the early church was their habit of pressing on into unreached territory. Every frontier was a challenge, and into those frontiers they pressed with zeal and vigor. A frontier was not a barrier to them but a challenge and an open door. However closed the door might appear from the human vantage point they pressed through it that they might reach the unreached.

Principally the energies of the early church were concentrated in key places. Approaching their evangelistic problem for systematic coverage, they worked in the great cities. From the cities the gospel was purveyed into outlying districts and rural areas in waves of varying intensity. The wisdom of this approach cannot be denied. The rural areas had in them fewer people, they were more difficult to reach, and they never were rallying points for further evangelism. The cities on the other hand were urban, progressive, less superstitious, and the number of people larger. The leadership of the ancient church based their operations on the large cities. A seventh factor explaining the dramatic spread of the faith was the leadership itself. The men in that leadership were strong men, men of spiritual power who persevered. These men possessed the qualities of leadership needed for the hard job they engaged in.

Less tangible, but significant nonetheless, was the part prayer and the fulness of the Holy Spirit played in this remarkable advance. The whole spirit and tone of the New

Testament breathes the spirit of prayer. Everywhere prayer without ceasing was made. Always did these men and women believe that prayer changes things and that the power of the sovereign God is released and His energies made available to those who bring their needs and problems to Him in prayer.

They knew and experienced, too, the power of the Holy Spirit in their lives. The Spirit of God was not described as an influence but a person. They believed themselves to be indwelt by that third person of the Trinity and conceived His residence in their hearts to be more than feeling; it was His actual presence. Partakers of the divine nature and indwelt by the living Spirit of God they experienced His dynamic, and drew on His resources and power. Their witness was empowered and the results assured because they enjoyed these divine and supernatural elements which were denied to other human beings not in contact with the true God via Jesus Christ. And it is here that one cannot overlook the sameness of need in the hearts of missionaries for prayer and the infilling of the Spirit of God. In a sense these two elements may be denominated as prerequisites for successful evangelism taking precedence over knowledge of the people and of the Bible. But since prayer and the work of the Holy Spirit undergird all missions and is principial to the entire enterprise, not being limited to evangelism *per se,* it is better to reserve this for further discussion in a separate section.

Meanwhile, another question should be asked, "What is the significance of the reasons given above for the success of the early church? How do they influence and affect the work the church is seeking to do now?" This can be said. What the early church did should prove a stimulus to the church today and should give it light as it formulates policies for evangelism. The early successes should encourage the church in these dark days when doors are closing and when persecution and opposition are rife. Whatever the hazards of missionary work today, they are no greater than those encountered by Christians in ages past. In addition the church has at its command equipment and facilities which, if Christians had possessed them in the first century, would have enabled them to do a better job than they did with their limited facilities. Enjoying these incomparable boons for the dissemination of the gospel, the church should envision the potential and the possibility of what it can do. In short, it needs a new vision comparable to that of the apostolic church. Today's missionary must recapture the conceptions embraced by the early Christians and fill his heart with their zeal and enthusiasm.

One of the most encouraging signs of the times has been the new emphasis on evangelism. Sparked by Youth for Christ, Billy Graham, and a host of lesser lights, the church today is experiencing a revival of evangelism. The older denominations have been moved by the same emphasis. Thus some of them have called for new approaches and new emphases on evangelism within their fellowships. The old Federal Council of the Churches of Christ in America, now known under the title of the National Council of the Churches of Christ in the U.S.A. has been touched by the same movement. For many years the word evangelism was anathema to this group, and the social gospel was the popular panacea for the ills of mankind. But in late years the appointment of "Chuck" Templeton as official evangelist for the NCCCA reveals the changing scene relevant to evangelism. The removal of Templeton from the NCCCA to a top evangelistic post in the Presbyterian Church U.S.A. again proclaims the changing direction of emphasis for evangelism. The Methodist Church which at one time was among the most successful evangelistic segments of Christianity has again moved in the direction of evangelism. Their program of the Seventy in which young men and women are sent out under the direction of the church and encouraged to engage in evangelistic work during the summer is a sign of this trend. For years before this remarkable revival of evangelistic emphasis a few intrepid souls never lost sight of the apostolic norm and kept the fires of evangelism burning. Among them have been Charles E. Fuller of the Old-Fashioned Revival Hour, R. A. Torry, Mel Trotter, Billy Sunday and Wilbur Chapman.

In conclusion, one cannot escape the observation that effective missionary work must be evangelistic. And evangelism itself is the prime form or method by which the gospel of Christ should be mediated to men. If and when evangelism dies, all other forms of missionary work will die along with it. And when evangelism awakens out of its lethargy, all other forms of missionary work will be energized and quickened by the renewed emphasis and will take on new leases of life. Evangelism must be kept before every member of Christ's body, and the responsibility of each Christian to be an evangelist in one form or another must be made relevant to life. When this happens, the present day church will have recaptured the idea of what God in Christ meant for the church to be and what the apostolic church actually was in practice.

CHAPTER XI

The Means by Which the Task Is Accomplished

II EDUCATION

CHRISTIAN EDUCATION IS THE SECOND METHOD FOR REACHING men with the gospel. It is a segment of the whole missionary endeavor involving human and divine forces cooperating together for the purpose of evangelizing the world.

Educational missions cannot be separated from evangelism, and if the term "educational missions" is used solely to delineate secular educational processes without religious content, it is inconsistent with missionary purposes. Here it is taken to mean one particular phase or method of getting the gospel to men. As a department or operational device it is an essential part of missionary tactics. But it must not be forgotten that educational missions do not stand in a class apart from other departments. Educational missions are related to and integrated with evangelism, medicine and literature.

Educational missions like evangelism and medicine constitute a segment of a united corporate effort that has one clear cut and exclusive aim—the gospel of Christ to the whole world or the evangelization of the world with all that this concept entails. Educational work may be carried on as an end or goal in itself. So also may this be done for medical, agricultural, and literary work. But that would not make it missionary nor can it ever be thought of as missionary unless it embraces as its primary goal the bringing of men to Jesus Christ and the establishment of His church.

In the ideal sense true education is evangelistic. True education proposes to get at the heart of things in order to dissolve error, for error obstructs the conquest of truth. Education is the communication of truth and all truth is one truth, the truth of Him who is all in all. Thus whatever dispels darkness, whatever lets in light and truth into the minds of men is essentially evangelistic. Any education which purposes to train the mind of man and does not treat the soul of man in his relationship to his creator is not true education. It is secular education designed for one dimension of life. But education in its truest and best sense is designed for every dimension of life, and to the extent it fails to touch any given dimension to that extent it is not true education and falls under the judgment of God.

The word "educate" means to lead forth. Obviously one can be educated in the sense of possessing knowledge. One can command the field of physics and entertain vast knowledge regarding nuclear fission. Two men may possess this identical knowledge one using it for the destruction of mankind in hydrogen and cobalt bombs while the other uses his knowledge for the help of mankind in constructive ways. The difference between them is found not in the knowledge they possess in the field of physics for in that dimension they are equivalent. The difference comes in the other dimensions of life. Educational missions sounds forth the viewpoint that the acquisition of knowledge in the field of physics is not true education unless it is related to spiritual values, and ethical and moral standards of life. The framework of reference for all education, whether it be medical, scientific, or sociological is the spiritual. Whereas men are and always will be uneducated in some dimensions (e.g. one cannot anticipate that all men will be able to command exhaustive knowledge in all fields, and perchance only in one and that rarely) whatever education they secure, must, in order to be true education, be properly integrated with at least one other dimension of life, the spiritual.

At this point a warning should be sounded. The impression must not prevail that the spiritual is but one dimension of life and that it runs in a parallel line with other dimensions. Rather, the spiritual cuts across every other dimension vertically and penetrates into these other dimensions which run horizontally. To the extent that the spiritual successfully performs this function, to that extent shall these other dimensions be related to the spiritual. In cutting across the lines vertically the spiritual does not simply influence and affect the dimensions into which it cuts, but it actually becomes a part of them. The reason for this is simple. The source of *all* truth is God. The truths of biology, physics, chemistry and sociology are God's truths, and since they are God's truths, the spiritual is in the warp and woof of them because they are true.

Undoubtedly the presuppositions undergirding the philosophy just propounded will be attacked by those who vigorously oppose the teaching of religion in the public schools. Proponents of the separation of church and state cannot help being unhappy with the viewpoint presented, because it leads to the conclusion that if true education *must* include the spiritual, then either of two methods for implementing this conclusion must result: either religion must be taught in the public schools in conjunction with secular subjects or a widespread system of parochial education must be procured, established, and supported.

But there is a third alternative and this we believe to be valid. The home and the church must recognize their role in the educational processes and not leave either the formal or informal education of young people to the public schools alone. Knowing that true education cannot be given apart from the spiritual approach, the home and the church will fill in and supplement and relate the spiritual to the secular in order to provide a balanced education. Obviously it is preferable to educate people in the direct framework and context of the spiritual and the secular, each integrated to the other in a total philosophy of life, but if the realities of the situation make this impossible, and if parochial education is not the best answer, then the compromise in which the state provides the secular arm of education and the church and home provide the religious is the best alternative. But this is true only when the secular educators do not try to break down, destroy, and undercut the spiritual approach as though the one were in direct competition with the other when they are actually complementary and have no real meaning apart from each other.

Educational missions have enjoyed prominence as an avenue for reaching the lost and dying for a number of reasons. As an evangelistic agency they have exercised a profound influence on every mission field and when properly used and applied have demonstrated their merit. Educational missions have not been employed by all agencies equally nor has missionary education been approved in principle by all groups. The chief exponents of educational missions in America have been the large denominations. Among them the Presbyterians, Anglicans, Congregationalists and Methodists have been prominent. Contrariwise, educational missions have been employed reluctantly if at all by leaders of faith missions. To this hour some faith missions are repelled by the thought of educational missions and express discontent with any other method than that of evangelism. A large proportion of the faith boards who have operated for half a century or more have reached a state in their development where they realize the value of educational missions and are now engaged in promoting them although not on a munificent basis. They have also limited educational missions and have kept its purposes more in line with strictly evangelistic endeavor than has been true with denominational education.

Why then can it be said that educational missions are indispensable and by what rules can the church justify this existence? Educational missions have generally given access to peoples and groups who could not be reached any other way. Closed doors became open doors via this medium. This method operates continuously and therefore exercises a more embracing and pervasive power. Evangelism is more spasmodic and less continuous. But education brings men and women before the educator in an unbroken succession of personal encounters which yield proportionate opportunities.

Educational missions constitute an indirect attack whereas evangelism is a frontal one. By indirection the ultimate results may be greater and the gospel commend itself with less trouble. As a flanking movement, educational missions can bore in appreciably while its obvious intent is more obscure. This does not mean that educational missions should be employed as a fifth column method or as a deliberately deceptive device, doing one job outwardly but really having in mind something entirely different and thus employing subterfuge. Educational missions should not be dishonest but make it plain that the educational opportunities which are offered, are offered within the context of the Christian gospel and that no one may enjoy the educational opportunities without being immersed in the hazards of exposure to the gospel at the same time.

Educational missions are justified by the needs of the indigenous church for leadership. Local provisions for education have never been adequate nor satisfactory, and today most of them still are inadequate for missionary purposes. Only through the school can missionaries train the national assistants and co-workers who are needed. The development of an indigenous leadership cannot be divorced from educational processes of some kind, and the demands for this leadership preeminently require educational missions. More than this the spread of the gospel produces a Christian community, and this community needs training. The nature of the training may differ vastly from that of the western world, and the requirements may vary for each field, but the basic need for training will exist always. People usually want education, and they normally look to the missionaries to provide that education. And while the missionary should think in terms of devolution and ultimately of dispensing with his services entirely, he is the key for the beginning of an educational system. Education helps to conserve the fruits of evangelism too. It gives greater permanence to the work and lends a stability which insures its perpetuation and continuity.

Education has been intrinsic in the genius of Protestantism and while this cannot be educed to justify educational missions, it does help us to understand why it has played so large a part in missionary operations across the last two centuries.

In our day, political changes so radical in nature as to appall thinking Christians have brought educational missions into purview for re-examination. This fresh look at educational missions, forced by circumstances, is both necessary and timely. No harm can come from appraising this work and setting our sights for the ideal in a new perspective. Such an examination may call for radical readjustments in the thinking, approaches and understanding of the church. No method is sacrosanct, and each course of action should be recharted from time to time so that the church may be sure it has not left the proper course which will direct it to the goal it has chosen to pursue.

Much thought has gone into the problems of educational missions in recent years. Because denominational boards have been deeply committed with money and manpower, they have re-explored the situation with more vigor than have the faith boards. The latter group has never been as heavily committed and consequently their problems have not become as acute as have those of the denominational boards although one should not discount the possibility that the faith boards will face similar problems in the years to come should they pursue the same policies as the denominational boards.

On every hand missionary statesmen are asking themselves questions about educational missions. And some of these leaders have come to feel that they may have to abandon educational missions to a large degree. And why do they say this? In the first place, the great educational institutions are in a precarious condition today. And this situation prevails for a number of reasons. National Christians today are not always able to support financially institutions created by foreign missionaries who spent large sums of money which are no longer available. And when the institutions have reverted to the nationals for support, it has created economic chaos. The decline of financial assistance rendered by the missionary agencies has in turn helped the institutions to become second and third rate. In the second place, many of the great educational institutions have long since lost their relevancy to missionary work. They have become secularized to a degree and extent that is amazing. From their doors have come graduates who instead of having been reached effectively for Christ have become arch opponents of the Christian faith and have leveled their sights for the destruction of missionary work. And they were trained in the very schools created to produce Christians! It is true that there is a normal hazard in educating those who may not become Christian, but when the institutions turn out a significant number of graduates who become the leaders of movements opposed to Christianity, the natural question arises whether educational missions should not be destroyed entirely or at least that such institutions be made to operate within boundaries which will insure no repetition of this unfortunate result in the years ahead.

Another problem that is vexing missionary statesmen about educational missions is the seizure of these schools by hostile governments. In China, for example, the schools have been taken over by the government, and their Christian and missionary nature has been perverted. Their original missionary purposes have been forgotten. The investments have been lost, and their usefulness is gone. Wherever communism has succeeded in gaining ascendancy, Christian schools have been among the first institutions to be absorbed by the conquerors and used against the Christian faith and for the evil purposes of communism.

Communism is not the only enemy of the Christian institutions. In many countries where communism has not become the way of life, the educational institutions have been hampered and their usefulness seriously curtailed. Government regulations and restrictions have cut down the institutions in many places to the point where they have ceased to be missionary in any real sense of that word. Imagine Christian institutions which are forbidden to hold chapel services and where, for the institution to be recognized by the government or registered, it is necessary both to delete the teaching of religion (i.e. the Christian religion) and chapel services. Some institutions dropped chapel and the teaching of religion in order to qualify for government recognition. Others retained these strategic distinctives and were not recognized or else were placed in an inferior category which in turn prevented their graduates from enrolling in institutions of higher learning operated by the government. Any Christian desiring graduate training in some field for which no training was offered in a Christian institution would be forced from the beginning to attend secular rather than Christian schools. In effect, policies like these have made Christian institutions "B-grade" schools whereas for decades they were the leading institutions.

In cases where educational work has not resulted in training those actively opposed to the Christian faith, other problems have plagued the institutions. In Korea a survey showed that more than eighty per cent of the student enrollment in Christian schools were non-Christians, and this figure is probably representative of most institutions on the mission fields. In those areas where government pressures have prevented the teaching of religion and the holding of chapel services, the vast majority of graduates have left the institutions without being converted and while not hostile to the gospel have been neither hot nor cold but lukewarm. Where government regulations have not interfered with the teaching of religion, the results have not been much better. Having a great majority of students who are not Christians has secularized the "tone" of the institutions and reduced the Christian impact and influence to insignificant dimensions. The leavening effect has been tremendous and when the alumni of a Christian school are largely unbelievers, however well disposed they may be, their religious unbelief will manifest itself in their pressures for a secular program. Missionary leaders experience constantly the frustration of being asked for large sums of money to support institutions which have long ago lost their relevancy to missionary work. The mere existence of an institution is often thought to be sufficient reason in itself for continued financial aid even when the institution is no longer vitally related to the church and when through the presence of unregenerate faculty members and a student body substantially non-Christian the school has ceased to be a witness for the gospel.

At the Willingen meeting of the International Missionary Council in 1952 the delegates wrestled with the problems of educational missions. They recommended that the place and value of educational institutions in missionary work be determined by the application of the following criteria to them:

(a) Is the institution of first-rate quality professionally and spiritually? Has it such a proportion of Christian staff or students as to ensure that its work can truly be called Christian?

(b) Do staff and students participate in the life of the local church? Does it give training for Christian responsibility and service in the church and in the community? Is it of such a pattern that the church can take some responsibility for it and share in its management?

(c) Does the institution make such a contribution to the total Christian cause that the continued use of Christian personnel and resources in this enterprise is justified as compared with use in alternative undertakings which may be more important?

(d) Is it possible for the union of two or more institutions to give a more effective Christian witness and to serve the church and community better?*

From the criteria above, it may be deduced that the delegates at Willingen were willing to draw inferences when the questions, as stated, had been answered satisfactorily. If the school is not spiritually and professionally acceptable, and if the proportion of students and faculty make it less than a Christian institution, it ought to be abandoned. If the institution is not related to church life, and faculty and students alike find no outlets for Christian service, then it ought to be abandoned. If the school does not make a contribution commensurate with the money being invested in it, then it should be abandoned. These inferences must be drawn from the criteria if the answers to the questions are in the negative.

The major question before all those interested in missions is this. Should the church continue to employ educational missions as a major method for propagating the gospel and if the answer is "yes," what should be the standards and program for this endeavor in the future? In answer to the first part of the question, the author must reply that educational missions are necessary and essential. By no stretch of the imagination can it be supposed that educational missions should be discarded. They must be retained. And this may mean a reappraisal of what they ought to be and may include a drastic change from what they presently are. Redirection and even curtailment may result, but this is only a realignment of the method and a reshaping of it rather than the disposal of it.

Educational work must go back to basic principles and com-

* Norman Goodall, ed., *Missions Under the Cross* (London, Edinburgh Press House, 1953), pp. 221-2.

mence again on foundations which have proven operable and satisfactory. And the basic principle governing all such work is this: that the educational work shall be in its ideal and in its output evangelistic. And if it cannot be evangelistic, then it has no place in the missionary program and should be discarded. Missions is not a social service enterprise, and however much the church may be concerned with social service, neither time, nor money, nor manpower is available to perform services and conduct institutions which are unrelated to the major enterprise which is to preach the gospel to every creature and to secure the conversion of men and women. Both in its ideal and output, then, educational missions must be evangelistic and if not then its usefulness is open to serious question. To educate for the good which education in itself may bring does not square with good missionary philosophy, and this attitude must stand under the judgment of the cross in the light of the missionary imperative and the response of the church of Jesus Christ to unite its corporate efforts to the end that men shall be saved.

A second governing principle for educational missions is the employment of proper personnel for the conduct of the enterprise. The teaching personnel must have adequate educational preparation of their own. No specific course of action can be laid down here, because the course will differ depending upon the type of teaching which is to be done. But insistence upon well-trained people with satisfactory academic pedigree is required. Beyond the formal preparation come those qualities which partly transcend formal preparation and without which no one should become a missionary teacher however great the formal qualifications. In the teacher must be resident certain qualities. These include sincerity, genuine interest in the job and the students, love, compassion, and the sacrificial surrender of the life of the teacher to the aim in view. These qualities will be more important than the attainment of the highest academic standards. It is better to employ a missionary teacher who enjoys these personal qualities but whose academic work is somewhat inferior to that of another teacher who is lacking in the vital qualities which make him an ideal representative of Jesus Christ. All other gifts and abilities being equal, the man who possesses the ideal qualities and who can be an incarnate representative of Jesus Christ is the only selection. If a choice must be made between sacrificing the spiritual or the academic, the sacrifice cannot be made at the level of the spiritual and, of course, it is to be hoped that it need not be made at the academic level. But if the choice must be made between the two, the lesser of the two evils must rule and the spiritual ideal in the teacher be maintained.

When it is stated that educational missions must be evangelistic and that the personnel must be Christian and spiritual, one runs head on into divergent philosophies governing the whole concept of missionary education. And it is here and at this point that a definite judgment must be expressed whether it will meet with universal approval or not. For decades a twofold objective has characterized educational missions. The one is that of leavening society with Christian ideals and the other that of training children from Christian homes to become leaders of the churches or key laymen. Many missionary statesmen have not regarded these two aims as being mutually exclusive and have felt that both could be stressed without harm to either. But the history of educational missions brings out the dangers which lurk in the background and which do injure the cause of missions. One of the two objectives will, by conscious or unconscious decision, become the ruling aim with the other secondary. And as one becomes more dominant the other will become more secondary. The history of late years has demonstrated quite plainly that the leavening of society with Christian ideals has become the main emphasis to the detriment of the training of young people from Christian homes. And for that reason a recasting of educational missions seems necessary in the opinion of the author.

Since past history does not give sufficient evidence to warrant the assumption that both objectives can be sustained, then a choice must be made. And the choice should be in favor of training the children of Christian nationals for lay and clerical leadership in the churches. This does not preclude the training of some non-Christian pupils, but it does mean that they will be in the minority and that the institution will not exist for them but for the Christian pupils. And instead of the Christian pupils being taught in a nominal Christian environment the non-Christians will be taught in a vital Christian environment. To enjoy a vital Christian environment, the institutions must have an entirely Christian faculty. No unbelievers shall be permitted to teach, for their introduction immediately gives an anti-Christian tone and brings in influences which are at odds with the ideal. The student body should be predominantly Christian. The institution exists primarily for the Christians, and they should constitute the greater percentage of the pupils. Thus the unbelievers who secure training in this atmosphere will be placed under a constraining influence which will bring them to a place of decision for Jesus Christ. Approximately eighty-five per cent of the student body should come from Christian sources, and this percentage should be kept in this bracket in order to retain the distinctive and unique Christian atmosphere. And ever and always should the tone and atmosphere of the school be definitely and dynamically Christian. If this means that some non-Christians will stay away, the sacrifice of the ideal for the increase of the student body and the diminishing of the positive influence of the Christian faith is too high a price to pay and ultimately will result in decay. If it means that the institutions will be smaller in relation to the student bodies and physical plants and even teaching personnel, it is better for this to be true than to have greater size without a completely

Christian faculty, a predominantly Christian student body, and a positive Christian atmosphere.

Assuming that the institutions will be evangelistic and that the teachers will be spiritual and well trained, what other suggestions should be made about the policies and operations of educational missionary institutions? Perhaps one very important observation is that institutions should follow rather than precede the establishment of a Christian community. And with the creation of a Christian community as the need arises institutions should be founded. This probably will mean that first there will be schools on the primary and secondary levels followed ultimately by institutions of collegiate level and for specialized training.

The schools should be built and developed in line with the needs and physical and financial circumstances of the people. As far as possible they should be erected by the nationals themselves and should be consonant with their ability financially to pay for them. For the mission group to construct buildings which they expect the nationals to control as soon as possible in an indigenous framework automatically means trouble if the mission pays for the buildings and then erects structures on the scale and style of western culture. Let the nationals decide what style of building they will have and let them pay for the construction of the buildings which they will appreciate more if they do it themselves. And if in so doing, academic standards suffer temporarily so long as a vital spiritual testimony is maintained this is far more important than the temporary sacrifice of academic ideals.

The students who come to the schools should not be underwritten by the mission. They should be self-supporting either through the agency of the local churches or by self-support. Those who truly desire that which the institution has to offer will find a way to secure that training. Too often people have been attracted to mission schools for purposes and with motives which have been unworthy. But they have come because they were invited to do so at the expense of the mission. And a free education which is paid for by someone else is always attractive to the unbelieving heart. Funds which have been spent in this fashion have ordinarily been poor investments with no permanent spiritual returns.

Missionary institutions need a flexibility not common to western schools. The pattern which has been developed in the western world is not necessarily the pattern for the mission fields. The standards set up in Europe and America for ordination and for other positions of service in the churches cannot prevail on all foreign fields without modification. The paucity of Christians hearing the call of God to serve Him in the churches is sometimes dismaying, and the fact that many communities of Christians, particularly in those areas where ordination is a necessity for the employment of the sacraments of baptism and the Lord's Supper, are deprived of the benefits of baptism and the Lord's Supper is unfortunate. Even among churches formed by Baptist groups who do not insist upon the need for ordination to enjoy the ordinances of baptism and the Lord's table it still has been a problem. Allen (see bibliography) has dealt with this difficulty in his studies on the indigenous church and recommends that a native ministry be created regardless of formal education until such time as the educational processes have caught up with the need. But in the meantime the need should be cared for by the immediate creation of a clergy. For western missionaries to transplant intact their systems and insist upon their standards is unwise as is becoming clear to all who are studying this problem and working their way through it.

The institutions must be thoroughly evangelistic in two senses. For that small portion of the student body coming from non-Christian homes and themselves non-Christians, there should be exerted definite efforts to win them and their families to Jesus Christ. This cannot be accomplished haphazardly as though the simple presence of non-Christians in a predominantly Christian school will solve the problem. They are to be reached personally and worked with individually. Their families should be approached and contacts established so that the gospel may be preached to them. But the Christian students must also be reached in a true evangelistic sense. Their lives must be deepened; they must be instructed and built up in the holy faith until they are conformed to the image of God's Son. Their problems must be faced and solutions arrived at, for no Christian is exempted from the difficulties which confront normally developing Christian young people.

Enrollments in missionary institutions should never exceed the capacities of the schools or the ability of the Christian teaching staff to handle them. While this may restrict the number enrolled, in the long run the product graduated will be superior, and the restrictions will prove profitable. The curriculum of the school must be adjusted to institutions of higher levels so that there is harmony and proper functioning without unnecessary overlapping. The work itself should be thorough and adapted to the needs and characteristics of the people. This implies a flexibility previously suggested, for mission fields vary and the needs of one will not be identical with the needs of another.

Education should cover different levels depending upon the requirements of a given field. Thus primary and secondary education may be the extent of the training offered in some fields. In others there may be in addition Bible schools, colleges, theological seminaries, medical schools, industrial schools and agricultural schools. The latter institutions require careful supervision to guarantee that they are not diverted from the primary goal and thus descend to the level of the secular losing sight of the spiritual. Some missionary leaders will question the advisability of having industrial or agricultural schools of any kind. But if and when they are employed, the same general rules for other institutions should apply—that they should emphasize evangelism, have Christian teachers, and be predominantly Christian in student body composition.

Whatever form of educational work is undertaken, periodic surveys of the work should be made. These surveys should ask penetrating questions, the answers to which will determine what further support shall be given or whether the institutions have ceased to be worthy of any support. The surveys must determine whether the original aims are being perpetuated, whether the program in operation is conducive to the attainment of those aims and what changes shall be made to bring the educational systems into closer conformity to the major objectives. And if the changes cannot be made, then the acid question is whether the board should discontinue its support of the work. But in it all, education still remains an important method for the propagation of the gospel and when rightly used is an invaluable tool. It need not be discarded because it has in it dangers or because it has been increasingly misused in given situations. Rather the direction of education should be changed, and the channelizing of the method in proper proportion and relationships made certain so that it may be more effectively used in the days ahead.

CHAPTER XII

The Means by Which the Task Is Accomplished

III. MEDICINE

MEDICINE IS THE THIRD MEANS FOR REACHING MEN WITH THE gospel. It has not always enjoyed popularity as a legitimate means however. Only slowly and against much opposition has it come into its own. Missionary medicine has come of age after this long struggle, and it is now recognized as a legitimate method of evangelization which its proponents have demonstrated beyond possible dispute.

The command of the Scriptures to go into all the world and preach the gospel to every creature is more comprehensive in its meaning and wider in its scope than sometimes appears to be true. Livingstone of Africa expressed the wider meaning of the commission in his observation that "God had only one Son and He gave Him to be a medical missionary." He further elaborated on this theme by stressing that being a missionary is more than carrying a Bible under one's arm and preaching the gospel by word of mouth. The missionary must maintain the form of sound words, but he must also engage in a practical manifestation of the spirit of the gospel with concern not only for the life which is to come but also for the life which now is.

In justifying medical missions, no higher ground can be adduced than that comprehended in the life of Jesus Christ Himself. Jesus so sympathized with suffering humanity that He healed the sick, fed the hungry, and went about doing good.

His life and His teaching alike included the principle that physical welfare, the welfare of the body, occupied an important place in the thinking of Him who placed the welfare of the soul first but who never neglected the second.

The Bible is replete with instances in which Jesus healed. He "withdrew himself from thence; and great multitudes followed him, and he healed them all" (Matt. 12:15). ". . . great multitudes came unto him, having with them those that were lame, blind, dumb, maimed, and many others, and cast them down at Jesus' feet; and he healed them" (Matt. 15:30). " . . . he . . . came into the coasts of Judæa beyond Jordan; And great multitudes followed him; and he healed them there" (Matt 19:1, 2). " . . . the blind and the lame came to him in the temple, and he healed them" (Matt. 21:14).

Did not the prophet of old write of Jesus: "He hath anointed me to preach the gospel to the poor, He hath sent me to heal the broken-hearted, to preach deliverance to the captives, and recovering of sight to the blind, to set at liberty them that are bruised, to preach the acceptable year of the Lord" (Isa. 61:1)? Did not Isaiah say, "Himself took our infirmities and bare our sicknesses" (Isa. 53:4)?

Beside the personal example of our Lord there are the direct commands which He gave to His followers. What He did Himself He commissioned His disciples and the first teachers of the Christian faith to do. "And when he had called unto him his twelve disciples, he gave them power against unclean spirits, to cast them out, and to heal all manner of sickness and all manner of disease" (Matt. 10:1). "After these things the Lord appointed other seventy also, and sent them two and two before his face into every city and place, whither he himself would come. . . . And into whatsoever city ye enter, . . . heal the sick that are therein, and say unto them, The kingdom of God is come nigh unto you" (Luke 10:1, 8, 9).

When the Apostles began preaching the gospel subsequent to the ascension of Jesus, healing played a large part in their early ministry. "And by the hands of the apostles were many signs and wonders wrought among the people; . . . Insomuch that they brought forth the sick into the streets, and laid them on beds and couches, that at least the shadow of Peter passing by might overshadow some of them. There came also a multitude out of the cities round about unto Jerusalem, bringing sick folks, and them that were vexed with unclean spirits; and they were healed every one" (Acts 5:12, 15, 16). And so on through the ministry of the apostles in the early church were these miracles of healing wrought.

Today many will contend that the gift of healing is no longer available and that this argument for medical missions is based on shifting sands. It is true that miracles of healing were attestations of the divinity of Jesus Christ and that they were evidences of the apostolic office in the Acts of the Apostles. But they were more than this. They were a practical manifestation of the spirit of compassion in the ministry to suffering people. Can it not be said without apology that the healing art in the service of the gospel of Christ is in line with the methods and intentions of God Himself? Christ and the disciples preached the gospel by word and deed, and the church today ought to do the same.

A casual examination of the New Testament should convince any gainsayer that teaching, preaching, and healing are so inter-related in the Bible narrative as to be indistinguishable. Luke traveled with Paul the Apostle, and there is every reason to believe that he employed usefully his art. He was not called "the beloved physician" by accident.

In advancing arguments in favor of medicine, no one should suppose that it is an end in itself. Nothing could be farther from the truth. It is simply a form of missionary effort which must subserve the one great purpose, which is carrying the gospel to every creature. As a means to this end, it is legitimate and has a rightful place in the missionary enterprise. Jesus Himself used healing as a means to gather an audience and bring into a saving relationship people who first were healed and who through this healing looked upon Him with gratitude and gladly heard what He had to say. Strangely enough the healing ministry of Jesus is emphasized more than people suspect and in particular as it stands in the context of the Sermon on the Mount. Before Jesus began this sermon in Matthew 5, He is exercising His healing powers. And when He concluded this sermon in Chapter 7, He immediately resumed His ministry of healing.

In years gone by, mission boards have asserted that they did not feel any responsibility to support medical missions. They were in the business of preaching the gospel to the heathen. This attitude no longer prevails except in isolated cases. Faith mission boards which have resisted medical missions more than denominational boards are today thoroughly committed to medical missions. The unfortunate predicament into which missions have fallen in some cases is the decline of medical missions to a merely humanitarian service with the tendency for men to conceive of it as a philanthropic agency. This predicament has made its largest inroads among the denominational boards and has not really touched the faith boards.

Traditionally medical missions have not been philanthropic or just humanitarian. The philosophy undergirding this form of missionary work has been the idea that it is an agency which bears the stamp of divine approval and embodies the spirit of the gospel, enabling men to further the work of reconciling man to God. The function of the medical missionary was held to be that of an evangelist.

The first four decades of the twentieth century have done much to dispel the early notions of the function of the medical missionary. The high-water mark of this discontent and recanvassing of this form of missionary labor was reached in the 1930's. The thinking which most appropriately expressed the new approach was embodied in *Rethinking Missions* which was published in 1932 under the name of the chairman William Ernest Hocking of Harvard. Speaking for the committee, Hocking observed that "The use of medical skill for ulterior ends has been rightly challenged, in our judgment, by social and religious leaders in India and China, and a statement of objectives should meet this challenge fairly. The general aims of Christian medical work should include:" And then Hocking enumerates a list of objectives for medical missions which does not include anything that resembles missionary work and which, if found acceptable, would make of medical missions a purely philanthropic and humanitarian enterprise divorced from evangelism and proselyting.

Further on Hocking says that "It is not easy to find ground unassailable by those on the one side who charged that the hospitals are being conducted for propagandist ends, and those on the other who are convinced that any mission institution in which the spoken message is not given has degenerated to the level of a devitalized humanitarianism." And then when enunciating principles to undergird any spiritual approach via medical missions the suggestion contains these words: "But the use of medical or other professional services as a direct means of making converts, or public services in wards and dispensaries from which the patients cannot escape, is subtly coercive, and improper." In a summary of principal conclusions this laymen's group recommended that "the time has come to set the educational and other philanthropic aspects of mission work free from organized responsibility to the work of conscious and direct evangelism. We must work with greater faith in invisible successes, be willing to give largely without any preaching, to cooperate whole-heartedly with non-Christian agencies for social improvement, and to foster the initiative of the Orient in defining ways in which we shall be invited to help."

The Hocking thesis has not won the day, however, for missionary statesmen in the main have rejected this viewpoint and have clung to the evangelistic function of the medical missionary. What the laymen's committee did not understand was that the support for medical missions came from people who were usually committed to the view that they were supporting agents whose concern was primarily for the souls of men or for their spiritual welfare. When medical missions were reduced to a philanthropic enterprise, these people were not willing to make sacrifices for that end. When medicine is divorced from Christianity, there is so much work to be done at home in healing the sick that one need not go abroad. But when going abroad to heal is inextricably bound up in the judgment that by doing this you will save the soul for eternity a bias for passion and sacrifice is inculcated in the hearts of people for the support of such a program.

The church must assume from the beginning that medicine (and education too) is a means to an end. It is not and never should be an end in itself. It involves proselyting for proselyting is basic to the spread of the Christian faith as it is to the spread of any other faith. And every means at the command of the church to spread the gospel involves ulterior motivation. When men are taught to read via the Laubach literacy program, it is with an ulterior motive in view; that by learning to read they may read the Word of God. When missionaries go among the unreached tribes to reduce their spoken language to writing, they do so with the idea that the Word of God shall come to them in their own tongue. And, of course, the plain and unvarnished truth is that any means or agency which does not include the determined effort to make disciples and to present Christ is not missionary work and is therefore not to be included within the scope of missionary endeavor. If some other agency or group not connected with missionary agencies wishes to engage in activities unrelated to spiritual goals, they have the privilege of doing so. But so long as the church is committed to engage in missionary work let it be certain that it is missionary and that the money given for these purposes is not misused in being spent for purposes other than those for which it was given in the first place.

The idea has crept into the thinking of missionary critics that medical missions as a means to an end is somehow unethical. They believe that it should be divorced from direct missionary activity and be an indirect approach to the problem of spiritual values. Two things should be said in reply to this difficulty. The first is directed toward the idea that it is incipiently wrong to use medicine as a means to another end. Obviously the end does not justify the means. The means must in themselves be proper and ethical. Thus the commission of murder cannot be justified as a suitable means to obtain a goal however exalted the goal may be. A lie is not justifiable although it may be told to produce a good result. A good end must be obtained through the use of proper means.

Medical missions has never obscured its true purposes. From its inception missionary organizations have indicated that behind medical means lies a spiritual goal. The gospel was being brought to the lost and dying spiritually via this or any other outreach which would open doors and make the preaching of this gospel possible. And if by using a lancet or a hypodermic needle, men will listen to the old, old story it is a cause for rejoicing. If, on the other hand, men and nations declare that they want medicine but under conditions which will not permit the gospel to be preached, the church must reply that if there can be no gospel there can be no medicine. This conclusion may sound harsh, but it is realistic. The nature of missionary endeavor demands this response, the stated purposes of missionary organizations responsible for sending medical missionaries require it, and it is consistent with the philosophy of the whole enterprise. Such a viewpoint will not prevent any individual from engaging in the practice of medicine in a framework divorced from missionary connections, but it will prevent a missionary organization from engaging in medical work when it must be divorced from missions proper. To lose sight of the spiritual goal of missionary work is to render the enterprise impotent, and to engage in operations which the nature of the enterprise forbids is inexcusable. If it is not missionary, it is wrong however much it might be good and acceptable in some other orientation or when considered by itself without missionary implications.

A hazard in the opposite direction persists for medical missions. This hazard comes when men so emphasize the spiritual in relation to medical missions that they forget the professional aspect of that calling. The true position and function of the medical missionary is that of an evangelist. But this does not allow us to underestimate the importance of strictly professional requirements. Boards do send out missionaries whose chief function is that of evangelist while the same personnel have acquired some minor skills in medicine. Many have neither enjoyed the benefits of a liberal arts education nor have they seen the inside of a medical college. Perhaps situations and circumstances justify sending out missionaries with a modicum of medical skill, and no one ought to criticize this policy but rather rejoice that God has used this to accomplish the primary goal. But this type of approach cannot be regarded as ideal and it must be recognized that it is a makeshift arrangement for the want of something better.

Medical missions is a calling in itself. The missionary who engages in the practice of medicine actually requires greater skill professionally, more self-reliance, and a deeper insight than his fellow workers at home. He is often an internist, a surgeon, a pediatrician, dispenser, consultant, nurse, architect, master-builder, and general superintendent of both hospital and dispensary. He must teach the principles and practices of his profession to the nationals if he is to secure relief from minor tasks. For this task a man with a little medical knowledge is a dangerous person. Men should not be sent out who are partially trained, and when mention is made of medical missions, it is with a two-fold qualification in mind. First the individual must be one who possesses the evangelistic gift and enjoys a true missionary spirit. But he must also have completed a systematic course of study leading to a medical degree, and he must have the legal qualifications to practice medicine.

The best is none too good for the mission field. And no medical man is too highly skilled or trained for this labor of love. The better physician he is, the greater will be the response which comes from his service all other things being equal. Good medicine is a means of access, of gaining entrance. Because of ignorance, superstition, prejudice, politics, or nationalism, evangelistic missionaries may not gain entrance into a country, or if they enter, they may not gain access to the hearts of the hearers. But the medical missionary can get a hearing that may be denied to all others. He is truly the person through whose skill the doors open wide to an effectual and permanent ministry.

The appointment of physicians for overseas service is a missionary appointment. While ordination is quite uncommon for physicians, they should not be denied some service which definitely and specifically sets them apart for this ministry. Normally, ordination as a minister would be impossible due to the lack of formal theological training, but some ecclesiastical status should be accorded the physician. It has been suggested that he be set apart as an evangelist. This would do two things for him. First, the sacredness of his task would be accorded formal recognition, and he would be incorporated into the program not as a pastor or teacher but as an evangelist. Second, this service would give him an ecclesiastical status in keeping with his peculiar functions, tying him into the structure of the missionary enterprise rather than leaving him in an odd relationship to it.

Once the medical missionary leaves for the field he faces problems some of which are the same as those faced by other missionaries and some of which are new and different. The nature of his work is such that the question of private practice on the foreign field becomes an issue. Money can be earned by physicians who will take private patients, and this money may either be a supplement for his own income or for the work of the mission. The second problem arises when the question of the salary of the physician is discussed. And to these problems answers are demanded.

Physicians' salaries for mission work cannot be different from the salaries of other missionaries. At home the average physician will earn four to twenty times what the average pastor will earn. Should not the same distinction prevail on the foreign field? In view of the long training and great financial sacrifice that the physician will make by going to the mission field ought he not be compensated for it? The answer must be a resounding "No." The reasons are several. First, the payment of different salaries on the foreign field will only be a real source of discontent among other workers. Friction, ill-will, and disharmony will prevail. Missions operate in a sinful world in which sanctification is a process, and knowing that weaknesses in the flesh are common, the payment of larger salaries to medical missionaries would fan discontent and produce reactions of a harmful nature. Second, larger salaries imply a half-hearted consecration. The missionary vocation does involve personal financial sacrifice. This is true for all missionaries whatever the form of labor in which they engage. The physician makes a larger financial sacrifice but not always. The minister perhaps could have been a business man and conceivably he could make more money at home than even the physician. But he has heard the call of God and has given up personal convenience and financial considerations. He becomes a minister and in doing so gladly makes whatever sacrifice is necessary. So should the physician. If he does not, he is giving himself partially and not with complete devotion. The loss he takes at the financial level will be repaid him by his Master, if not in this life then in the life to come. The physician faces the same choice that all other Christian workers face

—he must choose one of two paths. The one path is that of worldly advancement, and the other is the path of self-sacrifice and personal consecration. The physician who is unwilling to take the road of sacrifice or who measures his calling in terms of a stipend larger than that of his colleagues is not a suitable candidate for this most exacting of all works the missionary calling.

In reply to the second question the same type of answer must be forthcoming. A physician should not practice medicine on the side for financial return. As soon as he does, limitations of time force him either to neglect his primary work of missions while he neglects those who cannot pay, or he falls into the pit of mercenary considerations which produce a decline in his spiritual life. If private practice for financial gain is a major consideration, the physician would do well to remain at home. He goes because he has a call to go. His service is not to the people who can afford private medicine. His services is one that concerns the soul and eternal salvation. He cannot subject private patients to a forced hearing of the gospel. They are paying for medical services, and properly and ethically they have rights and privileges which the payment of money grants them. On the other hand when the physician is bringing to bear all of the skill and knowledge he possesses in the service of people from whom he gets no personal gain the situation changes. Knowing the conditions under which his labor is given and that it involves his primary purpose of being an evangelist, they can take or leave his medical ministrations as they please. But if they choose to take them, they do so with the knowledge that his service includes the ministry of the gospel for their souls as well as the ministry of healing for their bodies. For the few who might reject the combination, there will be hundreds and thousands to take their places without hesitation.

Someone may inquire whether the private practice of medicine for financial gain might not be satisfactory providing the missionary agency receives the money instead of the physician. And the answer is precisely the same. A mission board which engages the services of a medical missionary at a salary equal to that of other missionaries and which then uses his services for monetary gain for the mission is wrong. This is not to say that no charges for services rendered should be made but that when the practice of medicine has become a professional service based upon lucrative principles it is unethical to ask a physician to give his services for a meager stipend to benefit the mission board. This practice will bring to bear the same disenabling element which has been mentioned in connection with the physician who retains the fees personally— namely that you cannot expect patients who pay their own way not to resent what they may feel to be an intrusion into their personal privacy by the presentation of the gospel.

When the physician arrives on the field, he must learn the language. But because he is a physician he faces immediately the tension of withholding services that would save lives to the detriment of his language control. This first year for language study should be guarded sacredly and professional medicine kept in the background until the first language examination has been passed successfully. In order to accomplish this goal of language control, suggestions have been made that the physician learn the language some distance removed from the actual place of future service. Second, it has been recommended that his full medical and surgical equipment be deliberately kept from him until his language examination in the vernacular has been passed. Since his primary purpose is evangelistic, in which the physician uses the techniques of medicine as part of his equipment, it is essential for the medical missionary to learn the language. Understood properly it may be asserted that the language is more important than medicine itself, for all the medicine in the world unaccompanied by the ability to speak to the people about Jesus Christ is unavailing.

When the physician engages in his ministry of healing and evangelism, he should have as an active co-laborer at least one native evangelist. In a large station he may also have a number of missionary colleagues associated with him. But the medical missionary cannot engage in the follow-up work himself, so that help must be provided. The physician should endeavor to speak personally with every patient and should have evangelistic help in sufficient supply so that no patient is treated without also receiving the gospel. The object is the salvation of the soul, but the objective has not been attained when souls are won. They must be incorporated into a church for fellowship, instruction, and in accordance with the command of the Scriptures. There can be no isolated Christianity. But the physician who reaches the unsaved through medicine cannot perform functions which belong to the ministry proper. The work of conservation is as important as the work of conversion. The fruit of a medical ministry will be lost without that follow-up. Medicine is an evangelistic spearhead and as such has a proper function. But the work of the spearhead must be accompanied by the labor of coordinating personnel to conserve the gains. A discussion of the responsibilities and the means of accomplishing this further goal lie beyond the scope of the present consideration and is mentioned simply to acquaint the reader with the inter-relation that exists between medical missions and other missionary work.

Medical missions reaches beyond the unsaved into the community of the redeemed. This brings to the medical missionary a second function which, in the urgency of completing the Great Commission, should not be overlooked. He will have for patients those who have come to know Jesus Christ and whose families will come under his protecting wing for medical help. Immediately this suggests further problems. If the physician locates in a community highly populated by redeemed people, he may find that his time is preoccupied in service to them. If he commences work in a community without many Christians, time will fill in the gap and sooner or later the Christian community will become large enough to sap his energies and prevent him from reaching out to the unredeemed. This complication is unavoidable and sooner or later it must be faced and met by missionary strategy.

A third function of the medical missionary involves the service he renders to other missionaries and their families. The larger the body of resident missionaries and the larger the number of children the busier the physician will be with them. This is certainly a legitimate use of the services of a medical missionary, but it takes away time he might use for direct evangelistic missionary work through medicine. It is not hard to visualize a situation in which a missionary agency might secure the services of a medical missionary whose sole purpose it would be to serve the missionary family itself. This form of service would be a deviation from the pattern of medical missions as an evangelistic agency and place it in a non-classified bracket. But the same would be true for clerical workers, missionary treasurers and the like. They are essential to the proper operation of a large program in the present method of conducting that program. But they are not missionaries in the professional sense, because they do no direct missionary work. Missionary operations depend upon them, however, and their essential nature makes it impossible to divorce them from the enterprise. But these situations are the exception rather than the rule, and one should think of them as deviations rather than the normal.

A fertile field of service for the medical missionary may be that of sublimating his own missionary passions to a still higher goal. By training nationals for medical work the foreign medical missionary may enlarge the ultimate scope of his operations by multiplying the number of physicians who will serve the people. This higher goal served by the creation of a medical school for the training of national workers does connote or at least incipiently leaves the impression that by withholding good temporarily greater good can come from it. A physician may not be able to do the missionary work among the unreached that he so fervently desires, but through the multiplied ministries of scores of national physicians he may do far more than he could have done himself. Any thoughtful and significant program of medical missions should not overlook this opportunity in a world in which missionary doors in many lands are rapidly closing to medical as well as other forms of missionary work.

Training national nurses falls to the lot of medical missionaries. This again complicates the status of medical missions and places limitations on the service the physician can render to the non-Christians. But the training of nurses is necessary to a forward-looking program and warrants the limitations it puts on the time of the medical-evangelist whose ministry will be enlarged through the future usefulness of trained nurses.

The average medical missionary works in one of several ways. He can be an itinerant physician who travels from place to place on foot, or in an auto and with as much or as little equipment as circumstances permit. He will then remain in a given place for a limited length of time moving from place to place in this itinerant form of ministry. Opportunities come to him as he treats the ill. He preaches the gospel to those to whom he ministers. This is as close to an ideal medical-evangelist situation as one can come. Its shortcomings are obvious. The medical missionary who itinerates cannot have the same facilities at his command as one who works out of a permanent location. X-ray equipment, surgical amphitheatres, consultants, beds, nursing staff and kitchen with feeding facilities are missing. No anesthesiologist is available along with a thousand other items that the normal hospital situation has. But the physician comes as close to being an evangelist in this environment as in any.

The second way the average medical missionary works is through a hospital-dispensary combination. Normally this means that a hospital plant has been erected in a city of some size. Both inpatients and outpatients are treated. The latter will outnumber the former by far. Depending upon the number of beds in the hospital, the yearly number of inpatient cases will vary. This form of approach more nearly approximates that employed in the United States. It quickly becomes big business with all the implications that it entails. Administration becomes a complex factor, and the medical missionary must fit himself into that complexity. Duties and responsibilities fall upon his shoulders with great weight, and severe limitations beset him in his position as a medical-evangelist. The dual role is bound to be embarrassing and the complications many, but this neither implies that the office should be abolished or that the dual nature of the office should be separated into its component parts. The church must deal realistically with the problems and solve them as best it can despite the tensions which enter into the picture.

Medical missionaries have a contribution to make to the public health of the people they serve. In most of the mission fields, the nationals have strange ideas about sanitation. A true gospel witness brings enlightenment in the scientific realm. Ignorance of basic scientific truths can be attributed to the work of darkness, and the medical missionary brings with him knowledge of the sources and cures of disease on the level of community sanitation, hygiene, etc. When one considers that the average age at death in America is sixty-seven years, while in India it is twenty-seven years the disproportion is amazing. Of course infant mortality which reaches the staggering dimensions of thirty per cent of all babies dying before they are two weeks of age accounts for the lowering of the average age of death. But the advent of medical missions can do much to control this mortality and reduce the high death rate occasioned by ignorance, lack of sanitation, and general disregard for the practice of hygiene.

In summing up this section on medical missions it appears

justifiable to assert that this form of missionary work is here to stay. Whether it takes other forms, or is expressed later through the media of indigenous churches with nationals reaching their own people will in no wise diminish the validity of the principle or take away from the stature of medicine as a tried and true form of missionary endeavor. Modifications in the medical approach will undoubtedly come from time to time and within the compass of this form of missionary work vast changes may result with the passing of the years. But medicine is here to stay, and this emphasis must remain as an important segment of any real missionary program because it is an evangelistic spearhead and because a healthy body and mind are part of a redeemed Christian who would be at his best for Jesus Christ.

CHAPTER XIII

April 25, 1957

The Means by Which the Task Is Accomplished

~~~~~~

IV. LITERARY

A FOURTH GENERAL MEANS BY WHICH THE GOSPEL IS COMMUNI-
cated to men is the literary. In previous chapters evangelism,
education, and medicine have been discussed. Now comes the
last general form, the literary, which is not as specialized as the
others and which embraces within it a diversity of operations.
When this discussion of the means has been completed, the
last word has not been said. Other means outside the limits of
this presentation may exist, and in the future new means may
be devised. But so far as present missionary methods operate
the major means will have been covered. And the literary
means is one of them.

The division of missionary operations into compartments
like medicine and evangelism is made for the sake of expediency. Naturally the various means have an inter-dependence
above and beyond the unique aspects which identify them
separately. The literary, for example, is evangelistic. The
evangelistic in turn is related to translation work and the
printing press. None stands by itself although each has a place
by itself. They are all part of the common task of winning men
to Christ.

The aim of literary work is to bring to the nationals in their
own language a body of literature comparable in scope to the
literature at home but suited to the level of the given culture.

The body of literature might be thought of as written and embodied by print on paper, but here it has been extended to include ancillary means not included in previous discussions but which are closely allied to the literary in one way or another. What, specifically, are the items which make up this category of missionary means?

First and foremost among literary forms is translation work. This is twofold in scope. First, it includes the translation of all or parts of the Bible into the language of the people. Second, it includes the translation of Christian literature of many kinds, apart from the Bible itself, into the language of the people. Both of these fields of endeavor are basic to the preaching of the gospel and to the establishment of New Testament churches.

The translation of the Bible into the language of the people has, in one sense, been largely accomplished. As a result of the extensive labors of missionary scholars for hundreds of years, about ninety per cent of the people of the world today have all or some part of the Bible in their own language. The story of this accomplishment is fascinating. The New Testament was written in Greek. It was translated into Latin. Latin became an archaic tongue and ceased to be the vernacular of the people. For centuries the Bible reached only the small minority of people who were able to read and understand Latin. But the need for the Bible in the language of the people could not be obscured by the Roman Church in spite of its desire to keep the Bible from the people in the vernacular. Luther gave his people the Bible in the German tongue. In England, a terrible struggle was waged before the people got the Bible in their own tongue. Copies in English were smuggled into England from the Continent, men paying dearly for their efforts. Wyclif did much to spearhead the movement to secure the Bible in his mother tongue. This struggle eventuated in the King James version of the Bible which has served the English speaking peoples for almost three and a half centuries.

In the nineteenth century, the great missionary century, the principle of the Bible in the language of the people was firmly established in Protestant circles. Consequently, the first step of the pioneer missionary was to make the Scriptures available to the people he served in their own tongue. William Carey and his associates translated the Bible in whole or in part into more than thirty different dialects. Adoniram Judson translated the Bible into the Burmese tongue. Morison began the work of translating the Bible into Chinese. Henry Martyn did the same for the Arabic-speaking peoples. Wherever the missionaries went the story was the same. They simply had to translate the Bible into the tongue of the people to whom they ministered.

The work of the early missionaries was most difficult. They did not enjoy the advantages of modern linguistic discoveries. Each labored by himself amid terrible handicaps. Most of them first had to learn the language of the people via the inductive approach. Then they had to reduce the language to writing where this had not previously been done, teach the people to read their own spoken language, and give them the Bible to read in that language. Where the language was written the task was a little easier, but still it was formidable. When the translations were completed, they were revised across the years as language proficiency increased and an awareness of errors in translations developed. But this much should be clearly comprehended. Modern missionary effort today in most of the world is inextricably bound up in the translation work which is the foundation on which evangelism, education, and medicine rest.

Here it is purposeless to enter into a consideration of the complexities of translation work nor to give space to the problems of phonetics, phonemics, and linguistics. This is a technical and specialized discipline in itself. But the reader must be reminded that translation work is never final—and this for two reasons. First, there are languages which today (more than a thousand of them) have no portion of the Bible in translation. True it is that the Bible has been translated into more than a thousand tongues, but ten per cent of the world's population (estimated at nearly two and one-half billions) have no single book of the Bible. Second, language is always changing and translations must be brought up to date. Whatever one's personal opinion of the Revised Standard Version which was published recently under the auspices of the National Council of the Churches of Christ in the U.S.A., no one can object to the principle that the people must have the Bible in the current language of the day. Speech does change, and with the change old words can no longer be understood. New words enter the language. The Book must keep pace with changing language forms. The basic principle of Bible translation work is not beauty but clarity. Men must know what the Bible says and means. Beauty of language is most desirable, but perspicacity precedes beauty.

One can hardly approve of one translation or version as being the only usable Bible. Any version or translation will have its defects as well as its strong points. Consequently, men do well to have available for reference different translations of the Bible. Comparing one with another will help to impart a clearer understanding of the meaning of more obscure passages. Where one has perspicacity and another beauty, the good features of both may be retained by employing more than one translation.

Agencies today are working on both sides of the language need. Missionaries are revising translations which may be fifty or a hundred years old. New versions or translations are coming off the presses, and wherever it appears necessary and desirable, men are working over older translations to improve them. On the other side of the picture, agencies are engaged in the work of translating the Bible into languages which have no portion of the Word of God at present. In recent years the unprecedented growth of the Wycliffe Bible Translators has been amazing. This agency exists for the sole purpose of translating the Scriptures into languages which have no portion of the Bible today. With approximately four hundred workers they are leading the fight to eliminate this translation deficiency, and more than any other single agency they are working to bring the Word of God to men. The American Bible Society is active in this work also. Under the leadership of its versions secretary who for some years was connected with the Wycliffe Translators they are helping to make possible the ultimate dream of no language without some part of the Word of God in translation.

It is not amiss to mention that the Wycliffe Bible Translators have been operating language schools in America and other lands for prospective missionaries. These schools offer programs of study which facilitate the learning of any language and also prepare men to engage in translation work. Large numbers of missionary appointees from denominational and faith agencies have taken advantage of this unique opportunity to fit themselves for overseas service linguistically. Teaching missionaries how to learn languages which are not written and how to create language forms, and then how to teach the people to read their own written language is indicative of the renewed emphasis on a scientific approach to the missionary objective of reaching mankind with the Word of Life.

Closely associated with translation work is that of literacy. Frank Laubach has pioneered in this field and his contribution has been limitless. For years he was determined that illiteracy should be abolished wherever possible. He was convinced that since the great majority of the people have the Bible in their own languages, the one factor looming large against their getting the Bible was inability to read. He attacked this problem vigorously and has created over the years a method or approach to the problem which is rapidly eliminating illiteracy in many sections of the world.

Literacy is not an unmixed blessing, and the adverse side of it is frightening. The person who can read the Bible is able to read other material as well. In a world in which communism stands posed to strike, the threat is apparent. The Communists everywhere value the printed word as a medium for advancing the cause of communism. Millions upon millions of dollars have been poured into printed propaganda all over the world. This material has not been slanted in the same direction as the *Daily Worker,* but it has been carefully worked over to convey Communist ideology in a subtle manner. By infiltration, they have succeeded in arousing masses of people who might not have been aroused had they been unable to read. The promise of "pie in the sky" which is known to be spurious is nonetheless appealing to people who have no pie and to whom even the hope of something better is attractive.

The Christian church had better make up its own mind that if literacy is worthwhile, and the author believes it is, simply teaching people to read is hardly sufficient. They must be given something worth reading. And there must be enough material and a variety of material which will keep them interested and which will prevent communism from making drastic inroads with its insidious propaganda. A wealth of good reading material must flow from the presses to meet the need of the hour. The Sudan Interior Mission in Africa has caught a vision of this need and is doing something about it. They publish *Africa Challenge,* a magazine for the nationals which is Christian in its approach and yet has enough material to interest the average reader. Tens of thousands of copies of this magazine come off the presses each issue. The response has been gratifying, but it is only a beginning. The Evangelical Literature Overseas is still another agency working to fill the gap of the literary needs of increasing thousands of literate people. The children of light should not allow the children of darkness to steal away the opportunities which now exist and for which an answer ten years from now may be too little too late. Teaching people to read is risky, but it is a calculated risk which the missionary takes in the full assurance that the gospel of Jesus Christ can compete against other options and has power in itself to become a greater force for good than the opposing forces can become for evil.

Literary production does not cease with the publication of the Bible or of good Christian literature. A corpus of material follows naturally. In this the missionary must produce grammars, dictionaries, primers, and other literature. Educational work in every mission field hinges upon the creation of textbooks and materials which normally accompany educational effort. Moreover, hundreds of excellent books in the English language wait for translation into other tongues. The rich resources which have been the product of hundreds of years of Christian faith are of no avail to millions of people because they have not been translated.

Some missionaries should devote their lives exclusively to the production of printed materials for the nationals. In a long range program the effect of a life so dedicated may exceed that of a life given only to direct evangelism. Literary work is indirect to be sure, but it has a lasting quality about it which marks it as worthwhile. The works of Luther, Calvin, and Knox from the Reformation still are printed and still are sold after more than four hundred years, and from this the church should learn that it cannot afford to take a short-term viewpoint. When missionary leaders recall that Plato and Aristotle are read after more than two millennia, they should guard against any strategy which does not give literary work a place of primary importance.

No amount of literary work will survive without the printing press. When once the work of creation or translation is accomplished, the printing press conserves the values by the reproduction of exact copies of the work *ad infinitum.* Just a moment's consideration will convince anyone that the inven-

tion of the printing press was one of the key devices responsible for twentieth century civilization. Like the movable part,
which is the key to mass production and which accounts for
the highly-complex and intricate industrial system of the
United States, so the printing press is the key to the profound
changes which have been wrought in the intellectual sphere.

A thousand years ago the occupants of monasteries were
the guardians of culture and the copyists passed on to succeeding generations what they, by long hours and tedious work,
thought worthy of preservation. The existence of thousands of
manuscripts of the New Testament either in whole or in part
plague the scholar in this field. Variations of the text, notable
copyists errors, and the difficulty surrounding the deciphering
of the manuscripts give the scholars no rest. But the printing
press has changed all this. Now, once the type is set, there is
no occasion for further error. Identical copies of the same
book are made. And the number of copies may range from
five hundred to five million. And each is the same as the one
which preceded it. Is it then any wonder that the printing
press is the marvel of this age? Ideas are important. They are
weapons. Without them men perish. But ideas must be trans-
mitted to people. And the supreme agent for the transmission
of ideas is the printing press.

William Carey early saw the possibilities of the printing
press. Ward joined him as a printer, and he was one of the
first missionaries to use the printing press extensively. An ex-
tract from one of his letters tells vividly what the printing
press means. "You observe, laid out in cases, types in Arabic,
Persian, Nagari, Telugu, Panjabi, Bengali, Marathi, Chinese,
Oriya, Burmese, Nanarese, Greek, Hebrew and English. Hin-
dus, Mussulmans and Christian Indians are busy, composing,
correcting, distributing. Next are four men throwing off the
Scripture sheets in the different languages; others folding the
sheets and delivering them to the large store-room; and six
Mussulmans do the binding. Beyond the office are the varied

type-casters, besides a group of men making ink; and in the spacious open walled-round place, our paper mill, for we manufacture our own paper."*

The great fire in 1812 at the mission station of Carey wrought havoc. The fire consumed paper, type, buildings, and manuscripts. But the greatest loss was that of his manuscripts. Carey was the chief sufferer. Gone were portions of nearly all his Indian Scripture versions. Gone was his Kanarese New Testament. Gone were many pages of his Bengali Dictionary. Gone was all of his Telugu Grammar and much of the Panjabi. Gone was every page of the nearly-completed "Dictionary of Sanskrit and Its Indian Cognates," a work which his biographer describes as his *magnus opus*. One brother wrote, "A few hours ago all was full of promise—now all is rubbish and smoke." But this one example unfolds the grandeur of the work of translation and printing and opens our eyes to the breath taking significance of them in that day. Whatever may have been the possibilities then, the opportunities today are boundless and the future unlimited.

In our day a stream of literature comes from the printing presses. Bibles, books, tracts, newspapers, Sunday School material, dictionaries, grammars, textbooks, devotional literature, and magazines. What the copyist could not do in fifty years the printing press can do in a few days. Missionaries must catch a glimpse of this strategic weapon in this offensive warfare realizing that the printed word has power, a power so vast and immense that men have not yet fully understood its implications.

Another literary means is radio. Immediately someone will argue that radio is not logically a literary means. But it involves more aspects of the literary than any other missionary means, and for want of a better place to put it it can be fitted into this general category. A good argument for thinking of

* S. Pearce Carey, *William Carey* (Philadelphia, Judson Press, 1923), p. 283.

radio as a literary agency can be adduced which may justify its inclusion, however. Radio work involves the preparation of material for broadcasting, and this preparation is literary. No really good radio work is performed extempore. Careful preparation is the norm. Speakers for radio are not like public speakers who often can speak without the same prior preparation. Practically all radio work today is broadcast from material read or memorized. Music portions of a program are an exception, but missionary radio does not have for its aim the production of musical programs as such.

Missionary radio is an evangelistic arm whose major purpose is the outreach of the gospel. There is no rationale for its existence unless this aim is kept in the forefront. As an evangelistic arm and having for its main purpose the spread of the gospel, radio broadcasting is not and should not be limited to preaching. One of the chief values of radio is the attraction which comes from other than religious programs. Good music, well arranged soap-opera type programs, newscasts, and general interest programs give a station listening "pull." Religious themes worked into the total program probably accomplish more than what broadcasting exclusively devoted to religion will do. No radio broadcasting agency today is equipped to operate an exclusively religious network functioning ten hours a day. The amount of labor connected with a daily, ten-hour series of religious broadcasts is prohibitive. "Canned" music, tape recordings, and other devices lift this burden from the broadcasting station and undoubtedly increases its listening audience which may be attracted first by the so-called secular subjects and then by the religious programs. The secular offerings are a means to an end—which is to get people to hear the gospel when it is presented and to commit their lives to Jesus Christ for salvation.

Radio has advantages which are unique. Men who would never enter a church building will listen to the radio. It reaches places where the missionary normally could never gain entrance. It brings within the scope of the gospel out-reach thousands of people and gains admission to homes inex-pensively. The per capita cost of radio for the listening audi-ence is small. For a fraction of the cost of the work of an individual missionary, people may be reached. Radio is what may be termed a "constant." It is a faithful guardian which op-erates silently yet persistently. No minister or missionary can hope to speak to the same people or to as many people day in and day out. But radio does this.

Radio is not a substitute for direct evangelistic work con-ducted by individuals who come face to face with men. But it is an arm of evangelism which breaks down prejudices, reaches the unreached and leads men to Christ so that they will come out to the churches and public meetings. Its chief weakness is the divorce of voice from personal presence, but this weakness is more than overcome by its other values.

A number of agencies are engaged in radio broadcasting to-day. The best known radio agency is HCJB, a short-wave sta-tion located in Quito, Ecuador. Led by the vision-inspired Clarence Jones who has gathered together a splendid staff of co-laborers this station is literally girdling the globe with its gospel messages. Its amazing outreach through the years has brought rich fruits in conversions and in building up believers in the faith. The Far East Broadcasting Co., Inc. is a recent entry into the field of specialized religious broadcasting for the Orient. This agency derives its origin from World War II when so many of our soldiers fought overseas. This over-seas excursion gave thousands of soldiers a chance to see for-eign mission fields and to get a vision of what needed to be done. In the case of this agency the progress has been steady and they have had to work against real obstacles. With China no longer an open door to missionaries, radio broadcasting is one of the live options in answer to communism and the closed door. The ether waves cannot be dominated by the enemy nor can he always prevent people from listening. The future of the Far East Broadcasting Company is excellent. The Sudan Interior Mission has opened a radio station in Africa, purposing to reach more people with the Word of Life. In North Africa, International Evangelism Inc. operates "The Voice of Tangier" twenty-three miles from Gibraltar reaching forty-two million short-wave sets. Insufficient time has elapsed to evaluate the progress and the ultimate worth of these latter agencies, but they are a step in the right direction.

For some unknown reason, denominational missions have not done as much at the broadcasting level as have independent agencies. Yet these agencies without the support of well-defined and substantial constituencies have gone forward successfully. The shape of the future in the light of present events would seem to make it desirable for all missionary agencies to look into radio as a missionary arm when doors are closing and when the time of the white missionary may be running out. Radio is an unexploited method, and it is deserving of greater attention and use in the future.

A new method which has been listed under literary devices is that of gospel recordings. It resembles radio in some ways and in others it is more directly related to the literary. The length of time this means has been in operation is short, but the value of the work has amply demonstrated its worth as an agency for propagating the gospel. The group which has explored this medium is known as Gospel Recordings, Inc. The leadership in its initial stages was provided by Joy Ridderhof who returned from the mission field because of ill health. Catching a glimpse of the opportunities, she pioneered in this work which has reached sizable proportions in the post-war period.

The idea behind gospel records is that missionaries who do not know the language may still be able to act in a missionary way. Simply by carrying a small phonograph anyone can play records for nationals to listen to. The phonographs themselves may be utterly simple so that the power is provided by a handle and the handle powered by the human arm, or they can be more complex, using electricity where it is available. But the premise is that with or without other help than the human arm the message may be taken to men everywhere. The platters are made on field trips into areas where the need is great. Of course the recordings can be made in the United States if someone who knows the language happens to be available. But much of the work must be done on the field and through the services of nationals whose ability to handle the language is unquestioned. The tape recordings are transferred and edited, and then a die is cast from which the platters are made. These platters are shipped to missionaries who are laboring where the given language is spoken. In turn the missionary or national workers carry the small phonographs to the villages and into the highways and byways, playing the records for the people. The records tell the story of redeeming grace, and through this method thousands of people have accepted the gospel invitation.

This group, Gospel Recordings, Inc., works as a faith agency, making no charge for their products. They send out thousands of records each year all over the world. Those who ask for the records have the privilege of paying for them if they wish to do so, but the work itself is supported by prayer through the gifts of the people of God. Prayer and praise letters are sent out to an enlarging constituency of interested and participating people, but no requests for gifts are made. The cost of this program for phonographs and records is small in comparison to the values received. The personnel work without remuneration other than their ordinary expenses. The enterprise is one of cooperative self-sacrifice springing out of a vision which has introduced a new element into missionary methods. Since the program does involve literary problems in the preparation of the thoughts to be conveyed by the language specialists, it is closely tied into this fourth general means for the promotion of the gospel of Christ.

Finally, some mention should be made of one or two types of work which fall into the general classification of literacy means. One is the work of agencies like the American Bible Society, the British and Foreign Bible Society, and the American Tract Society. The second is the work often done by these societies but also done by others under the title of colporteur work.

The Bible societies are specialists in the field of translation and in the printing of the Word of God in other languages. They frequently work, not as direct missionary agencies, but as co-workers with mission boards for whom they act and to whom they render service. Missionaries who have translated the Bible into new tongues find these societies ready to print the Bibles or books of the Bible, and they do it inexpensively. The function of the Bible societies is to get the Bible into the hands of men in their own tongues. This they do well, and they have done it for many decades.

Colporteurs are book peddlers—distributors of religious books and tracts as well as the Bible. They go from place to place with their wares. They sell their products either for no gain at all or for a small profit. They are not in business to make money but are missionaries in the best sense of the word. Whereas Bible societies may employ colporteurs to sell Bibles, the word connotes generally a larger work than that of selling Bibles alone. In this sense the work differs somewhat from the work of Bible Societies and deserves special mention.

Colporteur work is difficult. The standing of the seller is not that of a missionary. His life is endangered in lands where forces are geared to prevent the sale of Protestant religious literature. He has no certain bed and is a migrant who travels here and there. Enlargement of this colporteur work has come in the form of religious bookstores which exist for the sake of distributing Christian literature. In the last two decades religious bookstores have increased in number throughout the world. Missionaries today have discovered that a small bookstore on the field is invaluable for promoting the work of Christ. The bookstore has the advantage of permanency without the hazards of travel, exposure, and special trials. But it must be located in a sizable city, and it suffers from the disadvantage of limitation in its usefulness. The colporteur benefits from his tactile advantage of mobility which enables him to reach more people and especially those in isolated places.

In conclusion, the prediction may be ventured that the literary demands have not decreased although the number of languages into which the Word of God has been translated has increased. There has been a widening demand for more literature and the ancillary components included under this category press upon missionaries more insistently than ever. The field is wide open and the opportunities tremendous. Will the churches buy up these opportunities before the night comes?

CHAPTER XIV

The Spiritual Life of the Missionary on the Field

MISSIONARIES ARE PEOPLE. HOW STRANGE THIS MAY SEEM TO Christians who are not missionaries but how true it is nonetheless. Taking a sea voyage does not make a missionary and becoming a missionary does not mean that all of life's problems disappear to trouble and vex no more. Simply because missionaries are people and thus human, they are beset by all the problems which bedevil Christians whose occupations are apparently more mundane.

The truth should be widely publicized that missionary endeavor is not an exotic enterprise. Missionaries are not on a glorious never-ending vacation. The glamour of which the books speak and the beauties and glories of other religions and life of which some authors make much is sheer fancy. The Taj Mahal is beautiful and the jade of China is not to be excelled, but the Taj Mahal and jade do not begin to represent either land and are the exceptions and not the general rule. Disease, filth, ignorance, lack of sanitation, and ten thousand other evils abound. Into the midst of them a missionary is thrown. The physical conditions which surround the average missionary are gross, and the terrific stresses and strains of missionary life defy description.

One-third to one-half of the first-term missionaries do not return to the foreign field for a second term. This mortality is not due to death alone but mostly to other factors. Ill health, inability to adjust to conditions on the field, psychological tensions, disillusionment, failure to learn the language, inability to get along harmoniously with colleagues, and dissatisfaction of the board itself with the services of the missionary are among the causes for mortality in mission ranks.

All of this suggests that a missionary is subjected to pressures which, if he does not rise above them, will lead to shipwreck so far as his missionary usefulness is concerned. But in order to grasp more fully the actual conditions which militate against the missionary, additional observations should be made.

Climatic environment is against the missionary. In Africa, India, China and many other places the heat, humidity, and differing climatic seasons foreign to his homeland work against him. When summer heat rises to more than one hundred degrees with no relief, no beaches for relaxation, no air conditioning to help, the missionary undergoes grueling tests on his physical man.

The customs of the people add to the force of the powers working against him. In a strange milieu, among people of a different language as well as a different culture, he is lost. How easy for irritation and vexation to creep into his soul as he blunders into one mistake after another. How hard to be patient and understanding of the ways of life of others when he is confirmed in his views that he has a better way of life which they neither understand nor appear to want. How often does he want to take the ever-present language book and throw it as far away as possible. What nerves of iron and oaken will are required to learn tonal tongues and to muster the grammar and the written as well as the spoken word! The horror of heathen customs, the depressing monotony of the routine, seeing from day to day the hardships of the people, all work against him.

Margaret Hickey, writing her personal observations in the *Ladies Home Journal* after a trip to India in connection with the Point Four Program, stated in an article "New Diplomacy in India," what any missionary knows by heart. "After eight months in India, Bill broods disconsolately as he remembers the comforts of the Middle Western college town he calls home. He feels that the Indian officials resent his suggestions. He himself resents the questions they often pose to test a new-comer: 'Is American aid designed to reduce India to the status of a colonial possession?' 'Are negroes allowed to go to school in the United States?' Worst of all Bill's wife hates their big, rambling cottage, which seems to absorb heat and dampness alike. She longs for congenial Americans to talk to. Like all Americans abroad, they live under constant scrutiny, and both sense an undercurrent of antagonism, reflecting the Indians' fears of 'strings attached' to American aid. Bill is the type of man who cannot teach without seeming to 'show off' Ameri-can methods. This is the gravest of drawbacks to any accom-plishment in India. Progress anywhere begins with people and grows only as their mutual understanding increases." The questions addressed to a missionary may differ slightly, but they can sting no less and the suspicion, weight of century-old customs, and lack of understanding are prevalent for him.

The problems that plague the missionary are in part de-rived from his own colleagues. This is especially true for the new missionary. He comes out on fire with energy and high hopes. He wants to see things accomplished. The earth must be moved overnight. Then he settles down to an existence under which he chafes, having to follow customs set up by his predecessors and having to employ methods he may feel to be antiquated and worthless not to mention time consuming. How to keep his mouth closed for the first three years until he gains an understanding and appreciation of methods and poli-cies on the field is fundamental to his future career as a mis-sionary.

Whatever the handicaps of the foreign missionary and how-ever grave the problems he faces, his is a spiritual work and should be carried on with spiritual foundations which enable him to meet the tests of his field and to emerge triumphant. A man who does not possess a strong spiritual life at home will not have a strong spiritual life abroad unless something dramatic happens to change him. Again, a sea voyage will not alter one's character, and the man who cannot meet the problems of life at home cannot meet them abroad. But a man who may get by at home will be exposed to sufficient additional testings abroad which will result in his downfall unless he has spiritual foundations to carry him through.

The devastating problem which faces missionary administrators is the mortality among missionaries who seemingly have adequate spiritual foundations but who still "wash out" when the way is hard and the road long and arduous. While it is relatively simple to assume that all who fail lack spiritual foundations deep enough to carry them though, the unhappy truth is that many who fail seemingly have those foundations and consequently the explanation for such failures takes on proportions which defy analysis. The main consideration here is not to account for those who wash out in spite of splendid spiritual foundations, but to deal with those who will prevail if their foundations are adequate.

Spiritual life even for a missionary is not a static experience. One cannot hope for some cataclysmic experience which will carry him through life without regard to the feeding, nourishing and encouraging of spiritual life. Spiritual foundations are dynamic and are based upon the truism that no initial experience can carry a man through life. His soul's food must be sought day after day. The missionary has deeper problems because of the nature and circumstances of his life's work. He has less opportunity to refuel abroad, because there are fewer contacts, fewer meetings for fellowship, no home church services, and not so many summer conferences with "big names" and first-rate Bible expositors.

The missionary abroad is constantly exposed to professionalism. He goes through the motions because that is what he is supposed to do. He reads the Bible because it is his "business." "They made me the keeper of the vineyards, but mine own vineyard have I not kept." Why it should be supposed that a missionary automatically is exempted from the same temptations which beset all Christians is hard to explain. Indeed, he is beset by all that others experience, and he has a few more besides. He cannot insure for himself spiritual vitality because of his initial experience. He cannot live on what happened to him when he met Christ yesterday. Spiritual life does not resemble the storage battery in which energy can be kept until needed for use. It will not stay in the life unless it is renewed day by day. For an ample outgo or output of spiritual power there must be an ample intake from the divine resources on which he can draw day by day but which like the manna given to the children of Israel in the wilderness must be drawn each day with nothing remaining for the next no matter how much is gathered on any given day.

To use the term "backslidden" as an appellative which could describe a missionary may seem harsh. Normally the term conjures up some Christian who has sunk into deep sin and who has cut himself off from the church and has fallen into the world and its tinselled sins. But there is a backsliding which never manifests itself in the outward elements. The person still gives the appearance of unchanging fealty to the things of God, but the heart is not right with God. It is this form of backsliding which insidiously attacks the missionary. Like the termites that ruin the internal nature withal leaving the external appearance unchanged, so spiritual vitality can be exhausted and unrepleted by the absence of adequate spiritual foundations in the field service of the missionary. If a missionary is in the throes of such defeat, how can he be delivered from it and by what means shall his deliverance come? And if the missionary has not yet been defeated, how can he prevent this evil from gaining control over his life? These are the practical questions for which creative solutions must be found.

The Bible is the first resource of the missionary for the maintenance of his spiritual life. The danger in the use of the Bible derives from its employment for professional purposes. The missionary necessarily employs the Word of God in his business of evangelizing men and building them up in the holy faith. He preaches from it, exhorts with it, and applies its principles to practical problems. It is his guide and textbook. To him it becomes like the hammer to the carpenter and the trowel to the mason; but unlike them he must use it for personal development and the preservation of inner life when the carpenter and the mason have put aside the hammer and the trowel until another day. The carpenter and the mason use the Bible aside and apart from their hammers and trowels; the missionary uses the Bible all over again. It is his tool both for the work of his life and for the spirituality of his soul.

Then the missionary is faced with the complexities of life as they relate to what he preaches and to what he practices. He is forever telling other people what they ought to do and be. This, in turn, he finds warrant for doing from the Word of God. But his own conduct does not always meet the exacting demands of the Scriptures and what he preaches does not find its full flower in his own experience. And it is here that the Bible must work and operate in his life to provide him with the grace and power to make his life conform to the standard he preaches. So the missionary must know that the Bible is his devotional book for personal life and ministry. No matter how much he studies it for use in the pulpit or the streets, he still must find time to use it for the nourishment of his own soul so that God may speak to him through the Word of truth.

No missionary can hope to keep the springs of his own life supplied with fresh water without taking time every day for devotional use of the Bible. A "quiet time" alone with God when God can speak to his heart through the searchlight of the Word itself is a vital ingredient for that spiritual foundation which will keep and preserve the missionary and his ministry from backsliding and defeat. How much he should read and how much time he should spend will naturally vary according to habits, circumstances and individual differences. But whether it is ten minutes or two hours the reading should continue until God has spoken something to the soul. Since God is at least as desirous of meeting men as men are of meeting Him, he can be assured that God will speak to the hearts of men if they wait on Him and give Him the opportunity.

While the Bible is the keystone to listening for and hearing the voice of God, devotional literature is another "must" for the missionary. To have a devotional book in hand all the time and to learn from the experiences and the mistakes of others is priceless. Any good Christian bookstore can supply a missionary with any number of the great devotional classics which have benefited Christians over the years. But the literature should be chosen from among the Christian classics and not from among the popular, light and often non-beneficial literature which floods the market. Books which have stood the test of time and which have lasted through the years are probably best for the person who does not have too much money to invest in the first place and who considers weight and space precious when traveling.

When using the Bible, it should be observed that some portions of the Scriptures are more important than others. All Scripture is inspired but all Scripture is not equal in importance and some parts of the Word of God are to be read over and over again. The Psalms are among the books which should be read and chewed and digested for the spiritual health of the believer. The New Testament is to be preferred in general over the Old Testament, and the Sermon on the Mount to portions of the New Testament which are not as pertinent to life and ministry. The didactic portions that aid personal living are to be preferred in general devotional usage to the apoc-

alyptic which certainly are to be studied and expounded on
occasion but which often have less value to the mundane realities of living.

The Bible may be perused for devotional life in varying
ways and with different goals in mind. One may use it devotionally by perusing a book at a time. It may be wise to follow
through and track down the great themes of the Word of God
like grace, salvation, and sanctification. Key words may be
traced through the Bible. The lives of men and women may
be looked into for help and a better understanding of the
strengths and weaknesses of human personality. But however
one wishes to approach the Bible, it must be used for undergirding the missionary's life and giving him strength and resources to survive the temptations which he encounters. His
first line of defense is the Word of God devotionally.

The second line of defense for the missionary in spiritual
foundations is his prayer life. So much has been written and
so much said about prayer that it almost seems presumptuous
to say anthing more. In fact one sometimes wonders whether
there is anything new to be said on this subject. The consensus
of Christian leadership identifies itself with the conviction
that prayer is truly the Christian's vital breath and that a lack
of prayer or perfunctory prayer is as dangerous to the maintenance of the missionary's spiritual life as anything else.

The average missionary on the field encounters problems
and meets with demands which call for all the time he has and
more. It is utterly impossible for any one worker to meet fully
the demands which are made on his limited physical and spa-
tial resources. The failure to comprehend this has sent num-
berless missionaries home forever or to an early grave. Literally they have been worn out in service by the free gift of
themselves without stint or limitation. The wearing out has
included in it neglect of those resources which would have
helped to prevent the debacle, but which neglect was posited
upon the need to render more service to the people on the

field. Foresight and a better philosophic orientation would have shown the missionary the wisdom of preserving his own spiritual foundations whatever else might be neglected. All missionaries can exhaust themselves in their work. No matter how diligently they labor there is more than they can do, and when they have done all they could, the measure of what still remains appears limitless.

The paradox prevails by which it is possible for a missionary really to accomplish more despite spending less time so long as he gives enough time to devotional use of the Word of God and prayer. What is done will be done better and more will be accomplished. Prayer is not for the benefit of the heathen alone. The missionary needs prayer for his own sake and for that spiritual power in public which is increased largely by one's own personal devotions. When a man is alone with God, then he gets God's message for others. Truly he who prays benefits himself, his work and other people.

Personal or private prayer is the first prayer resource. It should be engaged in at stated or particular times. The Old Testament Jews left a good example of prayer three times a day at stated times. When the Mohammedan call to prayer comes, all else is forgotten and the worshiper attends to that function of life. The twin dangers of fixing set times for prayer and praying frequently leading to sterility is to be anticipated, but there is more danger when prayer becomes haphazard and irregular.

Private prayer may be implemented through the use of a prayer book. In it can be placed items for daily intercession and those items which one might not want to remember every day but at intervals. The use of a book will aid the memory and give coherence and structure to daily praying. One section may be marked off for items which require specific answers with a column indicating the date when first the item was prayed for and another column to show when the prayer was answered or when, for some good reason, it no longer requires further prayer.

No Christian ever need fear that any item for prayer is too small to bring before the throne of God for attention or that any matter is beyond His ability to provide help and a satisfactory solution. But asking for things will not supply the spiritual undergirding needed for successful missionary labor. As much as it is important to ask for things, the highest benefit of prayer for the missionary's own personal life is the establishment of that communion with God which supplies him with spiritual water and heavenly bread so that he neither thirsts nor does he hunger. The tired soul will find its rest in communion with God; the disappointed soul will gather strength to rise and fight again; the perplexed soul will rest in the bosom of the One whose ways are not our ways and whose thoughts are higher than our thoughts; and the soul whose heart has been stricken with the thorns of a never-ending cross will find grace to bear with fortitude, and to endure without losing sweetness in order that Christ may be exalted and His will be done.

The mystical element of prayer is indefinable, yet it exists in a delicate tension which defies logical explanation. Its depths have not yet been plumbed but living examples whose lives of courage, fortitude, patience, and longsuffering portray its reality speak to Christians of the intangible and the illusive which are none the less a part of life and reality itself. Life's deepest problems and distresses when brought into focus through prayer give meaning and integration to existence and enable the believer to live above the commonplace and by some process of sublimation to bring forth unexpected and unanticipated nuggets of character made of pure gold. And prayer is the catalytic agent which transmutes the base and the vile into the good and the pure.

Beyond private prayer is corporate prayer in assembly where a number of people are gathered together in joint communion before God. National believers may attend this type of prayer meeting although the need for smaller gatherings of missionaries alone is not thereby preempted. Corporate prayer effort is recommended in the Scriptures, and the example of the disciples and other believers who were engaged in holy intercession for the ten days between the ascension of our Lord and Pentecost is a good example. Christ Himself intimates that when hearts are in agreement as touching specific items their prayers carry weight and secure from God a hearing and a response. Any endeavor be it missionary, educational, or something else loses more than human mind can imagine through failure to employ this divine provision for the bulwarking of an endeavor and for the release of divine power and grace to accomplish the result desired for the labor employed.

The intimate relationship of faith to prayer should be assessed. Prayer in itself is not nor can it be an effective agency unless it is salted with faith. To pray without faith is as profitless as believing without praying. They form two links in a chain wherein the weakness or the breaking of either link negates the value of its component member.

When the life of a believer is properly balanced, a healthy interaction exists between prayer and faith. Each in its place stimulates and improves both the quality and the performance of the other. Thus when a man prays, prayer in itself is likely to stimulate within the person praying a spirit of faith. When a Christian has faith, that in turn is likely to propel him into active intercession. The converse of this proposition is also valid. Lack of faith will tend to quench the spirit of prayer, and the failure to pray will vitiate and render useless the measure of faith.

A study of the lives of the great saints of God demonstrates the truth of the propositions advanced. Great saints cannot be found who were strong in faith and weak in prayer or strong in prayer and weak in faith. Strength in both of these areas commonly characterized the lives of God's great servants. Men

speak of the faith of George Müller, but the most casual examination of his life will evidence his possession of a magnificent
and compelling prayer life. The two went hand in hand. J.
Hudson Taylor's life further illustrates the uniformity by
which this principle operates. Certainly he was a man of faith.
Again and again he believed that God would provide the personnel and supply the material needs of the mission. Five years
before his death there were seven hundred and fifty missionaries within the family of the China Inland Mission. These
had come in response to the faith of the founder, but his faith
generated his praying, and it was the combination of both
which accounts for the victory. Perhaps the latter side of the
combination can best be shown by the financial policies of the
mission. From the outset Taylor determined that he would
not ask men for money nor would he make the financial needs
known to men. Rather the needs would be made known to
God alone trusting that God would move the hearts of His
servants to provide the sinews of war. Thus unceasing prayer
was made for the supply of financial needs while the missionaries waited in complete dependence upon God. But here the
prayer aspect was stressed so that they continued to wait upon
the Lord God as they asked Him to supply their needs. But
again prayer would have been unavailing had it not been accompanied by a lively faith. As they prayed they believed, and
their faith led them to lay hold of God in prayer unceasing.

One aspect of the problem relating to prayer in the spiritual
life of the missionary on the field requires further clarification. This has to do with the effects and power of prayer which
cannot be seen or measured. Scientifically it would be impossible to gauge with any degree of accuracy this intangible and
immeasurable benefit. Discerning Christians know and understand that prayer is positive in that benefits which are re-
quested are granted in a tangible fashion. The one who prays
asks for specific items and in time he may know that God has
heard and answered his prayers, and he is able to recite for

the benefit of others exactly and specifically how God has helped him. But the other side of this picture takes into account those situations which never arise and those circumstances which never eventuate because prayer was made. Many events which would have transpired do not transpire for the simple reason that prayer prevented them from arising, and the missionary was saved in a preventive sense from troubles which would have been of the first magnitude had they come into his experience. Thus prayer as the Christian's vital breath may well prevent illness from overtaking him in the first place; it may keep ugly circumstances from arising which would ruin and hinder his work; it may keep him from spiritual backsliding.

No one can say that because he did pray that such and so did not happen. Nevertheless, the values and benefits of such prayer are real although intangible and immeasurable. The missionary may not be able to catalog the results of this kind of praying nor is he able to know with certainty what might have happened had he not prayed. But he can be sure that prayer does have value as a preventive as well as a therapeutic and that it is one of the first lines of defense for a proper foundation in the spiritual life on the field.

Beyond the use of the Scriptures and prayer lies the person and work of the Holy Spirit in the life of the missionary. Reliance on the Holy Spirit is a bulwark which provides energy, wisdom, power, and sufficiency for the tasks ahead. As important as the use of the Bible and prayer are in the life of the missionary, more important is the person of the Spirit. The happiness and efficiency of missionary service will be in direct proportion to the manner in which the missionary experiences the rich fulness of the Holy Spirit in his life.

The Holy Spirit indwells the Christian heart from the moment of salvation. Every believer is sealed by that Holy Spirit of promise who takes up His abode in the heart. But being sealed by the Spirit is different from having the Spirit's fulness. And the fulness of the Holy Spirit is the *sine qua non* for a successful ministry. Perhaps one of the chief reasons why missionaries do not return for a second term of field service lies in the absence of the Spirit's fulness.

Oftentimes Christians perceive that something is amiss in their lives without knowing what the particular lack is. They experience defeat and depression, desiring a victory they cannot seem to obtain. Not always does defeat rise from a life of carelessness and sin. Sin is always producing its own brand of defeat, and missionaries do return home because of this problem. But while sin is positive in that it admits of active choice on the part of the missionary, the absence of the fulness of the Holy Spirit is often due, not to sin, but to ignorance. Knowing that something is missing, the defeat is just as real and the results almost identical as though gross sin had been committed.

The ignorance which accounts for the lack of the Spirit's fulness may be overcome by instruction and teaching which will open new doors and new horizons to the missionary who does not have adequate spiritual foundations for continued field service. And it is precisely at this point that another error intrudes itself into the picture. One may not be ignorant of the need for the fulness of the Spirit, but at the same time he may not know how to obtain it. The knowledge of the need is insufficient in itself unless one also possesses the knowledge of how the blessing may be obtained. And once the Spirit's fulness is a living reality in the life a missionary is far less apt to be a casualty.

Being filled with the Holy Spirit may be termed living "life on the highest plane," or it may be called a "life of victory." This overcoming will do much to offset the negative aspects of missionary labor which have been described earlier in this discussion. It certainly will provide rich resources enabling the possessor to work and to live "not somehow but triumphantly." By reaching new levels in the Christian experience, added strength and power will be available to the missionary which will not remove other difficulties but which will permit him to be triumphant in the midst of them.

How this blessing may be obtained is no secret. Christ has come to give His people abundant life here and now. All true believers have eternal life but not all possess abundant life. And the abundant life proceeds from the Holy Spirit. Jesus said, "He that believeth on me, as the scripture hath said, out of his belly shall flow rivers of living water. (But this spake he of the Spirit, which they that believe on him should receive: for the Holy Ghost was not yet given; because that Jesus was not yet glorified)" (John 7:38–9). In Acts 6, the early Christians knew that some Christians were full of the Holy Spirit and that others were not. Thus when the office of deacon was to be filled the command was given, ". . . look ye out from among you seven men of honest report, full of the Holy Ghost and wisdom . . ." (Acts 6:3). Paul later specifically enjoined, ". . . be not drunk with wine, wherein is excess; but be filled with the Spirit" (Eph. 5:18). This Pauline injunction is as useless as that in the Acts of the Apostles if it be true that all Christians are full of the Holy Spirit.

All men ought to be saved, and all Christians ought to be filled with the Spirit. All men are not saved, however, and all Christians are not filled with the Spirit—some because they do not know how either of these two desirable objectives may be obtained and others because they do not wish to obtain them. In the former case the defect is one of ignorance, whereas in the latter it is a want of will or disposition. Once a man knows he ought to be filled with the Holy Spirit (assuming him to be a believer) even this knowledge does not suffice unless two factors stand out in bold relief. One is that he must then know how a man may be filled and the second that he must be led to take whatever step of will and volition is needed to reach the estate he desires.

A man may be filled with the Holy Spirit and have the life

of victory so essential to missionary life in the following manner. The Holy Spirit being holy will not fill any unclean vessel. The first step for filling is emptying. Emptying is putting under the cover of the righteousness of Christ all known sin. This includes confession, restitution, and a holy desire to forsake these sins. The cleansing of the heart is absolutely essential as a prerequisite to filling.

Following the cleansing process comes yielding. This is the giving of self to God. It means that the undivided control and possession of self and all that one has, is, and hopes to be is laid upon the altar of sacrifice. This surrender of self to God is voluntary and final. It implies that once there comes this moment when the heart of a man is forever committed to this irrevocable decision.

Cleansing and surrender are followed by an act of faith in that having met the conditions for filling, the believer now accepts the fact that God, of necessity, is as good as His promises and will have filled him. There may or may not be an emotional experience, a feeling or an immediate and apparent change in the individual. But with or without them God will do His part and fill the individual with His Holy Spirit.

The power of the Holy Spirit in the life of the missionary is essential. And prayer and devotional use of the Bible is not enough in itself. Reliance on the Spirit will incalculably add to the spiritual foundation and resources of the missionary. The deep riches of the Spirit are always available to the person who has thus been filled, and he can go from depth to depth until filled with all fulness. Perhaps the words of David Brainerd convey the vital message behind this insight. "This I say, that when a soul loves God with a supreme love, God's interests and his are become one; it is no matter when or where or how Christ should send me, nor what trials He should exercise me with, if I am prepared for His work and will." Thus are missionary spirits fortified and prepared and enabled to stand firm amid the changing tides and storms of life with the Word, prayer, and reliance upon the Holy Spirit.

To the items already discussed must be added the human equation. The will of the individual in decisive moral action must be coordinated with these other factors or elements. To some extent, will is involved in praying, studying the Bible, and securing the fulness of the Holy Spirit. But in the area of human conduct and in the application of the principles found through meditation and prayer and the guidance of the Spirit daily decisions must be made. These decisions reveal how much grit, perseverance, and spiritual fortitude the believer possesses. If the particular problem is rising at a given hour in the morning, one does not need to pray that the Lord will awaken him. Just set the alarm clock and when it goes off, get up!

Conformity to the will of God or the actual doing of it is as important as surrendering the will and resolving to do that will. The making and passing of resolutions means little unless men implement these resolutions by action and conduct. To will to do precedes doing, but sometimes the will to do does not produce what the will to do desired. The effective exercise of grit and carry-through, then, becomes all important for as Jesus says, "Not every one that saith unto me, Lord, Lord, shall enter the kingdom of heaven; but he that doeth the will of my Father which is in heaven."

The life of Adoniram Judson reflects both the victories and the problems surrounding the doing part of a spiritual foundation. He laid down for himself rules of life which he determined to follow. Among the various items placed on paper from time to time were promises never to spend a moment in mere idleness, always to be diligent in secret prayer, to suppress every emotion of anger or ill will. Others were to rise with the sun, and still others to seek opportunities to make sacrifices and to rejoice in every loss and suffering. All of them manifested the mind and heart of Judson. They show his consciousness of his defects and an acute awareness of his needs. Had Judson normally and naturally enjoyed these rules of life he would have had no need to adopt them for himself. The adoption in itself portrays his awareness and his need at the same time.

In Judson's life the passing of the years and the renewal and restatement of the rules of life which he determined to follow open a window on another facet of his own life. He repeats certain rules of life manifestly showing that even with the passing of the years he still needed to seek victory earnestly in some areas of his life. It was a struggle, unremitting and difficult. In 1819 he expresses the wish to suppress every emotion of anger and ill will. In 1842 he is saying again that he wishes to be sweet in temper, face and word. More than twenty years later he is still struggling to maintain the ideal expressed in 1819. In 1842 he is still saying that he ought not to indulge in resentful feelings toward any person.

A résumé of the maintenance of ideals is not amiss in dealing with the spiritual life of the missionary on the field. Ideals are related to spiritual achievement and one cannot divorce the secular portion of missionary life from the spiritual. They do not operate independent of each other but work in a co-operative framework because they are interdependent. Therefore, the missionary on the field must set up for himself certain ideals and work assiduously to maintain them. He will depend both upon the power and help of the Holy Spirit and upon his own grit and stamina and exertions as he faithfully follows the code laid down for himself.

The maintenance of ideals have to do first with one's person and appearance. It includes eating, dress, the courtesies of life, attitudes and personality. On the mission field, habits of dress often become a stumbling block of sizable proportions. In tropical climates deterioration is rapid and standards tend to be lowered. The same is true for the home and for the table. A home easily becomes a hovel and eating habits can suffer when the standards on the field vary widely from the standards at home. Any missionary must set for himself optimum standards, not in a legal sense, but as a wholesome corrective and preventive measure against the inevitable downward drag of the normal field experience.

Whatever has to do with one's person, appearance, and table habits has also to do with the home in its personal relationships. Habits of courtesy abroad and at home do differ. All men are subjected to the temptation of "letting down the bars" on the home level which they would never dream of doing before their fellowmen. The sharp voice at home might never be displayed abroad; the irritated replies to routine problems can be masked easily outside the living room; words which the missionary would never think of using to his children before strangers he employs within the sacred precincts of the home. Why? Perhaps because even the missionary who is supposed to express the ideal has within him the tensions of a sinful nature which find expression at the point of least resistance; and the least resistance is always the home and the wife and the children.

What is true for a wife and children or for a wife in relation to her husband and children is true for servants. How easy it is to be polite to one's equals; how easy to treat strangers with care! But how hard to maintain the ideal relationship between master and servant; between missionary and domestic workers. To become demanding, officious, and bossy with servants is easy. And because the contacts are continuous and in a familial pattern the human weaknesses and frailties shine through. Countless missionaries have discovered too late that their home attitudes toward servants have limited their usefulness away from home because of the reputations acquired in the minds of servants who have not hesitated to spread far and wide what they have observed. Some missionaries have acquired through conduct at home nicknames which are appropriate but at the same time destructive to their labors for

Christ. Appellatives similar to "loud mouth," "big shot," or "bully" in the national language do the missionary no good. The ideal in the home must be cultivated and practiced because the home of the missionary is under scrutiny always. In the home the missionary should incarnate the life of Christ by his actions, and he can do more to attract unbelievers to Christ this way than by the powerful sermons he might preach. Probably no home can stand the searching scrutiny of unbelievers at all points and all the time, but the maintenance of the appropriate ideal can disarm the critics and afford them no basis for condemning the missionary as a hypocrite. To treat each other in the home with grace and decency and to retain the respect and love of servants is no mean accomplishment.

Then there is the spiritual ideal. This includes the expectation and hope of trying to produce the best in people; of calling forth from them hidden reserves of greatness, sweetness, and other graces. The missionary must possess these spiritual ideals and then have insight to find them even in an undeveloped state in the people with whom he has to deal. The cultivation of these gifts in the lives of men will in itself call forth the best within the missionary and challenge him in the use of all his latent capacities. What is done in and through the lives of the people with whom the missionary is in contact must first be done in his own life. Water cannot rise higher than its source, and the missionary in a real sense is the source from which new Christians take their ideal. He must therefore retain and build up his own spiritual ideals that in turn this ideal may be properly reflected in the lives and hearts of those who know Jesus Christ through him. The lowering of ideals in the life of the missionary will sooner or later manifest itself in the lowering of the ideals among the converts. To keep the spiritual ideals of the converts high the ideals of the missionary must be kept high.

All men either consciously or unconsciously adopt an attitude toward the work they are performing. The fact that a man is engaged in missionary work does not preclude him from having an attitude toward his work too. The individual who is engaged in vocational Christian service should not be expected to have a higher concept of his calling than the man in the street, because every calling is of God and is subject to the laws of God and is under the judgment of God. But in a world of human frailty the worker in the factory is not looked upon with the same critical attitude as the missionary or minister. Thus it behooves the latter class of servants of God to embrace with consistency the ideal and to maintain it with vigor. Laziness is destructive of this ideal and even missionaries are tempted to fall into this sin. They should be careful to spend the proper amount of time on their work. Deviations from the correct pattern inescapably bring reactions from the people to whom the missionary ministers, and his slothfulness will hinder his testimony before them. Quality is related to attitudes toward one's work, and the missionary must have that intuitional sense which speaks to him about the fitness of his work and which generates in him the feeling that it is adequate. This should exist within patterns of normality with the consciousness that there is a perfectionism which exhibits disease just as there is a careless and slovenly approach in the opposite direction. But within the wholesomeness of a well-rounded personality, the work should evidence quality and perseverance together with genuine satisfaction on the part of the worker.

Compounded within the ideal toward one's work is the missionary ideal itself. In this broad category are items, the adherence to which, will mark off the excellent from the average missionary. Since the obvious labor of the missionary is the ingathering of souls through a conversion experience, he must have a passion for the souls of men. However this word may have been abused, it stands for a genuine sense of commitment with an urgency which compels the possessor to leave no stone unturned and no work undone which will bring men to a saving knowledge of Jesus Christ. A missionary without this passion or a missionary who has lost the edge of such passion has also lost the missionary ideal. Subjoined to such passion is a continuing earnestness which should characterize the demeanor of the missionary. No suggestion should be entertained that the missionary is to be "sour" or that he should manifest a spirit of dull despondency or evidence a lack of outward cheeriness and happiness. Far from it! But with all this he must be earnest without the casual frivolity and lightness of aspect which bespeaks the life of a man who is engaged in not too serious business. As an ambassador of God, he is to represent that earnestness of approach which signifies the utter solemnity and seriousness of his task.

The same missionary ideal connotes a continuing interest in the work with a consequent zest for its fulfillment. So must God and Jesus Christ be lifted before national eyes day by day that neither one's relationship to them nor concepts of them are abridged. Missionary ideals can quickly be brought low by failing to keep before the person the highest concepts of God's love, holiness, power, and knowledge. And these in turn cannot be separated from the personal relationship which exists between God and the individual.

A final word will give perspective to the area of ideals. The word is sin. For the lowering of the ideal in any area is sin, and sin in turn always lowers the ideal which when unchecked reduces the ideal still further. Sin does not enter in its worst and most prohibitive forms at first. Gross manifestation of sin most Christians do not succumb to in the beginning. But small and seemingly inconsequential ones open the floodgates to larger ones until the barriers have been broken down and the flood waters sweep away the victim. Sin must be dealt with firmly and vigorously. It must be put away with stress being laid on positive righteousness.

Missionaries with failing health are sent home promptly. They become a hindrance both to the work and to themselves.

No administrator would think of permitting a sick missionary to remain on the field if it were possible to bring him home. But this is not always true for missionaries whose spiritual lives have declined to a point where they are useless or nearly so to themselves and to the work. This ailment is not as perceptible in the first place and brings complications which physical ills never produce from the constituency, friends, and defenders. The missionary who has lost out on the spiritual foundation should return home. And if he will not do so voluntarily, some method must be discovered by which the same result can be secured with the least repercussion and damage to the individual and to the work. But the work is larger and more important than the individual, and no missionary is fit to continue in service who has lost his spiritual foundation abroad.

Missionaries are people. They are subject to the same problems which all Christians face. No missionary, however, can be truly successful on the field unless he possesses a firm spiritual foundation. No substitutes will do. Therefore, let each one determine with the help of God to do whatever is required to insure a satisfactory spiritual life for the success of the mission, the ministry, and the individual missionary.

CHAPTER XV

Anthropology and Missions

~~~~~~

THE DOMINANT PURPOSE OF MISSIONS IS TO REACH PEOPLE WITH the gospel. The people who are reached will be different from the people who reach them. This is true today since the chief source of missionary personnel is the white race while the multitudes to whom they minister are non-white for the most part. Naturally there will be a difference between the "reachers" and the "reached" which may extend from the unappreciable to the almost irreconcilable.

For the missionary, any effort to understand the people to whom he ministers is almost bound to be unilateral. He is trying to reach "them." "They" are not trying to reach him. What he has to offer may not be attractive to his hearers, and he runs the personal risk of being a most unattractive person to them. The missionary is convinced in his own thinking that the gospel which he offers is absolutely necessary for the persons to whom he offers it. In fact he is quite convinced that the failure to enjoy what he brings is an irreparable loss for them in this life and in the life to come. Therefore, one of the primary problems for the missionary is the wrapping in which he brings the gospel, and his personal understanding of the people and his ability to adapt himself to their environment rather than their adapting themselves to his.

The science which has to do with the problem above is anthropology. This science is roughly divided into two major forms, one physical and the other cultural. Physical anthropology may hold the academic attention of the missionary, but it is not his primary concern. While he may be interested in evolution, genetics, racial divisions, skin color, and the measurements of the physical characteristics of men this is incidental to his true occupation. He is much more interested in cultural anthropology. He wants to know what men do, why they do it, and how he may adapt himself to their way of life.

It may be stated somewhat dogmatically that the best missionaries have been good anthropologists. Perhaps they knew little or nothing about the formal side of the science, but they had an intuitive grasp of the science without formal schooling in it. Thousands of missionaries have employed the science of anthropology subconsciously while many others have aided materially in the development of the science too. Few, if any, missionaries at any time in the past and certainly not today have taken the gospel of Christ to people in a vacuum as though the culture of the people to whom the gospel was taken was irrelevant. The few who might have thought that the gospel operates irrespective of the societal environment would either have been unsuccessful or have become discouraged by the failure of their message to take hold.

Missionaries are bound by the cultures in which they have been raised, and all other cultures are foreign to them. The temptation for mortal men is to regard their particular culture as sacrosanct and to think of all other cultures as "queer." More than that, many people think of their culture as being "right" and suppose that those who do things some other way are "wrong." Since the missionary is human, the chances are that he, too, will tend to think and to evaluate other cultures against his background and with the unspoken assumption that whatever is not in agreement with his culture is somehow suspect.

Many missionaries come from cultures in which bath tubs, automobiles, running tap water, and central heating are thought to be expressions of a "high" culture by the white man. Any culture which does not enjoy these "advantages" is labelled "primitive." Unfortunately the word "primitive" too often means only that people do not do things the way the missionary has been accustomed to doing them and therefore these people are "primitive." Somehow it is difficult to suppose that the absence of automobiles and central heating can possibly go along with a high culture and this idea in itself displays the provincial approach. Maybe the presence of some of these appendages of "modern" civilization may be more detrimental than helpful if the facts were properly analyzed.

If it be true that men generally are prone to pronounce judgment against other cultures, it is also true that they entertain ideas of their own racial superiority. Thus the white man is tempted to suppose that the negro race is inferior to the white race. His conclusions will be based, not so much upon evidence, as upon a prior conception which he later validates by any passing fact which comes to his attention. The defense of slavery in America before 1860 was supported by arguments such as the one that the Negro had never built a great culture in Africa nor had he produced the same tools or civilization as the white man had. This in turn was used to prove that he was inferior in status and should therefore remain in an inferior relationship to those who were his intellectual masters. The facts adduced were employed to bulwark a conclusion, not to establish one. And most people are susceptible to that form of reasoning which is based upon prejudice.

Racial prejudice is not limited to criticisms of people whose skin is a different color. Indeed, prejudice exists in many forms within the same races. Who has not heard the popular myth that the southern European races (Italians, etc.) are not the equals of the Nordic peoples? Have not the Germans regarded the Poles and the Russians as inferior people for centuries despite their coming from the same racial group? Who can escape the indictment of having been anti-Semitic in one form or another at some time with prejudice the chief factor causing it?

The missionary who comes to serve a nation with the idea that what he does is right and that what is not in accord with his standards is wrong is due for trouble. He is in very hot water when he infers that western culture and the gospel are synonymous. When he attempts to implement the gospel with the insistence upon standards of western culture, his efforts are bound to fail, and his failure at the level of western culture may result in the failure of the gospel to take root too. A proper appreciation of cultural anthropology will render him more effective as an exponent of Christianity, and it will give him a perspective which will enable him to discriminate between those things which are irrelevant and not principal as over against those things which are primary.

Individuals are apt to experience a keen sense of annoyance when they move into the arena of other cultures. If the average American could adapt himself to the French idea and method of fishing, he would be a genius. To accustom oneself to driving automobiles on the left side of the road instead of the right is not too easy. Harder still is the effort to convince oneself that the person who drives on the other side of the road is actually "normal." To the average American, the French custom of kissing each other first on one side of the face and then the other is hard to appreciate. Doubtlessly they regard our vigorous pumping of the hand as less than civilized in many places.

The missionary, in a special sense, must be acutely aware of the importance of anthropology in his profession. He is not a tourist who can gape at these exotic cultures and then return home with a hundred slides to show his friends. He does not visit any country as a superior creature, pleasure bound and with large sums of money in his pocket. Instead of being a master, he is a servant. Instead of others serving him and being subservient to his every wish, he is there to serve them.

And he cannot serve well the people he does not understand. Nor can he develop a liaison or a camaraderie with them unless they understand and appreciate him.

The best way for a missionary to be understood and appreciated by other races is to become one of them. He becomes one when he becomes like them. And he becomes like them only when he knows their ways, understands the pattern into which they fit, and has an honest appreciation of their culture. He is not there to sit in judgment upon the culture, nor can he afford to condemn the culture. No attitude is more distressing than that of the Pharisee who measures conduct and life by his own standard and who never makes a sincere effort to get to the bottom of the standards and conduct of other men. Christ consistently pronounced judgment upon Phariseeism and exposed its sham and hypocrisy. This does not presuppose that everything in any culture is perfect, but that there is a difference in attitude or approach which is all important.

The proper attitude for the missionary is to discard the crude and distorting lenses of western culture, beginning his pilgrimage with the intention of learning, not judging. First he must find out what the people do, then why they do it, and then he must learn what changes are taking place; for all cultures operate within a dynamic rather than a static tension. He must understand taboos and forces which hold cultures together. And perhaps for the first time he will examine his own culture against the backdrop of another culture, and he may be amazed to discover that his culture is not as good as he thought it to be. And he will discover that even the worst of the so-called "primitives" have something to teach him if he wishes to learn from them.

Nida in his volume, *Customs and Cultures,* points up that type of attitude which sometimes characterizes missionaries in their approach to cultural problems. A missionary in the Congo felt that the believers associated with his group were "worldly" and "unbecoming" in their conduct when they used crushed moth balls and palm oil as a kind of perfume or cologne. Before they could enter the church building, a "smeller" would admit or refuse them admission depending upon whether there was even the faintest odor of moth balls. Even among the most exacting fundamentalists in America no one would think of smelling a man to see whether he had been smoking a cigarette or imbibing the convivial bottle before he would be admitted to a church service. Jesus Himself would probably have been the first to insist that He did not come to call the righteous but sinners to repentance. And the church is precisely the place where a man who needs regeneration and reformation ought to go. His conduct and behavior cannot be influenced by denying him admission to the building as much as it can be by getting him under the hearing of the gospel so that he gets spiritual understanding which will enable him to discriminate between those things which please God and those which offend Him.

One of the first lessons for the new missionary to learn is that of values. Every culture has its own set of values, and they are sure to differ from that of the missionary. Some cultures have no interest in the acquisition of "things" as such. If a man has one pair of pants, he does not need a second pair. After all, he can only wear one at a time anyhow. He will work to secure one pair, but no one can get him to work for a second pair so long as the one pair he has serves him satisfactorily. American culture is a culture in which success is stressed. Success means the amount of money a man has, the kind of home he lives in, and the make of automobile he drives. The average American is not satisfied with one pair of trousers, and he spends his days working to give his wife another dress for "she has nothing to wear," and to give his children clothes, toys, bicycles, and the thousand other incidentals which make up the lives of American young people.

Men everywhere disagree about the nature of values too. One culture may regard silver and gold inestimably valuable.

They will fight and kill to have them. Another culture may look upon them with disdain. Beads in one culture, stones in another, and cows in still another may represent the highest values. In Western civilization an art museum will pay large sums of money for an oil painting which has been painted by an old master. Men will visit a museum to gaze upon a "priceless" Gutenburg Bible. Some other cultures would probably regard both of these as valueless, and from the vantage point of intrinsic value they would be correct in their evaluation.

Across the pages of history one encounters innumerable cases where men have made excellent "bargains" in their dealings with foreigners solely because of value differences. One race would hold precious what another one despised. And the one would sell to the other items on, what seemed to both of them, most satisfactory terms. The sale of Manhattan Island by the Indians for some beads was looked upon by the Dutch as the epitome of a bargain—and it was for them. The Indians probably felt that they had outsmarted the white man and that in return for a little land they had secured something far exceeding the land in value.

No missionary can hope to enjoy a satisfactory ministry among any people whose sense of values he has not come to understand and appreciate. The heart of a people will somehow be exposed by what they hold valuable, and the missionary who has a keen perception of their sense of values within the strands of the total culture will be a better missionary. Without this appreciation he inevitably is bound to fail.

Culture is not a series of isolated acts performed by people accidentally. Nor is it the accumulation of a given number of traits. Culture has pattern and symmetry so that the individual strands which go to make up the culture are part of an integrated and systematic whole. The function of culture is to make society operate. The operation in itself is a complexity of seemingly unrelated factors which, despite their apparent unrelatedness, are definitely related were we able to understand in full the operation of that given culture.

Perhaps the most difficult experience for the missionary is to understand those aspects of culture for which he finds no real need. In South America among some tribes, the husband must rest for days or weeks following the birth of his baby. Anyone familiar with the routine of reproduction knows that this kind of rest for the husband is not based upon a real but upon an imaginary need. But real or imaginary it is a part of the culture, and the missionary must not only recognize that it is part of the culture but he must also have a sympathetic understanding of it. At first he may be irritated by what is physically senseless until he realizes that the psychosomatic is just as real as the physical.

The westerner has in his culture many elements which he takes for granted. The missionary who is a westerner is no less likely to take the same elements for granted. But then he comes into contact with other cultures which do not take the same things for granted. Immediately the missionary is faced with a distinct cultural problem. If he retains his own ideas and refuses to think in terms of the culture to which he is ministering, he is headed for shipwreck. In western culture the position of women has been elevated over the centuries. A polite westerner would not think of asking his wife to follow after him. She precedes him. But in other cultures it is quite wrong for a woman to precede her husband. She must follow after him. For centuries western culture assumed the existence of the absolute and believed that truth was knowable. For an equal number of centuries other cultures have believed in the relative and have been certain that ultimate reality is ineffable. Things which one culture takes for granted are the exact opposite of what others assume, and the missionary meets this head on.

American life has been filled with clichés like "It's always darkest before the dawn," "Every cloud has a silver lining,"

"Every day in every way we're getting better and better." But other cultures take for granted a pessimistic approach to life. Still others believe in a rigid determinism which borders on a deep fatalism. The point of all this is simply that other cultures differ beyond basic values, moving deeply into the area of things one culture assumes which other cultures do not assume. And no missionary will be a good missionary finally who does not have an understanding of the elements of a culture which the person in that culture takes for granted.

Missionaries are apt to regard certain practices of a people to be wrong without knowing why they perform them in the first place. The missionary need not approve of every practice nor should he necessarily condone some of them, but at least he should know that they are not isolated from the rest of the culture but are an intrinsic part of it. The practice of infanticide does not commend itself to Christians, but this practice in some cultures is posited upon a very limited food supply which makes the sustaining of a growing population impossible. In America there has been an increasing pressure exerted in favor of euthanasia. Within western culture there have been those for and against the practice. But other cultures would regard this as an impossible practice while still others practice it right now. The strange phenomenon is the missionary who is righteously fighting the killing of elderly people on a mission field who has not lifted a finger to wage war against the concept developing within his own culture.

The problem of etiquette is a thorny one, and this is an anthropological question. In some instances etiquette may involve basic principles, but generally this is not so. Obviously where principle is at stake the missionary must work his way through the problem without compromising his Christian convictions. In connection with principle an observation should be dropped for the Anglo-Saxon who holds to the idea that decisions in the realm of ethics and morality are either "yes" or "no" and that there is no middle ground between. In the nature of the case life is tremendously complex and there are times when one must make decisions, not between the right and the wrong but between the lesser of two evils. If a missionary is about to be imprisoned or beheaded for a crime he did not commit but a choice is given to him which form of punishment to accept, he is placed in a position where he must choose the lesser of two evils, neither one of which, strictly speaking, is right in itself because he is not guilty to begin with. There is little chance that a missionary would accept death as over against imprisonment. And the acceptance of imprisonment outwardly, at least, would carry with it the idea of guilt, but the acceptance of the death penalty would carry with it the idea of guilt no less firmly, and whichever way the missionary chooses the same conclusion would be implicit in his choice.

But etiquette rarely poses the question of the lesser of two evils, for most of the time the problem is one of local custom without moral or ethical implications. Missionary strategy is simple. Just follow the customs of the people. This is particularly important for the custom itself may be tied to some concept, the violation of which would be extremely unfortunate in dealing with the nationals. For example, some people pass objects to other people with both hands. A seemingly irrelevant custom, it is linked to a concept which is very important in the minds of the people. To pass something with one hand is to imply that the person to whom the object is passed is like a dog or is being treated like a dog. This is offensive to the individual. The missionary should therefore pass objects with two hands, for no principle is at stake unless one thinks of the principle that missionaries are to be all things to all men, and this is one way in which they can fulfill this royal law. In China following the eating of a meal one is hardly polite if he does not belch aloud. The belching shows his appreciation of the dinner and is an expression which is most pleasing to the host. In the western world belching is not regarded as acceptable in polite society, but the rules for polite society differ depending upon whose polite society the missionary happens to be in. And when in Rome, do as the Romans do.

If it be true that the rules of etiquette and custom differ in one culture from another, it is also true that there are differences within approximately the same cultures. In America a large number of Christians are teetotalers and would no more think of serving wine or beer than they would of serving drugs. But in parts of Europe this is a common custom among the most select Christians, and it is not felt to be wrong. But the same homes in Europe which serve wine may think it extremely bad taste for women to wear lipstick, while the American women who refuse to serve alcoholic beverages think nothing of wearing lipstick.

In America no host would ever think of asking his guests to remove their shoes. But in Japan no guest would think of entering a home without removing his shoes. And the failure to do so would be most impolite. Likewise in some cultures it is impolite to correct or disagree with a guest. A stranger might leave such a home with the idea that all he said was agreed to by his host without knowing that national courtesy prohibited the host from disagreeing with his guest even though he really was not in accord with anything the guest said. The knowledge of conditions like these is important for the missionary who cannot succeed if he violates the simplest rules of social conduct and makes himself appear to be exactly what he does not wish to appear to be—a boor.

A missionary must not be contemptuous of another culture. But this is only the negative side to culture. Perhaps he may not be disdainful but he may not have any real appreciation of the culture either. He should be both interested in that culture and sympathetic towards it if he is to succeed. A genuine interest in what others do is necessary for the effective communication of what the missionary has to bring. He will not compromise his own position by being understanding, but he will almost surely compromise his ability to bring the gospel if he is not. The missionary should be uniquely equipped to find points of contact in other cultures rather than to point up the differences. The idea "Why, we do it this way too" is a tool of inestimable value to the missionary, for it places him on common ground with the nationals and serves to identify him as one of them. There are bound to be points of contact in ways of living which coincide with those of the nationals.

Habits of dress are anthropological problems. They are not often organically connected to sex. No missionary should assume that forms of dress are necessarily related to sex nor should he condemn every fashion with which he is in disagreement. In some cultures the woman whose breasts are covered is a street walker. In still another a woman whose ankles are exposed is lewd. In another a married woman will dress one way while a marriageable girl will dress in a different fashion. A proof that clothing does not in itself connote morality is patent from an examination of the culture of Eskimos. They wear a great deal of clothing—they have to because of climatic conditions. But the same Eskimos who are so well covered do not evince sexual morality so much greater than the Africans who go uncovered. In fact in some Eskimo cultures it is polite to share your wife with strangers, a privilege which is accorded you in return when you are a guest. There are cultures in which relative nakedness exists but in which sexual morality is no worse than in cultures wherein people go covered. If the Kinsey report is any index of the sexual morality of American culture, then clothing does not make as much difference as the minds of some would make it out to be.

The missionary who goes to a field where people are dressed so differently that it arouses within him feelings of concern should evaluate carefully what steps he should take toward national customs, and he should act without being precipitate. His first desire to force the nationals to cover their bodies may be unfortunate. And if the covering of the body is a matter of principle which the regenerate will practice, the missionary can well anticipate that the Holy Spirit will make that plain to the converts as time goes on. But to see a man of color in hot, humid Africa, dressed in the castoff overcoat of a man from America when the colored man needs no coat is not especially attractive. The important consideration for the missionary is not the way the nationals dress but what they will do with the gospel of Jesus Christ. Let them make that their first concern and try to develop a sense of perspective about the customs of dress.

The methods by which men secure their daily living vary much. In some places they are forced to work exceedingly hard to eke out a meager existence from the soil. In some of the islands of the sea, living is no problem. Fish from the ocean and plants which grow in exotic profusion serve to make life easy. To the missionary some national cultures will appear to be grossly indolent. He cannot understand why they do not make more of what they have or work harder to develop further their resources for security, etc. The missionary comes from a culture with a pattern which is different from that of the people to whom he brings the gospel. Culture patterns are not dogmas which have the exactitude of doctrinal revelation. The missionary's way of life is not an absolute. Let him beware of passing judgment on the other culture for the people of that culture may have developed a keener awareness of the briefness of life and the utter futility of adding to one's possessions those things he cannot take with him anyhow.

In the realm of religion people vary. The missionary must observe this from the beginning of his labors and seek out an exact knowledge of the religion of the group he is trying to reach. He has come to his place of service with the idea that all men are basically religious. And that is probably close to the truth. But having said that, sooner or later he will conclude that the similarities which are common to all religions just about stop there. It is correct that two groups may have elements common to both of their religions even though the groups are widely separated geographically. It is also correct that everything is not as it appears on the surface and the outward garb may hide meanings quite the opposite of what the missionary supposes. So the science of cultural anthropology comes to the forefront once more, and the missionary becomes a successful one in so far as he is able to bring this science to bear as a lever which will enable him to mediate the gospel to people who entertain religious ideas dissimilar to his own.

Religious differences may be defined broadly in dealing with blocs of human beings. There are those who believe in the supernatural and those who are antisupernaturalistic. There are those who believe in a divine revelation and those who do not. Some religions are moral and others amoral. Still others are inclusive, believing that all religions lead to the same God whereas others are exclusive, believing that all other religions are false. These differences may be extended *ad infinitum,* but the ones mentioned so far will demonstrate the complexity of the problem for the missionary who comes with the gospel and who must face these opposing religions which are embraced by people who are sincere, earnest, devoted, and convinced followers of the religious way of life.

In religious matters the missionary discovers quickly that the conclusions he may draw from his observations of the outward signs and symbols of the religious life do not always reflect the realities of the situation. One of the classic instances of this may be noted from a casual examination of the cultures into which Romanism was brought, and where the Roman Church covered the idolatry of heathenism with the external paraphernalia of crosses, incense, incantations, and prayers for the dead. When one probes beneath the surface, he soon discovers that so far as the nationals are concerned the outward façade is that of Romanism while the inward meaning has remained animistic.

If the problem exists for the missionary in his understanding of other religions, the problem is no less acute for the national who tries to understand the religion of the missionary. One or two illustrations will point this up. A missionary customarily knelt in prayer. He did this using a chair. Who can blame the uninformed national who supposed that the missionary worshiped the chair because he always knelt before it? Naturally the missionary would deny such a charge vigorously, but the person who could not see beneath the exterior would be correct in his appraisal until all of the facts in the case were known. Who can blame a national who thinks that church membership is like initiation into a secret society? And why condemn him for keeping the rules of the society simply so that he will not be thrown out of its membership? He is acting in accord with what he thinks is true. What the missionary assumes and takes for granted may be far removed from the interpretation placed upon it by the national. The good missionary, therefore, is aware of these problems and works to prevent misunderstandings which tend to vitiate his earnest endeavors.

In a survey work which is designed to orient an individual into the framework of missionary endeavor, there is not enough space to make a detailed study of the missionary and cultural anthropology. The best that can be done is to open the eyes of the reader to an awareness of the importance of this study for the would-be missionary. And for the individual who does not intend to become a foreign missionary, it should enlarge his appreciation of the perplexities which the missionaries who represent him have to face.

By way of summary, the following general propositions can be recommended to all:

1. Learn and understand the culture first hand.
2. Try to appreciate the culture and to exude a real sympathy, indeed to cultivate sympathy for that culture.

3. Never be shocked or outraged by what you see; and be sure that your reactions are not emotional and irrational.

4. Be patient in learning and responding. Do not make hurried decisions about matters until you are certain of your ground.

5. Work *with* the people and identify yourself *with* the people.

6. Beware of the competitive spirit between missions and missionaries to the detriment of the whole work of God.

7. Avoid the narrow spirit and cultivate the catholic approach which forbids dogmatism, self-righteousness, browbeating, superiority, and clamor.

8. Do not confuse the outward empirical manifestations of the Christian faith with the inward spiritual work of the Holy Spirit in the hearts and lives of men.

9. Remember that the greatest problem lies in the messenger and not in his message. He is the key to the endeavor for the message is an invariable, but the human instrument which brings the message is a variable.

10. Do not tear down and destroy without building up. Have a positive program of replacement for those parts of a culture which give way to the renewing power of the gospel so that the people may not be left in a vacuum for more devils to occupy the swept room than when first you came to destroy the works and the power of the Devil.

When all is said and done, any individual will be a good missionary (all other qualifications being equal) in proportion to his being a good anthropologist. Consciously or subconsciously, all missionaries employ the science of anthropology, and without this use of the science it is impossible ultimately to be a missionary. Therefore, cultural anthropology is integrally and inextricably related to missionary endeavor.

CHAPTER XVI

The Indigenous Church

THE AIM OR PURPOSE OF MISSIONS HAS BEEN STATED SEVERAL times. It is to bring the gospel to men so that they will commit themselves to Jesus Christ for personal salvation. But the salvation of the soul is not the final goal of missions. Beyond this immediate aim, the new Christian is then to be instructed in the holy faith and built up in that faith until he is conformed to the image of God's Son.

Has the goal of missions been fulfilled when men have been won to Christ and have been instructed in the holy faith? The answer is, of course, "No." The missionary has still another purpose in mind which, while it may not be chronologically primary, is organically related to missions in such a fashion that the failure to execute this part of God's program is to fail. He is to build churches. Indeed, every missionary is a church builder, and if he thinks of salvation for the individual in a dimension which relegates the establishment of a church to the periphery, he is sadly mistaken.

From the outset it must be crystal clear that the church of God exists before men are brought into its fellowship. The body into which new converts are brought does not need to be created; it already exists antecedently. The church, in this sense, is prior to the churches, and all of the churches put together do not make up the church. Immediately upon conversion, the individual becomes a member of the body of

Christ and thus enters into a spiritual relationship both with the Head and with all other members of that body. It is an anachronism for Christians of different churches in the same or even in widely-separated geographical areas to hold the same Head and not be in communion one with the other. It is biblically impossible in the ideal case for a Christian to have been baptized into Christ by faith and a good confession and not be in communion with all other baptized members of the body of which Jesus Christ is the Head. To be united to the Head is to be united with all other members of the same body who acknowledge the Head. And when the body is divided, it is sin—sin against the Holy Ghost.

When speaking of the division of the body and the consequent sin against the Holy Ghost, it does not mean that the visible churches must be organically united into one organization in order not to sin. Nothing could be further from the truth. Nor does it mean that all groups professing to be churches must be in communion with each other without regard to faith and practice. It does mean that to be out of communion with other members of the same body is most sinful unless the separation can be justified clearly on indisputable biblical grounds. And the grounds must be of such gravity that the very act of communion in itself would be a sin. To be in communion for any reason which is sinful is wrong, and to be out of communion for any other reason than that is sinful, too.

There is a church, then, into which all converts are brought by their saving faith and out of this body which comprises all believers there shall come churches. These churches have their roots in the church universal, and while they will never perfectly reflect the ideal, they will be the visible, empirical evidences of that universal body which owns the one Head. The visible churches are the creation of God, and the pattern or form of them has been determined by the Spirit of God Who is the vicegerent of Jesus Christ.

Missionaries have been entrusted with the task of building

churches. What they build will reflect what they are and how they think. The churches will naturally reflect (and rightly so) the pattern the missionary has in mind. This is no necessary handicap nor does it suppose that churches ought to differ greatly because of the personal views and idiosyncrasies of the founders. Church building presupposes a commitment by the missionary to the divine revelation in which is found the pattern for the creation of churches. And if the missionary grasps the pattern for the church in the New Testament, it is perfectly legitimate for the new churches to reflect what he has in mind—so long as what he has in mind is true to the apostolic norm.

Troubles do come because missionaries are human. Wide differences of ecclesiology have separated churches across the centuries. Some hold to episcopal forms, some to presbyterian, and some to congregational. Some mission groups place great stress on outward forms, ceremonies, and dress. Some depreciate church organization and grossly underestimate the necessity and value of it. Some groups work without having given any careful thought to the underlying philosophy of church planting and organizational forms; others have bogged down in a traditionalism and a formalism which have sacrificed the spiritual for the outward. The future calls for the establishment of a uniform biblical policy on church organization together with an adequate plan for leadership training.

The great mistake of western missionaries for more than a hundred years has occurred in connection with church planting. And the whirlwind is being reaped all too often because of the errors which were made consistently. One cannot speak harshly of the thousands of sincere and Godly men and women who laid down their lives on the mission fields, not counting those lives dear unto themselves. They were giants for the sake of Christ, and they did the best they could despite their tragic misunderstanding of the apostolic ideal of church building. They did not appreciate nor employ the indigenous method of church building except in isolated cases. They did not enjoy any real insight into the Pauline methods which the church enjoys today. The thinking of missionaries in the past has been quite parochial. They did not plant; they transplanted. And this fine distinction opens up a field of inquiry which is vast.

Missionaries in the past usually (known or unknown; openly or by implication) united a passion to take the gospel to the "heathen" with a passion for western ways and western superiority. They built satrapies and dependencies. They erected large and pretentious compounds, churches, schools, hospitals. The architecture was western, the money was western, the direction was western—and it was all done with the best motives and for the "good" of the people to whom they ministered. No reflection should be cast upon the efforts of those who have gone before if for no other reason than that today's missionaries in that orientation would have done no better.

Missionary policies of former days left indelible imprints in a thousand ways. The temptations in the western approach seduced many missionaries. Unconsciously they reflected an attitude of paternalism. The nationals were "our Christians, our Chinese, our Japanese." They often fell into an attitude of pride, and they generated in the minds of the people the idea that they were lords of the domain instead of undershepherds of the sheep and temporary workers who ought soon to be replaced by national leadership. Land ownership, large buildings and tremendous financial investments created all kinds of friction between national and westerner. Problems of upkeep, profits from sales and rentals, and the failure to allow the nationals to secure control and ownership of the properties all resulted in trouble.

Along with western money and buildings went western thought patterns. The occidental came face to face with the oriental and in the confrontation the occidental did not always manifest superiority. Unconscious mistakes alienated many nationals. Simple ones like wearing a second best suit to have dinner in a national home, failing to pay adequate respect to older nationals whose culture pattern demanded that even occidentals give them the deference their age and position required of younger nationals, and the discourtesy of westerners speaking to each other in the English tongue before their national brethren complicated the distress.

Missionaries did not always adapt themselves sufficiently to the culture and by the use of their money in the erection of large edifices also made the church a "foreign" one. It was not generally a national church. It "belonged" to the white masters and represented a form of religious imperialism or colonialism. It degraded the national and created within him feelings of hatred and distrust. The missionary held the money and paid the bills. The nationals were subjected to the indignity of "pay day" as vassals at the hand of the master when they were employed in the work of the mission. Authority rested in the hands of the missionary. Discipline came from him. When the missionary was gone, the work stagnated. In many stations the sacraments were denied the nationals because the particular ecclesiastical form demanded the presence of an ordained clergyman to administer them, and no national was thought worthy of ordination. Frequent requests for help were denied because there were no missionaries to send, and no one felt that the nations could go in place of the western missionary.

Instead of strong, autonomous, national churches, there were created weak, dependent churches which were small replicas of what the missionary had known at home. The national worshiped in a "foreign" structure, looked to a "foreign" voice for guidance and help, obeyed a "foreign" voice in discipline, and remained the vassal of a "foreign" lord. And it is in place of that kind of national situation that the suggestion is made in favor of indigenizing the church and creating a healthy, happy community of the redeemed in the apostolic tradition and with the apostolic power.

The Bible knows nothing of solitary Christianity, and as soon as there are several believers in any given area there is an incipient New Testament church. These believers should come together for worship, for the celebration of the ordinances or sacraments, and to perform the functions which belong to them as members of the body of Christ. This requires that an organization be created. And an organization is not *per se* an evil. Only the abuses of the legitimate constitute an evil, and God has ordained that there should be a visible church which should have organizational forms. Organization is required for definite reasons. Among them are the following: (1) The admission of new members to the fellowship demands standards of belief and experience which must be administered organizationally. (2) Standards of conduct must be decided upon for the body. (3) The members must be developed spiritually through instruction. (4) Discipline must be administered, and the procedures for its exercise and use must be developed. (5) Church government itself must be formulated and the church administered. (6) The extension of the church through the witnessing of the members requires organization. (7) Doctrinal standards must be agreed upon.

The foregoing needs of the new church in organizational form may best be met by the establishment of an indigenous church. What then is an indigenous church? An indigenous church is one which has become native to the land in which it has been planted. This growth will belie its source of origin save for the characteristics of the church which should be common to all churches. A national church influenced by the soil in which it grows will reflect the land and the people. It will have ties with the church universal, but it will express itself in a way which will mark it off from all other churches. It will not be an appendage to something else nor a carbon copy of its planters and their culture, but it will develop its own traditions, forms, and outward adornments. Above all it will have those three dominant of all characteristics which will mark it off as indigenous in that it will be self-governing, self-supporting and self-propagating.

From the beginning of his labors, the missionary must assume that his work is temporary. His biggest work is to make himself superfluous and to create a functioning church which does not require his presence, but which will operate well under the guidance of the nationals. The missionary must live his life from the beginning among the nationals as though he were to have no successor, and even more as though he were able to relinquish all responsibility of his own, not at the age of retirement but long before that time of life approaches. To this end he should practice retirement, and he should associate the people with him in all that he does to accustom them from the outset to the art of church management according to the plan of God. When he does this, the nationals will know that it is *their* church and what is more important still, the nonbelieving nationals will recognize too that it is not a "foreign" creation but one which belongs to their soil and to their people even though they may not be a part of it.

Basic to an indigenous church is the teaching which lays its foundation. Western Christianity has taken on, by accretion, trappings which are variables. They may or may not be worth imitating by another church. They are not intrinsic to the gospel in its fulness and purity. And they may be distinguished from the invariables which are constant and unchanging. A major variable is the profundity in which biblical concepts have been clothed by theologians through the centuries. Hairsplitting has been a scandal in the church (e.g., discussions about election, predestination, etc.), but even that which has not been splitting of hairs and which has become the heritage of the western church may be beyond the "younger" churches and should be carefully avoided. Therefore, the missionary who lays the foundation must lay one which is capable of being grasped by the people and understood by them. Truth which cannot be comprehended brings no light; truth which is so clothed that it cannot be retained is impermanent; truth which is obscure cannot be used; and truth which has not touched the warp and woof of the heart cannot be passed on. All teaching must be simple enough to be retained, used, and passed on by the hearer.

Any missionary who has in mind the use of the indigenous principle for missionary work must employ the strategy which is the normal accompaniment of committal to this principle. In locating a place for the beginning of his work, he will bear in mind that it should be a center of education, a trade center, a center of communication, and that it should show some promise of becoming a Christian center. This was apparent in the missionary strategy of the Apostle Paul as Allen points out so clearly. In his thinking a province took precedence over a town and a Roman province over a native state. He wanted to establish centers of light, and the places he chose in which to do this were centers of Roman administration, Greek culture, Jewish influence and trade. His selection took into account the future, for the establishment of a center was not an end in itself but a rallying point from which missionary activity radiated in circular fashion to encompass the surrounding unreached regions.

In its beginning, missionary work has for its object the conversion of men. And when men have been converted a church should be created, remembering that a church can come only from the prior creation which is the body into which men by believing faith have been baptized. The Lord's Supper must be celebrated. And, of course, the Word of God has already been preached. Where the Word is preached and the ordinances or sacraments celebrated, there is a true church. This church must have leadership, and it cannot wait for the leadership to obtain the kind of training the western mind regards as essential. Therefore, the missionary must see to it that from among the nationals there emerges at the earliest possible moment a leadership of their own. He will be associated with that leadership and that leadership with him, but he will not be the final authority and no man, either western or national, should occupy that place, for final authority rests in the church and not in an individual.

The organization which comes when men have been baptized and when they commune at the table of the Lord must be of such a character that the nationals understand it and see the need for it. It must be both natural and permanent. It behooves the missionary to see that nothing "foreign" creeps into it and that from its inception it belongs to the people. It must be *their* church, not his. He is only the planter and the seed which he plants belongs to God and is His seed. The product will be God's product, belonging to Him and not to the missionary.

From the outset, church responsibilities should be thrust upon the believers. From among themselves they should choose their own leaders. They will know and understand, far more than a missionary ever can know, who should be selected through prayer and the guidance of the Holy Spirit. It is not because the missionary does not have the same spiritual resources as the nationals but that they know each other better than the missionary can hope to know them after many years. And this advantage will enable them to lay hold of the mind of the Spirit better.

The problem of a church building will normally arise. This should be the problem for the church and not for the missionary. A building is not a church, and a church is not a building. A church is a group of God's people who are led of His Spirit whether they meet in an open field or in a home or in a building. When the people want a place of meeting (when *they* want it, not the missionary), then the responsibility for getting it should be theirs. The architectural forms, size, and the raising of the money are their problems. If they have no money, the missionary ought not to supply it. Let them devise ways of raising their own money, or let them build the place of worship with their own hands and materials. Let it be big or little as they wish. And let it reflect their own peculiar genius. The most important aspect of the place of worship is not that they have such a place, but that it be *their* house of worship and that it belongs to them. They should own the property and the building. The missionary has no stake in the building and no ties to bind him to it so as to create tensions and distrust.

Immediately upon the creation of a church and with the appointment of its officers (deacons and elders or bishops) the question of authority must be settled. Obviously the missionary and the people are tempted to regard the founder of their fellowship as the authoritative voice. Undoubtedly they will ask him to render decisions which he should refuse to do. Authority does not rest in the missionary nor in the officers of the church but in the church itself. It should be a responsible church from the first exercising churchly authority under the guidance of the Holy Spirit Who is the only authority above the church. This does not preclude the missionary from having his say, nor does it mean that his counsel is unworthy of consideration. But it does mean that he is not the ruler of God's people. The only appeal the missionary ever may have is that of a spiritual nature. He has neither the authority nor the right to legislate. He may argue, but even this must be only by moral and spiritual suasion.

If government is the function of the church, discipline is a function of all true government. Naturally discipline presupposes two things. One is a violation of the standards of the church and the second is based upon the first. The church must have standards to be violated. The Christian fellowship does not exist in a vacuum. It lives in this present evil world, and although it shall some day be perfect, perfection is not attained in this life, and it is the absence of perfection which requires standards, and discipline for the maintenance of those standards. Either without the other is impossible. To have standards without the means of enforcing them or to have a means of discipline without any standards does not make sense. The existence of a church in the world with its consequent tensions makes the exercise of discipline necessary, but forethought and care will in some cases make discipline unnecessary. If admission to the church is guarded carefully, individuals who might later be disciplined may be screened out in advance. This means that the church must have standards for admission. They should be thoughtfully formulated and prayerfully entered into. Above all admission into the fellowship should not be too easy. Admission into full membership should be preceded by a public confession of faith and by adequate instruction. After a period of time has elapsed following his conversion, the candidate should be examined by the church about his Christian experience, his faith, his life and his family. If his record of church attendance at the regular Sunday meetings and at the prayer services demonstrates his sincerity and earnestness, and if his profession of faith before the congregation is satisfactory, he should be baptized and permitted to become a member of the fellowship. At this point one cannot prescribe legalistically what the time period should be for probation. The details may vary in minutiae from place to place. But the chief point is that the church must guard its doors to prevent the undesirables from entering in order that it might not have to exercise discipline for recalcitrant members later.

In spite of all that the church may do to guard sacredly its fellowship from unbelief and sin, there will be those who will come under the scrutiny of the church for discipline. While the exercise of discipline may be minimized, it cannot be completely avoided. In America there has been an almost complete breakdown of discipline. This does not imply the absence of standards but rather the lack of moral rigor and an insensibility to sin about which the church does nothing.

When conditions arise which require discipline, it should be prompt, and it should be appropriate. Discipline has for its object the reclamation of the offender, the preservation of the purity of the church, and the good reputation of the fellowship before the world. Discipline is never punitive in itself save as the punishment is designed to reclaim the backslidden.

The exercise of discipline is a church function. It should not be the activity of the missionary or of the officers of the church alone. The missionary is peculiarly unable to make the wisest decisions about discipline, because he cannot know the background as well as the nationals themselves. For the missionary to be the disciplinary agent often creates anti-foreign feeling and the force and effect of communal participation is lost. Generally the nationals will administer discipline more severely than the missionary, contrary to his expectation of the opposite. They will do it in a way which will render their judgment more effective and create a preventive atmosphere which will keep others from falling into the same sins. The use of strong discipline lays a church open to the charge of legalism, but the truth is that strong discipline strengthens the witness of the church and makes its testimony before the world clear-cut and unequivocal. Before the unconverted it leaves a profound impression with a twofold implication: first, that one must be sincere in his original profession of faith and second, that his life must match his profession. When discipline has been administered by the church, the malefactor has no one individual against whom to complain and the concensus of the entire body is a crushing indictment of his guilt.

Discipline will vary according to the offense. A simple offense committed once may occasion not more than a private rebuke. Repeated offenses of the same kind may merit a public announcement before the congregation of the name of the individual and the offense he has committed. More serious offenses may cause the church to keep the individual from coming to the table of the Lord for a given period of time. Still more serious offenses may warrant excommunication of the offender and finally the erasure of his name from the rolls of the church when it becomes apparent that there is no repentance or a sincere turning to the Lord for forgiveness including whatever restitution needs to be made.

Standards cannot be divorced from discipline. Discipline itself as previously suggested implies that the church has standards. The first thought one entertains about standards is that they are doctrinal in nature. This is, of course, true because the church will have been founded upon the truths of the Scriptures. But, apart from the few fundamentals of the Christian faith, standards cover more ground and have vaster implications for more areas of life than simply doctrine. Standards have as much to do with conduct as with belief, and no one should suppose that the preservation of doctrinal standards is the greatest problem of the national churches.

The creation of standards is distinctly not a task for the missionary alone. He comes to the people with a western "set" of mind. He enjoys his own standards which are common to western culture, tradition and thinking. He is tempted to suppose that his standards are invariable in every case when they are actually quite variable and are related to culture patterns and not to the eternal gospel. The missionary will run afoul of the people if he tries to impose standards from without. They must come from within. He cannot understand fully the psychology and habits of the people. Their customs are permeated with superstitions and ancient traditions. These are often related to religion and have a peculiar significance. Only nationals who have been reared in this environment understand the significance and the relationship. The missionary must enjoy the help of the nationals in setting up standards of conduct for they alone will thoroughly appreciate the implications and bring to bear that form of guidance which will make the standards reliable and their use practicable.

In Africa a recurring problem is that of polygamy. The

question involved is not whether it is right or wrong. Christian conscience directs that polygamy is sin. The Madras Conference stated that "it (monogamy) is vital to the life of the Church and its value has been realized in its own experience; it was taught by the Lord Himself and has scriptural authority behind it." The real problem is how to deal with it and what standards to erect for the edification of the church. When a man has fifteen wives which he has taken prior to his conversion, shall he keep the first one and let the others go? What shall happen to the children? And to the wives he does not retain? These are questions which, in consultation with the nationals, the church must work out in the hope that succeeding generations will be freed from them since standards will always rule against the possibility of unmarried men taking more than one wife.

In western culture no one thinks it wrong to eat with his mother-in-law. But in some cultures this is taboo. Who, then, is to decide whether the church shall retain this custom which militates against eating with your mother-in-law? And is this matter one which deals with an invariable or only with a variable? Many areas of conduct involve problems which are definitely not matters of principle as such but matters about which two people from differing cultures could disagree without either of them being guilty of sin. In one culture it may be sinful for a man to wear pants and in another it may be wrong if he does not. The difference is not the important item. The important element is that each church shall forge out its own standards consonant with its culture and consistent with its traditions in the light of the divine revelation. And a self-governing church assisting the missionary in this task is a *sine qua non*.

An indigenous church is not only self-governing. It is self-supporting. This aspect of church building revolves around money. And in any culture money can cause a great deal of trouble. Fortunately all people do not regard the acquisition of money and goods the same way westerners do. But human nature is sufficiently similar so that it always will be a problem. The missionary must deal with money matters constantly, and he had better start the right way so as to avoid costly mistakes.

Coming from a home environment which stresses buildings, salaries, and increasing stipends, the missionary must overcome handicaps. His major temptation is eagerness to see things done. He wants results. While this characteristic of the western mind has worked for great good, the same characteristic can work real harm. The missionary wants a home. He wants a church building. He wants a school building. He wants colleagues (even when they are nationals) to assist in the work. This takes money. The nationals rarely have enough money to do what it has taken even western Christians years to do. But the missionary either has money or he can get money from a constituency at home because of their interest in "foreign" missions. He wants the folks at home to know that he has done something concrete. And what is more concrete than buildings which can be photographed, and large staffs which can be shown the friends at home who expect him to produce results and that quickly?

Dr. Nevius of Korea, who was a firm advocate of the indigenous church ideal, spoke frankly about western money in connection with missionary work. He never suggested that the missionary should disregard the sources of his own support, but he did say that the new churches should be self-supporting from the beginning. He advocated that foreign money should not be used to pay salaries or to construct church buildings, but that all monies required for these purposes should come from the nationals themselves. This idea included all necessary monies for carrying out the essential activities of the church too, and the maintenance of property.

At first blush such a "strict" policy appears inconsiderate particularly when there is money available from foreign sources. But the root of the matter derives from the truism that the people who pay the bills call the tune. And eventually the consequences of the free use of foreign money is more detrimental to the church across the years than the seemingly harsh policy of no financial assistance. Soltau in his volume *Missions at the Crossroads* gives an illustration of a Korean pastor who was the recipient of more subsidies than almost any other Korean pastor. He developed a spirit of lust and covetousness and also a sense of embitterment against all foreigners which made him one of the most outstanding anti-foreign members of the Korean General Assembly.

As long as money is supplied by the mission, the nationals will feel loathe to assume responsibility as they ought. Biting the hand that feeds them by expressing divergent opinions in open discussion makes it hard for nationals to speak their minds plainly lest they offend or perhaps even lose their jobs. Rarely will nationals take strong stands on the use of funds which originate overseas. On the other hand, if it is their own money which has come from their own people, their attitude will be different. They will develop quickly a sense of responsibility for that money, and they will have definite convictions about the use of it. Whereas a missionary might keep on his employed list men who are not doing what they ought to do or who are not all that they ought to be, the nationals as a group can dispense with the services of those they know to be inadequate and do it without embarrassment to the missionary who has left this responsibility in the hands of the people. A national cannot complain the same way about dismissal originating with his own people as he could about the missionary who is always a foreigner to him and against whom he could direct barbed attacks which would be hurtful to the work the missionary is trying to do.

Insisting upon the payment of the salaries by funds raised by the nationals helps in other ways too. Nationals will perform work which is just as significant as that of the missionary.

The question of the rate of pay for the "foreign" missionary and for the national worker is bound either to be raised openly or thought secretly. When the bills are being paid by money from overseas, the national whose stipend is from two to ten times lower than that of the missionary has a legitimate reason for misunderstanding. His grievance will be acute when he finds that the missionary is not willing to reduce his own salary (which in the sight of the national may be astronomical) in order to raise that of the national. But if the indigenous church is paying its own people out of its funds, the problem is not for the missionary but for the local church. And the missionary can always act on behalf of the aggrieved ones if, in point of fact, the church is not doing for its own workers what it ought to be doing.

Indigenous church planting means self-support and this in turn means that the mission will not provide funds for church buildings, or for paying national salaries of evangelists. It will not pay for the maintenance of properties or for the salaries of national school teachers or even school buildings. Immediately, the reader will sense that this prescription is seemingly in disagreement with previous discussions of education, for example, as a means of evangelization. In that section there was expressed an acute awareness of the educational buildings problem, but it was stated in the context of conditions on the mission fields as they are now known. Nothing said therein should be construed to mean that mission boards today should throw their resources into the construction of large hospitals, schools, etc. Boards will do well to employ physicians, and teachers, but they will also do well to look to the national churches to assume responsibility for these areas of national life as soon as possible.

When the nationals become conscious of their need for a church building, the missionary can tell them kindly but firmly that he is in agreement and ask them what *they* are going to do about it. When they see the need for a school, he

can tell them kindly but firmly that he is in agreement and
ask them what they are going to do to provide first a building
and then a teaching staff. Let them raise the money and provide the personnel. It will encourage them to stand on their
own feet; it will strengthen their testimony; it will make them
independent; it will develop their leadership; it will keep
them free from foreign domination; it will prepare them to
take over from the beginning the functions which normally
belong to the church and not to the missionary. The missionary will be surprised to observe that the nationals are capable
of managing their own financial affairs and that this management will prevent them from being paupers on charity and
will furnish them with opportunities to grow into maturity.
He is there to counsel and to advise, but they must make their
own decisions and be responsible for their own actions. When
the missionary carries out this policy firmly, the nationals will
respect him, and they will seek his counsel. But they will
know that he has no ulterior motives and that he is not seeking to dominate or control them. And above all he cannot be
accused of Christian colonialism or imperialism.

The indigenous principle is committed to a self-propagating church too. By this is meant a church which will perpetu-
ate itself through a national ministry via education, and a
church which will enter into its obligation to spread the gospel and be an evangelizing influence commensurate with New
Testament demands and standards. Without these no church
can rightly be called indigenous nor has the missionary been
successful who does not see this kind of church develop under
his tutelage.

An indigenous ministry must be educated to supply the
need for national leadership. This educative process should
be consistent with the needs and demands of the field. It does
not mean that the level of that education should be similar to
that of the western world. It need not imply formal education
in the same way the western world understands it. The office

of the elder or bishop is a spiritual office, and men who have good sense and the approval of their fellow Christians as qualified for and having the endowments of the office can be selected without hesitation. Different mission fields may require different standards, but whatever the field the need for an indigenous ministry is apparent. The ordinances or sacraments should not be kept from any people because of the lack of a foreign missionary. Standards for ordination should never be so rigid that they will exclude available national help. Even though it may result in the selection of men who are less educated, in a formal sense, than appears to be desirable the selection should be made with the realization that time will tend to correct the difficulty and that standards gradually will be raised as the church grows intellectually. The training of nationals for the assumption of church responsibility will be permeative, extending throughout the enlarging needs of the fellowship and reaching out into all of its minute ramifications.

A self-propagating church must be a witnessing church. This is consistent with the definition of what a church is and how it ought to function. The foreign missionary has come to bring the gospel. And when the gospel has taken root in a community, it becomes the business of those who have entered into the blessing of the gospel to assume the responsibility for the spread of that gospel to their countrymen. This implies that every missionary church should in turn become a missionary church and reach forth in an expanding fashion geographically with the gospel. The Great Commission becomes the immediate and compelling responsibility for new converts and churches. They are not to climb on the bandwagon, but they become a bandwagon which should move out toward the creation of new ones. The principle of cell division is here applicable. Just as the missionary has created a cell by his activity, the new cell must in turn create a cell which in turn will create more cells. The number of cells created from a preexistent cell can be infinite, and the moment a church or cell ceases to be re-creative, that moment it has lost its life and it becomes a dead or extinct body no matter how orthodox it may be. A church must remain alive, and the sign of life is its creative activity. So long as it reproduces it has life; when it ceases to reproduce, its life is gone and the rationale for its existence has virtually come to an end.

If the missionary does not embark upon this course of action in creating a self-propagating church, he will silence the gifts of the Spirit inherently given by Him for the work of the church. These gifts are imparted to men by His good pleasure. If the missionary does not encourage, indeed if he does not demand creative activity in witnessing and reproduction, he will silence the divine activity of the Spirit in the hearts of the new converts. Witnessing to others what God has done for them is as much a part of the experience of regeneration as breathing is a part of physical life. To quench this spirit which is structurally a part of regeneration is to kill the life-giving element which has been provided by the Spirit of God. Rather it should be helped and developed and strengthened and encouraged by the missionary for the cause of Christ.

Let the national church train its own workers, set its own standards for ordination and for other church offices. Let it educate its own people for service and do it with its own money and buildings and under its own church control. Let it send forth its evangelists, and pay them and oversee their activities. And let it create other cells or churches which enjoy the same rights and privileges which it has been accorded but all in the fellowship of the saints.

When the indigenous principle is applied, the results will be surprising. The national church will be a stronger and more aggressive church. It will grow rapidly, and it will reach out in ever-enlarging circles to encompass the rest of the field. The relationship between missionary and nationals will be wholesome and brotherly, and it will open more quickly new fields of service for the missionary who has not become a nursing mother of a sickly child but the father of a mature and responsible adult who has grown normally and naturally from babyhood to adulthood in a framework of the New Testament pattern which is definitive.

Whatever have been the errors of the past and however long it takes to correct these errors on fields already occupied, the new approach to the problem of world evangelization, in the opinion of the author, will best be served by the use of the indigenous method of the New Testament and particularly of the Apostle Paul.

CHAPTER XVII

Prayer and the Holy Spirit

~~~~~~

NO DISCUSSION OF MISSIONARY PRINCIPLES AND PRACTICE WOULD be complete without a section dealing with prayer and the Holy Spirit. The inclusion of both subjects within one chapter follows naturally because of the interrelation of one to the other. It is also appropriate because the two of them together form, inextricably, a combination guaranteeing the success of the missionary program. When either one of them is deleted from missions, by accident or by design, the result is tragic.

Prayer and the Holy Spirit, rightly understood, place all men on a plane where self is subordinated and God is exalted. Primacy is given to those elements which ought to be kept in the forefront and, as a consequence, the men who make use of them become secondary. All spiritual work suffers from the temptation of men to usurp the place and functions of God. Correctly understood, prayer and the Holy Spirit keep men in their right relationship to God so that He is able to accomplish through them what He intends.

Hundreds of books on prayer have been written. But the writing of books and the reading of books do not guarantee anything. The practice of prayer and the correct use of prayer principles count much. When men have been told what they ought to do and how to do it, all that they learn is valueless unless they actually do it.

314

Some of the ancient material on prayer will have to be reproduced here. Basic principles which every believer should know will be restated and suggestions will be made. It is hoped that something fresh will stand out in the midst of the tried and the true.

Robert Speer some years ago wrote about prayer in connection with missions. At that time he said, "In a supernatural cause, resting on a supernatural charter, led on by an omnipotent leader, with all His supernatural power pledged to its support on the conditions of consecration and prayer on the part of its human agents, a neglect of prayer is a denial of the Lord's leadership and a wilful limitation of success. For in all the missionary work of God, to take no wider ground—if there be any wider ground—all success and guidance are consequent only upon prayer."

The sacred record in the Old and New Testaments supports the thesis that spiritual progress and forward movement have been the result of effective prayer. A few examples will amply demonstrate this thesis. Moses prayed, and God declared that He would deliver His people from Egypt. Job prayed for his friends and found God's mighty deliverance for himself. Hannah prayed and God gave her a son. David prayed, and God forgave his sins of adultery and murder. Samson prayed, and God gave him back his strength. Elijah prayed, and the child was raised from the dead. He prayed again, and his sacrifice was consumed with fire from heaven. He prayed, and no rain fell for three years. He prayed again, and the rains came. Hezekiah prayed, and God slew one hundred and eighty-five thousand Assyrians in one night. Ezra prayed, and spiritual awakening and revival came to the remnant. Nehemiah's prayer turned the heart of Artaxerxes toward his return to the Holy City. Solomon prayed for wisdom, and God granted his request. Daniel prayed for wisdom and understanding, and God gave him the answer to Nebuchadnezzar's dream. Daniel's prayers landed him in the den of lions, but God delivered him. Jonah prayed, and the great fish gave up its prisoner who went to Nineveh to preach for God. These are simply tokens of prayer and its power as evidenced in the Old Testament record. In the New Testament records are manifold instances of effective prayer.

The life of Jesus is, of course, the supreme example of prayer because He so wonderfully demonstrated its underlying principles, but even more so because He showed its usefulness pragmatically. His life will not be discussed but rather the lives and ministries of His followers. Men expect great deeds from Jesus, but the answers to prayer in the experience of Jesus' followers is even more dramatic because they were without divinity.

The first and the last recorded acts of the apostles following the ascension of Jesus were prayers. When Pentecost came, the disciples were on their knees in prayer in an upper room. And when John writes the concluding sentences of the final revelation of God, he cries out in adoration and hope, "Even so, come, Lord Jesus." The three thousand souls who were converted through the mighty sermon of Peter at Pentecost were added to the church. The record significantly says that ". . . they continued steadfastly in the apostles' doctrine and fellowship, and in breaking of bread, and in *prayers*."

Matthias was chosen to fill the place of Judas Iscariot through prayer. The first deacons were chosen by prayer, and they were made deacons so that the apostles would have time to give themselves to prayer. Stephen the first Christian martyr died while he prayed, and the glory of his prayer is the spirit of forgiveness it emphasizes, ". . . Lord, lay not this sin to their charge. . . ." Ananias went at the request of God to visit with Saul of Tarsus. He was informed that he would find him praying. Peter prayed and Tabitha was raised from the dead. Cornelius at Cæsarea was praying, and Peter at Joppa was also praying. The one sends for the other in and through prayer, and this led to the conversion of Cornelius the Gentile. Peter was put into prison by Herod, and prayer without ceasing was made by the church to God for him. He was delivered in a miraculous fashion from the hands of his enemies. In the Philippian jail Paul and Silas prayed, and they were delivered by God from their imprisonment. Paul himself records that ". . . when I was come again to Jerusalem, even while I prayed in the temple, I was in a trance." And when Paul is on his way to Rome, he lands on Melita, healing the father of Publius through prayer. To the Colossians Paul says that we "do not cease to pray for you. . . ."

If the record of the Bible is not sufficient, the experience of two thousand years bears out the same truth—that prayer has power and that prayer is essential. The Moravian custom of maintaining a constant and unremitting twenty-four hour a day prayer vigil explains in part their missionary greatness. Calvin, Luther, and Knox attest to their lengthy prayer sessions. Any survey of the lives of Carey, Judson, Hudson Taylor, or "Praying" Hyde will manifest the same truth. They knew how to pray, and they prayed. In 1887 the China Inland Mission prayed out one hundred new missionaries. The American Board of Commissioners for Foreign Missions began with a haystack prayer meeting. Pastor Gossner the great German saint and missionary enthusiast was a prayer warrior. During his lifetime, he was responsible for the sending out of one hundred and forty-four missionaries. A single sentence from the final message delivered before his open tomb tells eloquently what he did through prayer. "He prayed up the walls of a hospital and the hearts of nurses; he prayed mission stations into being and missionaries into faith; he prayed open the hearts of the rich, and gold from the most distant lands."

A missionary once said, "I do desire to say, gravely and earnestly, that my missionary life has been successful so far as I have been prayerful and non-successful so far as in prayerfulness I have been lax." Adoniram Judson left behind him this statement: "I never was deeply interested in any project,

I never prayed sincerely and earnestly for anything, but it came at some time—no matter how distant the day—somehow in some shape, probably the last I should have devised—it came!" And who can forget the poignant picture of David Livingstone who was found asleep in Jesus on his knees before the King of kings?

God only knows how many missionaries have become missionaries because of the prayers of their parents, pastors, or Sunday School teachers. The words of the parents of Paton, one of the truly great missionaries illustrate this point. To Paton his parents said: "When you were given to us, we laid you upon the altar, our first born, to be consecrated, if God saw fit, as a missionary of the Cross; and it has been our constant prayer that you might be prepared, qualified, and led to this very decision."

As important as prayer is, prayer is no excuse for disobedience in life. Praying does not excuse those from going who are able to go. It does not relieve them of other responsibilities just because they pray. It is not a substitute for anything else. The man who says, "I cannot give, but I can pray" does not understand God's economy. He may not be able to give much, but if he gives as much as he can, then his observation about prayer is reasonable. Going and giving and praying are separate and distinct from each other with none of them a satisfactory substitute for any other one.

The suggestion is made elsewhere that prayer is dynamite; that it is the most powerful latent force in the universe. Prayer should be used in connection with every problem in life, but it is specially relevant to those areas where, humanly speaking, men have reached the end of their tether. There are many tasks in missionary work which cannot be performed today because forces are in operation which make it literally impossible for the church to do them. But the application of proper prayer to these problems will result in creative solutions by God Himself which will circumvent the forces working against missions. For example, China is a closed door today. But prayer can blast open this closed door. India is half-closed. But prayer can open it wide. More missionaries are needed if the job of world evangelization is to take place in the near future. Only prayer through the inworking power of the Holy Spirit can accomplish this task. Has not Jesus said ". . . pray ye therefore the Lord of the harvest, that he will send forth labourers into his harvest?"

When speaking of prayer and its power in relation to missions, it is not personal or devotional prayer that is meant. In the treatment of the spiritual foundation of the missionary on the field, the need for and use of prayer to keep the spiritual life dynamic and alert was stressed. But that treatment of prayer was only one facet of the larger subject. And it is to the larger one that reference is made here.

Prayer is so simple and so obvious that no mention of what it is should be needed. Because some people treat it as an esoteric and mystic complexity, however, a word should be said about its simplicity. Prayer is only speaking to God. This may be audible through voice and the spoken word. Or it may be inaudible. Or it may be ejaculatory and involuntary. The One to whom the Christian prays, knows and understands the deepest yearnings of the human heart. A believer may pray amiss without intention, but He Who knows the true need understands and is willing and able to grant his petitions. When he is hungry, he may ask for a crust of bread. God may send him something else. He knows that the prayer is for food, and He may choose to give him oatmeal instead of bread; or steak instead of hamburger.

Why it is that God has ordained that prayer shall be the means through which His work in the universe will be completed is not known. Surely He could do it by Himself without reference to men. But He has graciously ordained that by prayer men shall come under the convicting power of the Holy Spirit. Through prayer men will feel the call of God to full-time service. Through prayer evil men will make decisions which, unknown to them, will be precisely the decisions they would never have made had they known the ultimate outcome. Through prayer will come strength, understanding, insight, and spiritual power otherwise not obtainable. Regeneration will make men what they could not otherwise be, and prayer by regenerated believers will enliven their faculties and enable them to use what native gifts God has implanted to the fullest.

Prayer has for its end the glory of God and the exaltation of Jesus Christ. It is in and through Jesus Christ that prayer is possible. Because of what He did and of the relationship He has to the Father, Christians come to God in prayer. The name of Jesus alone assures them access to God and more than access their every answer from God springs from His satisfaction with His Son as their Mediator.

There is nothing that would be good for Christians which God does not wish to grant. But prayer has its own laws and even followers of Christ cannot treat prayer as a convenience subject to their own whims and idiosyncrasies. Precisely because they are creatures, and God is their Creator, prayer has its own laws and modes of operation according to the will of God. One of the chief laws of prayer is that they who do not ask shall not get. No matter how much God may love His children and how much He may shower them with blessings, there are many more things He would like to give but which He will not give unless they pray. God wants to call enough missionaries to complete the task of evangelization, but the very calling of men and women to world evangelization is in response to the prayer of God's people to the Lord of the harvest beseeching Him to thrust forth laborers into His harvest fields. No one possesses sufficient knowledge to appreciate fully what Christians have failed to do, because they did not pray or ask God to do great things.

A second law governing prayer is that which guarantees its

integrity. Before men lies a power so great that were an ungodly person able to obtain this power he could use it for evil purposes. But prayer cannot be used for ill. And whoever asks amiss—to satisfy evil lusts and passions—does not receive what he asks. Since prayer is designed to glorify God, no request which fails to do this can be assured of an answer.

A third law which governs prayer relates to the human factor. Prayer cannot be analyzed through the eyes of reason alone. If it could, men could not ask for the impossible and the miraculous. And it is the granting of the impossible (humanly speaking) which is the specialty of our God. Hezekiah prayed for deliverance from the hosts of Sennacherib when the situation was impossible. Yet God performed the impossible. Rain falls in accordance with the operation of natural law and is therefore regarded by some to be outside the realm of prayer. But Elijah prayed, and it did not rain for the space of three years. And when he prayed for rain, it came. Thus if prayer has value only for those requests thought to be humanly possible, and if it has no value for requests which human reason says are beyond normal expectation, then limitations have been imposed on prayer. Somewhere between the two poles of unbelief and credulity which looks for the world to disintegrate at the sound of the voice in prayer there is a happy meeting ground. And if there is honest doubt about the relevancy of prayer for a given matter, believers should never hesitate to give God the benefit of the doubt, letting Him decide what the answer shall be.

A fourth law governing prayer is that of works. Believers should pray as though they could do nothing and then work as though they had never prayed. Students should pray that God will help them in their studies, but there is nothing in the laws of prayer which should lead them to believe that success in study will come apart from human effort. Having prayed for the help of God in their studies, the individuals should then do their part by studying. Faith and prayer without works is dead. The history of Christian missions is filled with examples of God's great prayer warriors. Not one of them was great simply because he knew how to pray. Each also was a co-laborer with God who knew hard work. Carey, Judson, Morison, Taylor, and Nevius were all great men of prayer, but they were men of hard work who used every human gift to accomplish the ends to which God had called them. "Prayer *and pains* through faith can do anything" was the slogan of one great missionary. He joined prayer with pains.

The day is past when Christians can afford to pass resolutions about prayer or form prayer bands that never function. Prayer has to be more than lip service. It must become a passion within the heart. And when God can find a hundred people whose hearts are so impassioned to pray as the apostles prayed of old, a new era in missions will dawn and once again the holy power of revival quickening and worldwide conversion will take place.

The failure to pray is virtually a mandate to God to keep His kingdom from coming and to prevent the Holy Spirit from convicting and converting men. Prayerlessness will shut up the pocketbooks of the wealthy; it will close open doors on the field; it will inhibit the efforts of missionaries; it will allow millions to perish without Christ and without hope. And if this be true, why is it that countless men and women do not linger ceaselessly before the presence of God refusing to let Him go until the great goal of the age is accomplished, even the evangelization of the world?

Whereas prayer is man's work, the Holy Spirit is the third member of the Godhead and the personage around Whom the work of missions revolves in this age of the Spirit. Jesus said that it was expedient for Him to go away so that the Holy Spirit might come. The Holy Spirit was sent by the Father and the Son, and with His coming a new age or dispensation of the Holy Spirit began. It is, therefore, impossible to fulfil the commission or to understand this age without reference to the Holy Spirit. Before prayer comes the Person and work of the Spirit in missions.

Missions is a spiritual enterprise to begin with. As a spiritual business it has as its head the Holy Spirit. The conquest of the world and of the kingdoms of this world shall come through spiritual means. The Communists use force; others may employ social, political or financial means. The Christian is bound to honor the precept of God that ". . . Not by might nor by power, but by my Spirit, saith the Lord of Hosts." It is in and through the Spirit that the Great Commission shall be completed; that Jesus shall secure His rightful place in the hearts of men; that the church shall be the church.

The Spirit is the only One Who can keep the eyes of Christians fixed on the goal and Who can keep them from error. Today He is speaking to men afresh, and on every hand there is evidence that His voice is being heard in a new way. For years the institution of the church was exalted and missions given a place as an organ of the church. But once more men are seeing the truth that the church is the organ of missions. Missionary work is not a segment of the work of the church. Missionary work *is* the church, and the church exists precisely because of this. The Holy Spirit is the One Who alone has the power to make the church see its missionary character. He alone can prepare the world for the mission of the church.

When God's people understand that the desire of the world is not towards Christ and that the drift is in the other direction, they can then appreciate the other facet that the desire of Christ is towards the world. Only the Spirit can overcome the currents of opposition within the hearts of men and interpret to them the passion of Christ for the world. Christians cannot bring the world to Jesus Christ. When they try that, they operate against the deadening forces of unbelief, inertia, hostility, superstition, and the efforts of the Devil. But if, through the Spirit, they carry Christ to the world they do so with the

Spirit's power and fulness for this is the way of the Spirit whereas bringing the world to Christ is not.

Years ago A. J. Gordon stated that missionaries are "not to stand in the world and testify to Christ but stand in Christ and testify to the world." To stand in the world is to stand without the Spirit. This is defeat. To stand in Christ is to stand in the fulness and power of the Holy Spirit and this is victory. The early apostles stood in Christ, and by the power of His Spirit they were filled with missionary passion, led of Him, and they went out preaching Christ to the nations. The success of the early church has been repeated in missionary history whenever men, be it ever so small a company, have surrendered to the Spirit and have been filled by Him.

The proof both of the relationship of the Holy Spirit to missions and of His importance to the outcome of missionary endeavor is derived from a study of Pentecost. The great command of the risen Jesus is the commission to take the gospel to the ends of the earth. But this command is unalterably connected with the command to tarry for power. The command to go is linked with the command to tarry in such a fashion that one without the other is useless. To evangelize without first getting the power which comes from tarrying is to go in vain. But to tarry and get the power without going into all the world would make the tarrying of no effect. Pentecost and missions are inseparably connected. One writer graphically portrays the scene by remarking that Christ went up, the Spirit came down, and the disciples went out. The outgoing of the disciples was occasioned by the coming down of the Spirit which in turn was occasioned by the going up of Christ. The effect of the Spirit's fulness will be the going out of disciples with the gospel. It is a matter of cause and effect. And if the effect the church desires is not to be found today, then the obvious reason for the lack is the missing emphasis on the Holy Spirit.

When the church is consecrated to the task of Christ in its

fullest meaning and the Holy Spirit has His way, there will be a revival of missionary fires. The pulpit will sound forth the glories of missions; Christians will give of their children and their substance; prayer without ceasing will be made; tongues will speak of the accomplishments of missionaries instead of the light and frivolous things of the day; churches will find the money to send forth their best and their ablest young people. The Spirit is the only One who can lift the church from its slough of despond, calling forth its richest sacrifices, taking away its crassest selfishness, purifying its worldliest spirit, removing its worst corruptions, and sending forth its finest children. The Holy Spirit at Pentecost created a Pentecostal church with a Pentecostal commission, and gave to it Pentecostal power.

Briefly stated, the work of God in this age embraces two elements. The first is the witnessing element which is the responsibility of every Christian. God's program for the church is a witnessing program. Those who do witness are not to concern themselves with results. Their business is to do the bidding of their Master. And their Master says for them to witness. The second element is the outcalling of a people for His name —the *ecclesia*. The salvation of the world is not the goal of God's program. All men will not be saved, and never shall the world as we know it become Christian. But God does have a remnant in mind, and He is calling out this remnant during this age. The theological involvements relative to predestination and election are immaterial here. Whether men have free will or not does not matter. The cardinal fact is that God has a church, and His purpose is to bring into that fellowship those who should be saved. The witnessing of His messengers is the means by which this is accomplished, and the Holy Spirit is vital to the fulfillment of this program.

What is the work of the Holy Spirit in missions? To ask the question this way is to limit the answer automatically. The Spirit works and has worked in other ways which shall not be discussed. For example, the Spirit had a place in creation, in revelation, in the Incarnation, in Calvary, in prophecy, and in His consubstantial relation to the Trinity in eternity past. A complete examination of the work of the Spirit is not called for here, but only His work in relation to missions. That becomes a major interest now.

In this age, the Holy Spirit is the sponsor of foreign missions. As the vicegerent of Jesus Christ, He is the supreme commander of the church of which Jesus is Lord. The third person of the Godhead has assumed the non-communicable work of His office which He alone is able to fulfil.

The Holy Spirit will bring to mind the things of Christ in order that Christ might be glorified, and He will guide believers into all truth. There is no truth but God's truth, and the Spirit is the One who can make the truth of God plain to the hearts and minds of men. Truth is not only one of intellectual perception. It is also one of heart relationship and direction. The end of all truth is the glory of God, and the glory of God always means the exaltation of the Son of God Who is the Mediator. The Spirit brings men to the knowledge of truth, and truth's highest knowledge is about Jesus Christ and His redemption.

Second, the Spirit works as the convicting and converting Agent in redemption in the hearts of men. Believers are channels through which the Spirit works, but they are only channels and never principals. They are accessories after the fact. John wrote down the words of Jesus that the Spirit will "reprove the world of sin, and of righteousness, and of judgment." No man can come under conviction apart from the work of the Spirit. No matter how much preaching he hears and however fluent and gifted the speaker, the Spirit and the Spirit alone can bring conviction of sin. Men can pray that the Spirit will move hearts, and He will do this. But no man of himself or apart from the Spirit of God can expect to see true conviction wrought in the hearts of men. Furthermore, conviction of sin does not mean salvation. It is the first step in the direction of salvation and conviction must lead to conversion and regeneration. The Spirit both converts and regenerates. It is His work and any conversion or regeneration, so-called, is spurious unless it proceeds from the Spirit. This work of applying the gospel to the lost and dying is the sure guarantee of the gospel's effectiveness, because the Spirit has the power to break down prejudice, wipe out arguments, and melt the coldest heart.

Third, the Spirit of God calls and commissions workers for the special task of missions. The first deacons were chosen for their office by and through the aid of the Holy Spirit. Paul and Barnabas were called by the Spirit for their special work. Of them the Scriptures say that they were sent by the Holy Ghost. Jesus commands His followers to pray to the Lord of the harvest to thrust forth laborers into His harvest fields. The Lord of the harvest can only be the Holy Spirit. When believers pray to Him, He in turn speaks to the hearts of men about missions. All Christians are called of God and potentially empowered by the Spirit to be witnesses of Jesus Christ. But some men are called to special tasks as evangelists, deacons, and elders or bishops. In the early church some were called to be apostles. But whatever the calling it is derived from the work of the Holy Spirit. All callings are sacred and for each believer there is a life work for him to do under the guidance of the Holy Spirit.

In the calling of men to the service of God, the efforts and labors of interested parties cannot be discounted. Ziegenbalg's mother prepared the seed in the hearts of her children. She professed to leave them her Bible, every page of which she had wet with her tears for them. Is it any wonder that the Spirit was able to claim this man for the service of Jesus Christ. Christian Freidrich Schwartz's mother on her deathbed said to her husband, "I have dedicated our youngest son to God, for such service as He shall appoint. Assure me that when he hears the Lord's call you will not discourage it." And when the call of God through the Spirit came, the father of Schwartz struggled with God for three days before he gave up his youngest son for the service of the Galilean. And for forty-three years Schwartz was a power for God in the land of India. The life of Count Zinzendorf amply illustrates the same truth, for the preparation of home and kindred made him a fit subject for the calling power of the Holy Spirit. Time fails us to speak of J. Hudson Taylor, Harms, Gossner, Spener, Francke, Wesley, and a thousand others whose lives were touched by the Spirit because first they were conditioned by the prayers and consecration of others.

The Holy Spirit, in the fourth place, performs a mighty work of grace in the hearts of believers. They are transformed by His power to become what they were not and to do what they could not. Weak men became strong; stammering tongues were unloosed to speak with power; the frightened and fearful became unafraid. Even the unlearned and ignorant displayed a wisdom which came from above and not from within. The Apostle Peter when he denied his Lord had fallen into the sin of weakness and fear. But the Spirit at Pentecost made him strong so that he preached fearlessly and with mighty power. When the apostles spoke to their intellectual peers, it was perceived that they were unlearned and ignorant men upon whom the Spirit of God had come in mighty power. Uneducated as he was, William Carey's native powers were enlarged and energized so that he was able to translate the Word of God into more than thirty languages and dialects. The Karen bandit who was saved as a depraved and horrible specimen of humankind under the ministry of Judson was transformed by the Spirit into a glowing and powerful testimony for Jesus Christ unto the salvation of thousands of the hill people in that land.

Fifth, the Spirit controls and directs the labors of His servants, sending them where He wills and to do what He wants.

Paul tried to go into Bithynia, but the Spirit would not permit him to go. Instead he went into Europe with the gospel. C. T. Studd was furloughed out of China that God might later use him mightily in Africa. Judson was not permitted to remain in India that Burma might know the exceeding riches of God's grace. Livingstone was forbidden to go to China that Africa might become his graveyard. The great missionary statesman is the Holy Spirit. Human statesmanship is secondary to divine guidance. What men may think to be an excellent move may not be a good move unless the Spirit of God approves that move as good.

The Holy Spirit has at His command many means for the accomplishment of His desires. Sickness, circumstances, death, closed doors, and changed motivation are among the instruments which He commands. He can and does move the hearts of men in a hundred different ways to control missionary strategy. Human freedom and responsibility are not abridged, but this freedom and responsibility operate as a circle within the larger circle of His divine omnipotence to which all decisions and minds are subject in a voluntary fashion for the cooperative venture of the gospel to the world.

Sixth, the Holy Spirit should be the supreme Agent in the missionary councils which make decisions and arrive at concepts of strategy. "He should be" because the thought lingers that He frequently is not. Since He is the vicegerent and since He controls and directs the enterprise, every decision should be arrived at only with the consent of the Spirit of God. The chief example of this conciliar headship is the first missionary council which is delineated in Acts 15. The definitive word which comes is "For it seemed good to the Holy Ghost, and to us. . . ." The Holy Ghost preceded the "us," and the "us" was a decision made after the will of the Holy Ghost had been revealed. Walking in the light of His fulness, His decision was a fiat which they accepted and obeyed for His will was to be their will. The Spirit is sensitive, and He may easily be grieved by hardened hearts or the refusal to give Him first place in the councils of men. The loss of His presence means the loss of His power, His knowledge, and His wisdom which in turn means that these councils do not have the Pentecostal power they should normally enjoy regardless of the apparent success of the mission.

The Spirit, seventh, is the disciplining Agent in the Church. The power of the keys rests in the hands of the Holy Spirit and through Him in the hands of the church. As vicegerent of Christ no human being can usurp His power. Christ alone is Lord of the conscience, and the consciences of men cannot be bound save as they are bound by Christ through His Holy Spirit. To sin against the church is to sin against Christ and the Spirit.

The Spirit is in the church, and He acts as a restraining agent to prevent acts by people against the work of God. Through Him guilty sinners should be punished via the appointed means to insure the spiritual life and purity of the church. Unfortunately there are those who pervert the processes of justice and do violence to the ordained means of punishment acting as lords of men's consciences. The Spirit desires that erring men should be punished but only by spiritual punishment and not through the use of the secular arm of the government. Excommunication is the most serious form of punishment beyond which no church may go in bringing to bear spiritual forces upon the sinning and the recalcitrant. The objectives of the Spirit in punishment are the reclaiming of the erring brother, the preservation of the reputation and purity of the church, and the desire, by punishment of offenders, to prevent others from doing the same thing. Punishment always has for its object the change of the individual and his reclamation. The only occasion when this condition does not prevail is at the final judgment when the estate of men who have persistently rejected God will be eternal separation from His presence.

Last, the Holy Spirit is the final ecclesiastical power from whose decisions there is no appeal. He is the court of last appeal. Deacons and elders or bishops have been ordained of God for the peace and tranquillity of His church. These officers have selective functions which they are to perform. But in no sense do they constitute final authority and their decisions cannot be so considered. What they say and do and the decisions they make are subject to the decisions of the Holy Spirit. Insofar as the decisions of men are consistent with the decisions of the Spirit they are to be obeyed. The Holy Spirit is incapable of error but men are not. And when men make decisions inconsistent with the nature and work of the Spirit, they are to be resisted. But the means by which decisions rendered according to the mind of the Spirit may be enforced are spiritual.

It is most unfortunate that ecclesiastical powers always face the temptation of believing that their voices are the voice of God. It is worse when they employ non-spiritual means to enforce non-Spirit directed decisions or when they seek to enforce decisions which have come from the Holy Spirit but are being enforced by means which He cannot approve. In an episcopal form of government, employment of the threat of removal from office or the placing of financial pressures upon an individual to force him into conformity is unfortunate. To force upon men programs and measures of which they do not approve and about which there may well be a real difference of opinion is another sign of the use of carnal means to accomplish a purpose. Men should never stand in judgment on their brethren except as those judgments reflect the prior judgment of the Holy Spirit and are in accord with the divine revelation which is His product.

In these ways the Spirit operates today as the representative of Jesus Christ in this age. The lack of emphasis on the Spirit has been so apparent and glaring that one is surprised that it has taken men so long to correct this omission. One looks in vain for any real mention of the Holy Spirit in the Laymen's Inquiry or in *Rethinking Missions*. There is no single mention of the Spirit in the index of this book. Hendrick Kraemer wrote a profound volume entitled *The Christian Message in a Non-Christian World*. This book served as the backbone for the discussions at the Madras Conference in 1938. The index of Kraemer's work does not contain a single line on the Holy Spirit. In the seven volumes of the Madras Conference, almost every other subject is treated but not the Holy Spirit. The authority of the faith, the life of the church, the economic basis of the church, the church and the state, the church and the international order, evangelism and other kindred subjects are dealt with—but the Holy Spirit is left alone.

At Whitby in 1947, John A. Mackay spoke on the subject of the Holy Spirit. At Willingen in 1952, F. W. Dillistone spoke on "The Dispensation of the Spirit." These are but straws in the wind that the return to biblical theology has included a return to the person and work of the Holy Spirit in a trinitarian formula. If the large denominations represented in these international missionary conferences lost sight of the Spirit in the past few decades, the same cannot be said of the faith mission boards. They have continuously stressed the Holy Spirit, but the faith mission boards have been guilty of neglect within the pattern of recognition. It is insufficient to have a head knowledge of the Holy Spirit in relation to missions. Men must have His power too. He is the dynamic of the enterprise, and the ultimate success or failure of it depends upon their knowledge of, and appropriation of, the power and work of the Spirit of God. When believers once more enter into the fulness of the blessing of the Spirit, then missionary work shall assume proportions and make progress in the direction of missions' final goal—the evangelization of the world.

CHAPTER XVIII

The Local Pastor and Missions

THE PASTOR IS AN IMPORTANT KEY TO THE MISSIONARY PROB-
lem in the local church. This individual holds within his hand
powers which, when properly used, will make possible the
missionary advance and ultimately the completion of the commission that the church of Christ has been looking for these
many centuries.

If the pastors of the churches are the key to ultimate evangelization of the world in some generation, it is axiomatic that
the pastors by and large are products of theological seminaries.
As products they will reflect what they have learned and have
been taught in these institutions. The drive of the seminary,
its compelling challenges as expressed by its faculty, curriculum, and inner life will dominate the lives and ministry of its
graduates over the years. Exceptions to the rule will occur.
But the bulk of the men will reflect in general the ruling passions of the institutions at which they received their theological training.

A cursory examination of the curriculum of the average
theological seminary will demonstrate the thesis that it is not
particularly interested in foreign missions. Numerous institutions either have no professor of missions at all or relegate the
teaching of missions to the periphery of the seminary. If missions subjects are taught, a small minority of the students pursue them while the vast majority are untouched. The student

who wishes to become a missionary finds that practically no provision is made to equip him for that special field of service. Everywhere the curriculum reflects the unspoken assumption that the work of the seminary is to prepare men for the pulpit ministry or for other ministries such as Christian education at home. The life and work of the seminaries are definitely geared to that end, and in some cases they are geared to the production of teachers and scholars rather than to the production of men for the pulpit and church ministry.

On the other hand, the denominations, speaking either through their annual meetings or in conclaves such as those held by the International Missionary Council or the World Council of Churches, repeatedly emphasize the "mission" of the church which is to evangelize the world. Whether one consults the findings from Jerusalem, Madras, Whitby, Willingen, or the writings of individuals, the consensus is that the church exists for a purpose, and that purpose is its mission with the gospel to the ends of the earth. But the thinking as evidenced by these proclamations and writings has not percolated into seminary consciousness to any degree. A basic disjunction exists between the theory as expressed by segments of the various denominations and the actual practices of the seminaries. One critic of seminaries goes so far as to say that most institutions on this level do not know what philosophy of theological education they entertain in the first place, and that the courses of study when broken down into component parts reflect that the parts are unrelated to the whole. One department does not know what the other departments are doing and no department seems to know whether the subjects it teaches and the work it is doing is relevant to theological education. And if this can be said about theological education in general, it can be said with greater emphasis about seminary training in its relation to the missionary task of the church both in the production of pastors who will emphasize missions in their par-

ishes and in the training of those who will become missionaries.

Whatever training is offered by seminaries, that training is
not geared to the requirements of those who are interested in
becoming missionaries, and therefore is bound to be lop-sided.
Perhaps that is why institutions like the Kennedy School of
Missions in Hartford, Connecticut have been created to fill
the gap. The students who do not anticipate becoming missionaries are in a worse plight yet. A casual examination of the
average seminary product will show that he has a severely
limited and unenlightened point of view about the nature,
function, and design of the church. He has never faced the
question whether he himself should become a missionary nor
does he have any understanding of the missionary call. Uneducated in the operation of a suitable missionary program
and emphasis for his local church he enters the pastorate without the passion or the ability to create and sustain a missionary
program of prime quality.

Bible colleges and Bible institutes in the United States and
Canada have been more successful in their efforts to promote
missions. These institutions frequently have semi-professional
missionary courses on a post-high school level which provide
the kind of training that will fit a candidate for the mission
fields. And for those students who do not become missionaries,
the course of study and the non-academic impact of the institution on their lives leave an indelible imprint and eventuate
in a missionary bias which they carry into the fields of service
that they enter. The atmosphere of the Bible colleges and institutes is normally more missionary and in that atmosphere
young lives are challenged dynamically to devote themselves
to service abroad. The graduates of these institutions do not
find service overseas through denominational channels. Their
educational background is considered sub-standard by most of
the large denominational mission boards. Consequently, they
find an outlet for service through the faith mission boards.

During the last thirty years in America, all of the large denominations have retreated and retrenched. Only within the last few years have they been able to equal in money and personnel what they had in 1927. Meanwhile, the faith boards have been growing by leaps and bounds. One or two examples will suffice to show how true this has been.

The Presbyterian Church, U.S.A. has always been a missionary-minded denomination, and it represents a large and significant example of foreign missionary work among the larger denominations. In 1929 the foreign missionary budget ran approximately $4,400,000.00. By 1938 this budget, through the depression years, was reduced to $3,000,000.00. Not until the later 1940's had it returned to the position financially which it held in 1929. By 1953 recovery was completed and the budget projection for that year showed an increase of approximately fifty per cent more than in 1929. In 1953 the budget was almost $6,500,000.00.

Among the faith boards in the same period, a remarkable difference may be seen. The Sudan Interior Mission in 1925 had an income of $64,000.00. In 1952 the income had jumped to more than $2,200,000.00. In 1925 they had less than a hundred missionaries on their rolls. In 1952 this had jumped to 1,000. The Africa Inland Mission had an income of $115,-000.00 in 1925. By 1952 this had increased to almost $800,-000.00. The Wycliffe Bible Translators do not appear in the 1925 report by Beach and Fahs. In 1952 this organization reported an income of almost $600,000.00. The China Inland Mission had about $120,000.00 income in 1925. Their missionaries have been forced out of China, and the agency has undergone extensive reorientation in the last fifteen years, yet in 1952 this agency had an income for missionary work of $850,000.00. The Latin-American Mission which does not appear in the 1925 report had an income in the 1952 report of the Interdenominational Foreign Mission Association of North America of $190,000.00. The Scandinavian Alliance

Mission of North America, now known as the Evangelical Alliance Mission had an income of $107,000.00 in 1925 and in 1952 an income of almost $1,500,000.00.

If one were to list the agencies connected with the International Missionary Council today and check back into the number of missionaries employed by these agencies thirty years ago, the percentage of missionaries represented by them then would be far greater than the percentage today. One can only conclude that the agencies not found among the constituency of the International Missionary Council have made forward progress dynamically in a period when the other agencies were suffering setbacks or standing still. While it would be almost impossible to assert dogmatically that the primary reason for this lay in the failure of the seminaries to train their graduates with a missionary bias for service and for the parish ministry, yet there is some ground on which to rest such a case. The zeal and passion for missions has partly been lost on the pastoral level, and since the pastor is the key to missions, the whole enterprise has suffered because of it.

Placing blame upon the theological seminaries for the absence of a ruling missionary passion in the hearts of the ministers should not in any way relieve the individual minister of his personal responsibility. Whatever guilt belongs to the institutions in which a pastor receives his theological education the pastor himself still has the Bible. Any superficial reading of the Bible with open eyes will reveal the truth concerning missions apart from special emphasis on the part of the theological seminary. If the average pastor took seriously the New Testament teachings about the major function of the church, that in itself would motivate him in the direction of a passion for missions. The place where the average pastor will probably prove to be deficient even when he has grasped the New Testament idea of missions and embraced it will be in the area of implementation. He may know what he ought to do without having much knowledge how to go about it. It is at this point that the lack in his theological training will hurt most. But it is also at this point that most denominations, large and small, are defective too. Every one should have a packet of material which will inform the pastor about what he can do to keep a missionary program in his church operating. This is more than sending out occasional literature with a map and some statistics. A comprehensive and fully coordinated program should be laid before him for his guidance and help at the local church level.

The pastor is the key agent as has been suggested. He is the essential force reaching the people of his church who in turn will make possible the accomplishment of the program he places before them. He is the go-between through whose ministry the lives of men will be challenged to accomplish what the church has in view for missions. This raises the question of the obligation and responsibility of the pastor to his church for that kind of missionary program envisioned as ideal. What precisely is the function of the minister in a missionary program and how can he bring into being one which will elicit the full support of his people?

The minister as an educator leads his people out into something. The underlying assumption is that the people in moving into something else make a change for the better. To make them better the minister must know the answers to two questions. One is the question "what" and the other is the question "how." The "what" is a matter of what shall be given them or imparted to them and what the consequences of the program will be. The "how" is the means by which the objectives in view are implemented. These, as in other phases of communication, comprise the "what" and the "how" of the processes.

A pastor will be helped in his educational efforts if he and the congregation understand the need for missionary education. The foremost reason for educating a congregation is to acquaint them with the plan of God for the ages. No church can engage in a task of which it has no understanding. The people must be made to realize that Christ has a plan for His church, and they must see that perpetual propagation is required by the peculiar nature of the Christian faith. Men must be shown that if Christ means anything to them, and if He is honestly to be made regnant in their hearts, they must do all they can to make Him known and regnant in the hearts of men everywhere. This is surely the first step which a pastor must take in order to be an effective educator.

Second, the spiritual lives of Christians will be developed and heightened when missions are fundamental and not supplemental. No individual or church can be elevated, deepened, and inspired to that life on the highest plane apart from a thorough grounding in, and commitment to, foreign missions. And the pastor who would develop the spirituality of his people to its highest peak cannot do so without stress and emphasis on missions. So as an educator he must develop this spiritual life, and it can be done successfully through missionary channels.

Furthermore, the pastor imparts information because he knows that on the basis of information concrete results accrue. Psychologically the will cannot be moved until the heart has first been moved. And the heart is moved by information. One does not will to do something unless he first possesses a knowledge of the problem. And when the knowledge has touched his heart it will lead to action. Thus, for example, if a congregation is made aware of a specific need, such as the evangelization of the world, this knowledge must precede any act of will directed toward the accomplishment of that need.

Human nature does not change and education for missions must be continuous. To maintain enthusiasm and to recall to the minds of church members what they have forgotten requires constant reminders. The failure to keep the missionary bias before the people will produce a decline in the program, and the pastor is constrained for this reason to educate without interruption. Furthermore, giving is related to knowledge, and the supply of the financial needs for the work of missions is difficult unless someone makes the people conscious of the precise needs and challenges them to meet them. The pastor cannot be an effective agent unless he tells his people what the financial needs are and invites them to participate in meeting those needs.

What is true for money is true for prayer. Christians pray for those items which are prominent in their consciousness. They should remember people, not generalities. Who has not suffered from the bane of praying so generally as to make his praying ridiculous? Who can suppose that a prayer, "Lord, help all the missionaries," is an effective prayer? God, in effect, replies saying, "You want me to bless all the missionaries? Now name one specifically that you want me to bless. And what actually do you wish me to do for that missionary?" Much that passes for prayer is valueless, because it is not based upon the principles and precepts of prayer. Knowledge produces prayer. For when men know, they feel. And when they feel, they catch the vision and begin to ask God for particular persons and things. As an educator the pastor wants to get people both to give and to pray.

Missionary training will accomplish for the church what no substitute for it can do. The efficiency of the church will be increased. Indifference, selfishness, parochialism, and spiritual myopia will vanish. The work of every other department of the church will develop when missions flourish. More people will come to the Sunday School and to the church services; more money will flow into the coffers; more spirituality will be seen; more vision will come. The basic vitality of the work will increase, and the blessing of God will rest abundantly on that group of people.

What a pastor should encourage his people to do is obvious. He should get them to give and to pray. But knowledge of what ought to be done does not produce the results desired. A second level of consideration confronts him even when he has ascertained the answer to the question "what." How can he get people to give—to pray—to go? What are the means by which the pastor can educate his people? What tools ought he to employ in the promotion of missions?

The first answer to the question is plain. The pastor is a preacher, and the pulpit is his throne. That pulpit should ever reflect his passion and concern for missions. He should preach definite missionary sermons and do so regularly. His sermons not directly related to missions should include allusions to missions and illustrations taken from missionary experience. He should place before his people the needs of the world, the urgency of the task, the opportunities and open doors before their feet, the need for prayer, self-denial and consecration. The sermons themselves should ground the people in the basic principles, giving them the facts of the matter; they should show men what their duty is; they should bring them to the place where they will do something in response to all of the foregoing. Ultimately, all that is done and said is designed to secure results, and the results will demonstrate pragmatically whether what has been said is effective.

The missionary meetings of the church are another means for education. Instead of limiting them to the Women's Missionary Society, there ought to be missionary societies for the men, for the young people, and even for the children. Regular missionary meetings devoted exclusively to this subject should be held. These meetings must be planned and executed carefully. They should include the use of slides, movies, and other audio-visual aids. Through the Sunday School, approaches to the pupils can be made via missionary meetings too. It should allot four to eight sessions a year just to the subject of missions. Many Church schools set aside a number of Sundays for temperance lessons and surely as many Sundays for missions should be allowed as for temperance.

The church should develop a good missionary library. Biographies of leading missionaries, books on missionary life, preparation, call to service, comparative religions, and others should be placed in this collection. The books should be made available to the people and the people encouraged to read them. A lending library is the only kind of library collection to have. And this library should be supervised by an interested and competent librarian.

Many churches find a missions study class to be a good means of developing a rich program. Meetings should be held one night a week for several months a year, and a simple course of study designed for laymen is advisable. If the program of the church is a full one, it can be incorporated before or after the mid-week prayer service, or it can meet on the same night set apart for choir rehearsal. Using good materials, a missions study course will fill people with genuine insight and enthusiasm for the task. Added to this the pastor should make the church itself, in a physical sense, the medium for indirect missionary education. Maps on the walls showing the distribution of missionaries, the fields where they serve, and lighted spots on the map for the missionaries supported by the church itself will help. Collections of curios from the various mission fields, charts, magazines, pamphlets and a church missionary committee are helpful.

The pastor himself should keep posted. He should buy and read missionary volumes. He should keep and file missionary data. He should attend missionary conferences. And above all he should be filled with the spirit of missions. His live interest, alertness for taking advantage of new opportunities, and a consuming passion to make missions central in his ministry is a "must."

Missionary work is a spiritual work. But spiritual work requires money and money is an instrument of power. The present method of missionary endeavor requires money, great sums of money, to keep it going. Critics like Allen reprobate the present methodology and look for the day when missionary strategy will be revamped beyond present recognition.

Perhaps the thesis of Allen has merit but hard cold facts do not warrant the conclusion that the present strategy of foreign missionary work through denominational and faith agencies and boards is going to disappear in the immediate future. If and when the present agencies do disappear and some other method is employed, there will be a need for a new approach to the problem of money and the place of the pastor in being a financial agent implicated in the raising of money. Right now money is very important in the forward movement of the missionary program whether it be denominational or otherwise. And all agencies are circumscribed (with the exception, perhaps, but not entirely so of agencies which promote missions on a "faith" basis on the extreme right wing) by the amount of money available for them to spend. Faith mission boards operate in this bind as do denominational boards and literally hundreds of candidates are not serving on foreign mission fields today, and will not serve until some visible means of support become available to them. Money, therefore, is a vital element in the present missionary program, and it is right and proper to be interested in this element which helps to make or break the program.

No pastor should encourage his people to believe that money is a proper substitute for personal missionary service. But any Christian who knows that he has been called to some field other than that of vocational full-time Christian service should also know that his money may be used to parallel his own life work, and that he may have the privilege of supporting someone in his place and stead. Long after a man is dead the money he has given still speaks for him. And in the case of those who have left behind sums of money for use following their departure, this money speaks for them and is a testimony to their faithfulness before God. All the money that is needed to complete the job of world evangelization is available today. But little of the available money is spent on missions. Less than fifty per cent of the church members give any money toward foreign missions. And the average per capita gift of those who do support missionary programs is small indeed.

No one can determine accurately the per capita giving from independent churches or from the constituency supporting faith mission boards. For that reason no one can assume that the per capita giving in these cases is either better or worse than that of the denominations about which more information is available. In 1953 the Southern Baptist Convention in its Cooperative Program designated about three and one-half million dollars to its foreign mission board. With a constituency of more than seven millions of people, the per capita giving for the foreign mission board which represented about forty per cent of the total budget would be fifty cents. Fifty cents per member would be about one penny a week from each cooperating church member for foreign missions. Among the Northern Presbyterians the per capita giving was considerably better percentagewise, but not too much better when computed on a weekly basis. With a constituency of about two million six hundred thousand people, the budget requirements for the foreign mission board represented an average per capita gift of two dollars and fifty cents. This would bring the gifts to approximately five cents a week per capita which is five times better than the average of the Southern Baptist Convention, but five cents a week for missions can hardly be called generous. The American Baptist Convention for the year ending April 1953 had an income of one million eight hundred and fifty thousand dollars for the two foreign missionary societies. This figure divided by the constituency of a million and a half people means that the per capita giving was one dollar and twenty cents a year. That in turn means that the missionary giving for the two foreign boards was less than two and a half cents a week. Even when the receipts for the home mission boards of the American Baptist Convention are included in the total per capita weekly giving, the amount is still quite small. And again it should be stressed that missionary interest measured in terms of financial support is negligible among American Protestants, and the examples as given above are not a reflection against the denominations cited for they are in the same category with other groups and have been selected at random and not by design. The others are no better by and large.

In raising money for missions, the pastor of the church must lead that church in its financial efforts. He should educate his people properly in order to secure maximum results. He must stress principles for missionary giving. The first principle is personal stewardship in relation to the Lordship of Jesus Christ. Stewardship cannot mean less than tithing. The emphasis on tithing should reflect the truth that when a Christian tithes, by that act he admits that the other ninety per cent belongs to God, and that he has a stewardship which calls into account the use of everything God graciously lets him have.

In stressing principles a minister should carefully relegate the responsibility to the individual and not to people en masse. The church of Jesus Christ has a responsibility as a corporate body, but it is psychologically true that when the emphasis is placed on individual responsibility, the hearts of individuals are moved in a way they are not moved when the emphasis is general rather than specific.

Another principle is that of systematic giving. Far too many Christians are irregular in their support of missions. They give as the spirit moves them, and they often think they are doing more for missions than they actually are doing because they have given slightly larger sums at infrequent intervals. Regular and systematic support is the only satisfactory form of giving in a well-ordered financial program. In addition giving should be proportionate. This principle reflects the truth that the more one has the more one should give. The larger the annual income the larger should be the proportion of that income spent for the missionary program. In the

United States the man with a large income is able to give more because of the peculiar income tax arrangements. A man who has an income of one hundred thousand dollars a year is giving only twenty-eight dollars out of every one hundred. The government pays the remainder, seventy-two dollars, which normally would be eaten up by taxes. Thus after the tithe has been deducted, there is plenty of room for men with large incomes to give money at a net cost that is negligible. With new charitable exemption provisions in the income tax law allowing for thirty percent deductions, charitable giving is more attractive than ever before.

The pastor should inculcate in his people the conviction that the form of giving which produces the best results spiritually is that which is rooted in self-denial. To give from an abundance is one thing. To give liberally out of self-denial is quite another. Giving that does not bring with it a measure of self-denial cannot possibly produce the highest fruit. God honors the denial of self in giving, and the greater the denial the more blessing there is which comes to giver and receiver alike. Last, the principle of right motivation should be kept in the forefront of the thinking of the people. No matter how large the sum of money given, if the gift does not spring from right motives, it is without value in the sight of God. We are not to give because it is the thing to do and is popular. God's people are not to give in order that it might be seen and admired of men. They are not to give just to please the pastor. They are not to give because a committeeman waits on them. They are to give for reasons rooted and grounded in their relationship to Jesus Christ, and with an understanding of their responsibility to Him and for Him and because of what He has done for them. Anything less than this is grounded on self and is unworthy in the sight of God.

Having indicated what principles the pastor should stress, the second step is to specify the methods for eliciting money from people. This is the "how" of obtaining funds to keep the wheels of missions turning. Each church should adopt a businesslike, comprehensive plan which is adequate for its particular circumstances. This means that the members of the church will be expected to make regular gifts to missions. Yearly the membership will be canvassed with the request to designate how much they hope, in the providence of God, to be able to give for the coming year. In some sense this represents a pledge of which they will be reminded occasionally but which they will not be dunned for in order to collect it. During the year, in addition to the annual pledge paid systematically there should be thank offerings. These are over and above regular gifts and represent special times of blessing and opportunities to do more than what is ordinarily expected. As soon as a church, using this program, is able to support its own missionary it should do so. If the church is a small one, and the membership limited, partial support of a missionary can be the starting point, and the church can go on from that to full support and then it can take on additional missionaries as circumstances permit. Each year the church should aim to increase its giving. This may sound fantastic but the church which is faithful in its missionary giving will ordinarily experience an increase in its attendance and a rise in its spirituality. Both of these will make a financial increase not only possible but absolutely necessary, for further advance both in numbers and spirituality will be contingent upon missionary advance.

Some Christians question the advisability of asking for money. And this criticism is justified when a man is asking for himself. But the pastor of a church stands in the place of God ministering the things of God to His people. The minister is privileged and indeed should ask for money and should urge upon his people the desirability of giving money when he preaches. Sermons on stewardship and particularly missionary stewardship are quite in keeping with the legitimate biblical means for securing funds for mission work. Negatively speaking there is one "don't" which every pastor should keep before him. Do not employ questionable means for raising money. Bazaars and fairs and suppers are not the best means of raising money for missionary work. One can undoubtedly secure money in this fashion, but it is not a spiritual method and takes away the true blessing which comes from sacrificial giving.

The supreme method for raising funds is to promote the spirituality of the congregation. When men are spiritual, they will give. This is inevitable because it follows the spiritual laws of God. No man can be spiritual and not give. And when he is spiritual, he will give without being begged to do so. A parting injunction about raising money is the suggestion that the pastor give liberally himself. His own attitude and example are far stronger than a thousand words. And if he will lead the way, the people will follow. He sets the pattern.

In concluding this discussion of giving, it is not amiss to suggest that ministers do not overlook the possibility of obtaining large sums of money through their influence and counsel. Many Christians consult their pastor when they make their wills. And who is in a better position to recommend that they remember liberally the cause of missions when they dispose of their earthly possessions? And what better cause can they give it to than to missions, and what greater reward shall they have than in doing this? But the pastor should also in personal counseling seek to secure gifts from living donors before they die, for the work here and now. Even relatively poor people can do a great deal if approached properly and under the correct circumstances.

The responsibility in the local church for educating people and raising money falls to the pastor. But his responsibilities stretch further than that. He is also the logical person to enlist young people for missionary service. Every church should have coming forth from its membership some young people whose lives through the ministry of that church have been captured by God for His service. The church which does not have young people going out into the service of God in the foreign and home ministries is a church with a vital defect in its outreach. The failure of a church to propagate itself in personnel generally means that the church is not spiritually alert and is probably in a backslidden condition. That the pastor of the church is implicated in the situation is obvious for he has a duty to discover, enlist, and help arrange for the training of prospective candidates for full-time Christian service. Behind this responsibility of the pastor to enlist young people for missionary service lie harsh statistics, and these help to clarify the problem.

The churches do not have enough well-trained, able missionaries on the fields today. The workers on the field are calling for additional helpers all the time just to cover present needs without taking into consideration the additional personnel required to complete the task of evangelizing the world. Replacements for superannuated missionaries, for missionaries retiring from service because of illness, and for missionaries who have died on the field are constantly needed. And when boards move forward to occupy new fields, more workers are essential for the task. New missionaries who are eager to engage in pioneer endeavor are an ever-pressing necessity, and there is no real cessation of need for more candidates. In perusing a form letter from a mission board recently, their list of missionaries needed came to more than seventy-five for whom places of immediate service could be found without any difficulty whatever. Thus the pastor, who knows how great the need is for more missionaries and especially for well-educated, cultured men and women of broad outlook, infinite patience, ability, faith, and courage, becomes an important cog in the machinery designed for the purpose of locating new personnel.

Good people do not agree whether the church can supply enough missionary manpower to complete the evangelization of the world, or whether it will be accomplished finally through the agency of the indigenous church and a new concept of national responsibility on the field which will not require the extensive services of the white man. However, for our purposes, it must be assumed that the present direction of missionary operations will probably continue for some time as it has for the past fifty years. If this be true, it means that thousands of new personnel must be attracted if the church is to seek seriously to complete the job. On the whole it takes from twenty-five hundred to four thousand Christians to produce one missionary and to support one too. If the Moravian Church at its peak spiritually could enlist one missionary from each block of one hundred members or less, then America today has not begun to reach the goal with its less than twenty thousand missionaries. The churches of America theoretically are able to complete the work of evangelizing the world, and they should be able to enlist sufficient personnel to accomplish the task. And if this is to be accomplished, it will take place through the help of the pastors of local churches who see the vision and put their shoulders to the wheels in a recruiting program.

Young people do not become missionaries for a number of reasons. But no one can argue that he is not a missionary on the ground that God has not willed to call enough men to do the job. The reasons do not lie in the failure of God to call His people for the task. Rather, the reasons spring from within the hearts of God's children. What, then, are some of the reasons why Christians do not become missionaries? Often men are moved by considerations of business and money making. This challenge of a business career appeals to them, and they do not consider the mission field for it does not offer to them the same challenges of career and money. Some have gross misconceptions of missionary work. They do not know or they do not really believe that Christ is needed by the pagan world. Or they feel that the need at home is greater; or they do not know what a missionary call is or how they can recognize it when it comes. The churches at home sometimes lack a missionary bias, and they fail to develop missionary consecration early enough in life. Pastors do not give public appeals for consecration of life and talent, or they fail to speak in private with promising candidates who might heed their appeals. Pastors and relatives oppose consideration of missionary service and willingly consecrate the children of their friends but shrink at the thought of their own children becoming candidates for the foreign field. Many times young people are not able to reason conclusively or objectively, and without the aid of someone to guide them to a place of final and affirmative decision, they are lost to the missionary cause. But the pastor is the key figure in guiding his young people. What, then, can the pastor do to recruit his young people for God?

In his personal life a pastor will not be greatly used of God unless he himself has done certain things. First he must have a fixed and clear conviction about missions. If he is uncertain and if he wavers, he cannot enjoy the same positive relationship to his young people that he should have. He should be able to declare that he has faced the missionary call himself and perhaps he should set the standard by going himself. His children should be yielded to God for missionary service as an example to the congregation and with a real desire that God may have them if He chooses. In his private and public praying, he must lay hold of the Spirit of God to thrust forth laborers into the harvest fields.

In his life and ministry, the pastor should bring to the attention of his people the idea of definite missionary service with the expectation that the Holy Spirit will use his words and exhortations to call them forth to serve. He must show the congregation that the missionary calling is a noble, exalted, and honorable career—not a work for weaklings, the effeminate, and the untalented. Through missionary sermons the pastor will be able to maintain a missionary spirit, and to influence parents and children alike. By using missionaries on furlough and missionary candidates, their influence can be felt throughout the congregation. Missionary conventions, conferences and special meetings will further aid recruitment. The pastor should examine carefully the list of young people in his church, and by personal conferences and through any other means seek to bring the key young people to the place of commitment for service. Just a hand on a shoulder and a proper word at the correct moment may make the difference between a young man who enters business or who becomes a missionary. These means are at the command of the pastor, and if he is alert and eager to take advantage of his opportunities, there is no limit to the number of young people who will heed the call and yield their lives for His service overseas.

The pastor has a fourth responsibility in his work to engage the services of young people for the mission field. This fourth responsibility is a spiritual one for the pastor is a spiritual force for missions in the church. And there is a definite relation between a church's spirituality and missions. To reiterate that a spiritual church is a missionary church and that missionary churches are generally spiritual churches is worthwhile. Missionary history provides fitting examples of the relation between spirituality and missions. Moravian spirituality which gave rise to tremendous missionary passion is one example. The Pietism of Europe as exemplified in the lives of Spener and Francke and the great missionary advance arising from this movement is another. The Wesleyan awakening in England inevitably produced a missionary impetus which shook continents for God. William Carey's great missionary passion is not unrelated to the occasion when he disbanded his church and recommenced with a regenerate few which led to spiritual awakening and missionary endeavor. The spiritual quickening occasioned by the life and ministry of Dwight L. Moody gave rise to an increased missionary passion and vision. The Cambridge Seven owed much of their passion to the

Moody meetings. Mount Hermon in Massachusetts was the fruit of revival and in turn produced missionary passion of quality and quantity. The Student Volunteer Movement had its rise in this sequence, and this movement exerted a power for God that shook a generation of college men and women, and led to the greatest missionary advances since the days of the apostles.

As a spiritual force, the minister can do certain things which will insure a live missionary program. The first is to quicken the spiritual life of the congregation which in turn will lead to missionary outreach. By giving to the church a dynamic spiritual experience, this quickening will be easily channeled into missions. The missionary enterprise is simply the projection abroad of the church at home so the church at home needs to be quickened first. The result will be a missionary passion to create abroad the replica of what exists at home. This will not mean a replica in buildings, forms, rites and ceremonies, but it will reproduce a spiritual likeness recognizable despite outward, superficial differences.

The home church must become a praying church even before thinking of going and giving for missions. The source of any spiritual movement is God, and the power and energies of God are released in answer to believing prayer. Everything vital to missions hangs in one fashion or another on prayer. Men, money, and revival all come through prayer. Pray for the missionaries; pray for the native workers; pray for greater efficiency in missionary agencies. Prayer is the greatest force available in the world, and the church of Jesus Christ has power to wield this force for the glory of God. The pastor should preach on prayer—on intercessory prayer. His people should be encouraged to read books on prayer and to practice prayer by entreating God for specific items. Prayer meetings should be just that. Important as the exposition of the Word of God is, and singing, and testifying, a prayer meeting should major on praying and the saints should be given opportunities to join together in this holy service. The creation of prayer bands holding prayer meetings of the "cottage prayer meeting type" will also help. Prayer is not easy. It is hard and difficult work. But it will unlock doors, break down barriers, produce results, enlist, challenge and empower; and of course it will let loose the power of the Holy Spirit more than all the committee meetings, plans, speeches, trips, charts, and other things men might use. They are only accompaniments related to prayer but these things without prayer are ineffectual and impotent.

A last suggestion is in order. Every church should have an annual missionary conference. The conference should run for a week if possible, but if this cannot be done at first, the conference should last from Sunday through Wednesday or from Wednesday through Sunday. Visiting missionaries and missionary leaders should be imported. The people should be stirred. The purposes of such an annual series should be thought out and each series of meetings analyzed to discover whether the objectives have been attained. Briefly, the objectives are to stimulate the people spiritually, to enlist their prayer help, to secure financial aid, and to obtain missionary recruits for foreign service.

A missionary conference will take four to six years to develop but when once it has become an integral part of the church program, the membership will look forward eagerly to each new conference. New goals and higher goals will be reached year after year. The membership will increase; the Word of God will go out.

So the work of the pastor in missions is a big one. He is indeed the key to missionary interest and passion. He must lead his people into these green pastures for their own gain. And he must creatively work for missions until the church reflects his vision. After all, the average church is frequently a fair reflection of what the undershepherd of the sheep is like.

CHAPTER XIX

Missions and the Future

WHAT OF THE FUTURE? THIS IS A FINAL WORD. YET IT CANNOT be final because the future belongs to God, and what men say is but a guess. Limited to imperfect knowledge of the past and without great insight into the future, man can peer dimly into that dark glass and plot pathways conjecturally. Time will tell how accurately he has diagnosed situations and how well the panaceas suggested have worked. The Christian, in this otherwise obscure dimness, has a peculiar advantage over most others. Whereas he enters into that which is unknown to him, it is known to God. The believer need have no fear of that which is unknown to him because he realizes that the future is God's and that as His ally God will see him through, and He will ever be the God of history completing His eternal purposes for man.

The church of Jesus Christ is living between the times— between the time of its creation and the time of its consummation. It lives in tension as a witness to the grace of God so that its very nature presupposes that it will plan for and enter into the future with the expectation that its work will be needed until the end of history. The church must have its plans ready and its sights set. But the church must not be quiescent. The battle in which it is engaged is fluid. The objective does not change but strategy, methods, and deployments may change rapidly depending upon conditions on the field of battle at any given moment.

One can assume, all other factors being equal, that certain large-scale strategic plans will prevail for the battle in which the church is engaged. This plan of battle for the future will be outlined but with the reservation that the unexpected may eventuate which will require a complete renovation and reformulation of basic strategy and call for the adoption of an entirely new plan. Furthermore, missionary statesmen are not now agreed on one line of attack, although generally it may be said that two schools of thought exist.

One school of thought for missionary strategy is that which places its main reliance upon the indigenous method. Popularized by Roland Allen several decades ago, it has met with opposition in some quarters. In others it has been received favorably, but in the main it has been listened to and passed by. Often there has been tacit consent to the thesis but not enough has been done to implement it or carry it through. The chief content of the indigenous method has been given in the chapter covering that subject. Allen and others have contended that the employment of this method is the only means for completing the task of worldwide evangelization.

The use of the indigenous method in effect neutralizes the method of missionary strategy which has been in operation for more than one hundred years. This second strategy is one involving foreign missionary societies and looking to the completion of the task of world evangelization by the white man rather than by the nationals of the countries to be evangelized. Many administrators are loath to surrender the mode of operation which has worked for a hundred years and which certainly has produced remarkable results. They are not ready to suppose that by this method they are unable to finish the job nor are they convinced that the indigenous method is the answer.

In any discussion of the future, one or two facets gleam brightly amid the controversy of strategy. The first one is that the present strategy and present missionary agencies will continue for a long time to come. There is no apparent hope that there will be any overnight change to the indigenous method exclusively. If a change does come, it will come slowly and undramatically. Missions will move from one to the other over a period of time and as missionary statesmen are convinced and themselves implement these convictions concretely. Events beyond the control of men may force the issue at an early date and in terms which will shut up the church of Jesus Christ to the indigenous method exclusively. Thus China today does not present any strategic missionary opportunity for western societies, and whatever missionary work is being done within the confines of the bamboo curtain is being done indigenously and without the financial help or leadership of the western world.

This writer is convinced that the indigenous method is the ideal one and that world evangelization ultimately will transpire through the use of this method. This conviction springs from the simple arithmetic of personnel and money. Right now the church of Christ is unable to enlist a sufficient number of missionaries to accomplish the job. Instead of twenty or twenty-five thousand missionaries, a million would be needed. There is nothing on the horizon remotely suggesting the possibility that the church can recruit that many missionaries. The half-hearted financial support of the missionary program by the constituency does not indicate that the sinews of war for the support of one hundred thousand let alone one million missionaries is going to be forthcoming. If this be true, then missions will ultimately be shut up to the indigenous method.

Indigenous methods involve a transition for no missionary work can ever be indigenous in its beginnings. The introduction of the foreign missionary in itself is a denial of the indigenous concept, but the operation of an indigenous program must first be set up from the outside. This can only mean that the present missionary methodology must prevail with alterations until the adjustment is completed. In the event that missionary leadership is unable to adjust from the present imperialism and colonialism to autonomous self-governing, self-propagating, self-supporting churches, the result may well be disastrous.

The future of missions is wrapped up in strategy which has for its objective the evangelization of the world. The strategy suggested is posited upon the assumption that it will lead to the establishment of indigenous churches. No one can foretell what the length of time will be between the beginning of a work and the elimination of the foreign missionary from the picture. So complex is the picture and so involved because of fluctuating factors and geographical differences, no time sequence can be laid down with any guarantee that the objective can be accomplished within that time limit. It is known, however, that unless the indigenous concept is kept in the forefront and unless its promotion is expedited from the commencement of new missionary work it is highly likely that it will bog down in the morass of the older colonialism and Christian imperialism. It is known, further, that the most difficult job of all will not come in the areas where new work will be commenced but in those areas which are already steeped in colonialism and imperialism and where drastic changes will have to be made.

The hour is long since past when the white man can hope to dominate and control the churches around the world. The rise of a new nationalism and the desire of men of color to be freed from the shackles of white domination is a handwriting on the wall. And behind the handwriting is the very finger of God, for He never meant that mission churches should be satrapies and dependencies but that they should be equal to and on the same footing with the founding churches. Christians are all one in Christ and their differences are swept away when they kneel before the same cross and partake of the same supper. The International Missionary Council and the

World Council of Churches have expressed this awareness which is seeping through gradually but persistently when they speak of the "younger churches." Surely the older churches shall be, to the younger ones, brethren in the same household of faith, assisting but not controlling; suggesting but not dominating; recommending but not demanding.

In the light of these facts, what shall the strategy for the discernible future be? Whatever the plan is, it should be adequate in scope, adequate in thoroughness and adequate in detailed execution.

Missions today and tomorrow must plan a program which is adequate in scope. The field is the world and no nearsightedness should prevent statesmen from seeing the whole field. And then they must see the fields within the field.

A glance at any missionary map will disclose that there are many areas geographically which do not have a gospel witness. China, with the exception of Formosa, is closed to all missionary work. Parts of South America are either closed to missionaries or so restricted as to make missionary work most difficult. Afghanistan, Baluchistan, Nepal, Bhutan, Sinkiang and Russian Central Asia are closed to the gospel. All of the countries in Europe within the iron curtain are impenetrable, gospel-wise. Manchuria, Siberia, and Russia itself are unreachable. Any missionary plan must include these unoccupied fields. They are territories possessed by the enemy, and they must be conquered for Christ. These closed doors must be opened and the citadels attacked. It will be done at the cost of blood, and a new age of martyrs may have to dawn before victory is won. But so long as any gate stands closed in the night against the gospel witness an assault must be planned on that fortress.

On the fields which have been occupied and in which there is a gospel witness, the plan must include in its scope a suitable witness for segments of society which are unreached by the gospel. In a land where there are missionaries, they often limit their activities to certain spheres. They may reach the lower-class people or the middle-class people while they leave the other classes untouched. No plan is adequate in scope which does not include an assault structurally so as to cut across social and economic segmentation. To reach the poor but to leave the intelligentsia without a witness is inadequate. To touch the middle class without getting at the upper crust of a culture is inadequate. There must be a cross-section witness on any field.

An adequate plan must also take into special account the difficult fields. Some of them appear to be impregnable fortresses, whether they happen to be whole fields which are unreached or strands within a field or fields. The Mohammedan world has been among the most difficult to reach with the gospel. This world extends itself across national barriers into many nations, and this religion is embraced by men of many speech patterns. Fanatical in his convictions whether he is black of skin in Africa or yellow of skin in Indonesia the Mohammedan seems to be impregnable to the gospel. But this very impregnability is a challenge to the missionary which cannot go unheeded. Special attention must be afforded difficult fields for they are dangerous to the future of missions when neglected.

A second governing principle in an adequate plan for missions tomorrow is thoroughness. If the plan must be adequate in scope, it must also be thorough in its execution. From previous discussions, it is evident that in completing the commission at least two factors in that completion have been left indefinite. One is the extensiveness of the witness and the other its intensiveness. Whether every creature in a literal sense must hear the gospel, the Scriptures do not say. When they have heard the gospel is difficult to determine. But missions in the future must be thorough in both of these senses.

In dealing with thoroughness the problems of communication and relevancy rise to plague the missionary. He exists to bring a gospel witness to men. This witness has got to be relevant to the age in which he lives and it must reach people where they are. The missionary must communicate concepts like regeneration, justification, and the trinity to his people. The language in which these concepts were conveyed was Greek. They have been translated or communicated to him in the English language. He in turn translates them into the language of other men. Oftentimes the languages into which the translation is made do not have ready-made words for the terms he seeks to communicate. And if they have comparable words, the content or meaning may vary a shade.

Translation always involves intangible hazards. Instead of translation which means discovering an equivalence, there may be perversion. Instead of the gospel there may be an irrelevancy defined in terms of sociology, psychology, or politics. If missionaries seek to preserve the gospel pure and undefiled, they may fall into the pit of insulating that gospel esoterically so that while it is not perverted, it is still irrelevant to men. For any concepts which remain unchanged, but which cannot be made relevant to men and the age in which men live, are dead. This leads to the question whether missionaries who fall into this pit have ever really appropriated the gospel for themselves. Men must experience regeneration and then carry the objective and the subjective frameworks of reference to other men who in turn will be touched by the objective nature of the eternal and unchangeable gospel but who will also experience that gospel within the whole man.

Each missionary who is privileged to serve mankind as a witness must be absolutely sure that he is a witness. If, on the other hand, he brings with him that which men cannot comprehend and that which is non-intelligible to them, he is not a witness even though he may use terms and repeat phrases which are meaningful to him but meaningless to his hearers. He has to break through communicatively and relevantly before he is a true witness. And breaking through means that he conveys the core-truth unperverted in its objectivity and his personal subjective witness of a transformed life. Any witness which does not accomplish these two objectives is not thorough and is therefore inadequate.

In thoroughness the problem of the gospel witness is further complicated by that of the extent of the witness. When has the gospel been communicated to man is allied to the question "when has the job been done?" Missions today and tomorrow must put into operation some plan which has for its goal the completion of the task. Whatever plans are devised, unless they seek this goal they are not thorough. Obviously the church is presently limited so that within its current abilities it must be selective in what it does. There is not going to be any sudden mass offensive which will dramatically cover or circle the globe in a few days' or weeks' time. But the limitations imposed by insufficient personnel and money do not mean that long-term planning for the ultimate completing of the task should be forgotten. Step by step, moving forward irresistibly, the church must destroy every stronghold of the enemy until the witness has been completed.

Completing the task should not be confused with Christianizing the world. God is calling out for Himself a people, a church, an ecclesia. There shall be some from every kindred and people and tongue. But there shall be no worldwide conversion of all men. Rather it will be selective from within the races of men, cutting across lines of distinction in every direction. This preaching of the gospel should not be superficial, and it must embrace the idea that the church is reaching outward and onward, pressing forward step by step, advancing steadily until the goal is reached.

As each step forward is made, a national and indigenous church should be established which in turn should be equipped and certainly is obligated to exist as a witnessing church among its own people, freeing the missionary forces for the assault on the next stronghold. Unreached nations should be dealt within the scope of a policy for a worldwide gospel witness.

The execution of the missionary plan is a strategic operation, and in the methods and approach looking toward the completion of the plan there are principles which govern the strategy. The principles cannot be thought of as unchanging and are general in content rather than specific. Even when the principles appear to dictate a single course of action, compelling reasons not included within the principles examined may warrant the selection of another course of action. But generally the following criteria make possible a decision in an average situation.

The accessibility, openness, and willingness to receive the gospel message is a governing factor. When one finds a field where the doors are open and easily entered and where the people eagerly respond to the gospel message, this field should be given a high priority. A year from the time these conditions exist the situation may change for the worse. Immediate action with heavy assaults on the target which is ready to succumb is indicated. This is particularly true when the nationals respond in number to the preaching of the gospel and churches are easily founded.

The number of people in a geographical location will determine action. If there are places where men are concentrated, this is a place to go. In many areas today a key city will be the focal point for the gathering of nationals from the interior and the very concentration of men in one place implies that it is a spot which should be selected as a center for evangelistic outreach.

The condition of the field and the previous extent of gospel witness is a strategic consideration. If the field is unreached and the neglect is apparent, this in itself is good reason for giving it serious consideration. A field without any gospel witness after two thousand years deserves special concern. Usually such a field will be socially degraded, grossly ignorant, and in great spiritual need. Strategy would warrant throwing in missionary forces on such a battle front immediately.

Difficult fields, too, must be given special attention. It is easy to drift with the stream and there are always convenient reasons for following the pathway of the least resistance. But the missionary cannot allow this philosophy of life to dominate his strategic decisions. The more difficult the field the more thought should be given to entering that field quickly. When difficult fields have been entered and churches established, these churches normally prove rock-ribbed and display qualities reflected in the field in the first place so that in times of persecution and tribulation they stand firmer than those churches formed in easy fields.

Strategy includes a witness to nations which are providentially placed in terms of power and usefulness. Japan is obviously a strong and strategic nation in the Orient. No missionary program can afford to overlook this nation. As a key to the Pacific in a way even China is not, and in her relationships to the islands of the Pacific, Japan must not be forgotten. Standing as a leader among the oriental peoples, a strong gospel witness well received by this nation will react for good through the other nationals who look toward Japan either fearfully or as an ally in determining their destinies.

The principle of urgency should determine the gospel witness in some cases. Today India is a closing door. As long as that door is open, and since there are so many of the world's people involved, it behooves the church to give this country great attention. Even an island like Ceylon warrants reinforcements as the doors slowly shut. Ceylon has in force a policy which permits no new missionaries to enter the island, but this policy does allow for replacements of missionaries already there. One can anticipate that the restrictions will become more stringent in the years ahead and every step should be taken to insure the creation of a strong indigenous witness before the doors close. But in order to do this, steps must be taken now to prepare for the eventuality of the closed door. Reinforcements of personnel may be impossible even now, but there are other steps which can be taken to aid greatly the work of the missionaries who are there and those who replace retired or disabled ones. The urgency is obvious when the doors are being closed. Before the missionaries leave, they must establish a coordinated and permanent testimony which will stand the shock of their departure.

In any culture the stratification of society into classes is a phenomenon which is common. In so-called classless societies there are still echelons and classes. The denial of classes does not remove them and classless Russia is as solidly structurated as other nations. America is not divided into classes nearly so much as other countries, but America does have divisions. There is a laboring class; a capital class; a middle class; an upper class; and a lower class. The differences may not be as marked, and virtual freedom exists but there are semblances of class distinctions. Just as there are strategic nations and regions so there are strategic classes. Good missionary planning takes this into account and makes every effort to reach the classes first which will give Christianity a status and a standing and make possible the permeation of the whole structure of society with the gospel. Often the simple fact that one segment of a people will receive the gospel will make the gospel attractive to other segments of the same culture and cause those segments to turn to Christ in a remarkable fashion.

The deployment of missionary forces is a vital element in missionary planning. The proper distribution of missionary forces is determined by definite factors. The density of population may quickly reveal how many missionaries should be sent to the area. The less densely-populated places may require fewer missionaries. The state of the culture, the temperament of the people, and their religious beliefs will cause statesmen to deploy their available forces differently. The more intelligent and educated the people are, the greater the number of missionaries normally needed for the field. And the greater will be the demand for better-trained missionaries who will be able to meet the nationals on their own level.

How many national workers and their ability and skill will affect deployment of missionary forces. When national workers are numerous and when they have had adequate education (not necessarily equal to western standards but adequate for the field and their people) and are equipped to carry on the work indigenously, the number of foreign missionaries may be reduced to a minimum.

Whatever decisions are made, the missionary forces must be adjusted from time to time to reflect changing conditions on the field. Re-surveys of every field should be made periodically to see whether the maximum results are being secured from the investment in personnel and money. The results of these surveys will be reflected in readjustments. Naturally missionaries are subjected to lethargy like other people and personality problems may militate against sudden and dramatic field changes. But the work at large is of greater moment than the convenience or temperament of a single missionary. As much as one dislikes disturbing missionaries who are settled, the very nature of the missionary vocation presupposes that they are never to become settled and should be alert to devolution to an extent that they are ready to leave any field for another open door and to do this as quickly as it is feasible in the interests of the total thrust.

On the home front the greatest need of the future is for the church to become the church and to do what the Lord of the church wants done. Christians must somehow be made to see what the need of the world is, what they ought to do to meet that need, and then be challenged creatively so that the whole church will militantly and sacrificially get behind the task of world evangelization. Philosophies will come and go. Political systems will rise and fall. Nations will wax and wane.

These are all expendable. But there are some things which do not change. The church is one and the Great Commission another.

As the church goes forward, the presence of the Lord of the church will go with it. His is an abiding presence so that as His people go about their work He will never leave them nor forsake them. Because He is the same yesterday, today, and forever He is the unchanging amid the changing; the eternal amid the temporal; the absolute amid the relative. Besides His abiding presence, He gives to every co-worker His sufficient presence. With this goes the divine enablement by which men are made able to meet the challenges of every hour. With His sufficiency they can conquer the foe and vanquish darkness, bringing light and life and immortality.

And with it all goes the necessary presence of the Lord of the church without which presence the work cannot be done nor the goal reached. The failure to take Him into account or the failure to follow His directions will inevitably result in the failure to accomplish what He intended and will leave the worker without the blessing of the Lord of the church.

The darkness of night will never overtake His church, but as good stewards His people are to watch faithfully and work carefully knowing that the Master cometh before the dawning of the morning. And when He comes, that coming shall signal to all men the truth unchanging that "Jesus shall reign wheree'r the sun doth her successive journeys run. His kingdom spread from shore to shore, till moons shall wax and wane no more."

Bibliography

Aldama, Manuel Garrido. *From Roman Priest to Radio Evangelist.* Grand Rapids: Zondervan Publishing House, 1946.

Alden, Edmund K. *The Medical Arm of the Missionary Service.* Boston: Congregational House, 1898.

Allen, Belle Jane, Comp. *A Crusade of Compassion for the Healing of the Nations.* W. Medford, Mass.: Central Committee on the United Study of Foreign Missions, 1919.

Allen, Leonard B. "The Microphone and the Millions." *National Christian Council Review,* May, 1946.

Allen, Roland. *Educational Principles and Missionary Methods.* London: Scott, 1919.

——. *Missionary Methods, St. Paul's Or Ours?* London: Scott, 1912.

——. *Missionary Principles.* London: Scott, 1913.

——. "The Relation Between Medical, Educational and Evangelistic Work in Foreign Missions." *Church Missionary Review,* March, 1920.

——. *The Spontaneous Expansion of the Church and the Causes Which Hinder It.* London: World Dominion Press, 1927.

——. "The Whole and the Parts of Foreign Missionary Administration." *Church Missionary Review,* December, 1920.

Ashley-Montagu, Montague Francis. *Men's Most Dangerous Myth: The Fallacy of Race.* New York: Columbia University Press, 1952.

Ayers, T. W. *Healing and Missions.* Richmond, Va.: Educational Department Foreign Mission Board, 1930.

Báez Camargo, Gonzalo. *Christianity and the Race Problem: Christian Bases of World Order.* Missionary Education Movement, 1943.

Bailey, Ambrose Moody. *Evangelism in a Changing World.* New York: Round Table Press, 1936.

Baillie, John. "The Given Word: The Message of the Unvarying Gospel." *National Review of Missions,* October, 1947.

Barton, James L. *Educational Missions.* New York: Student Volunteer Movement for Foreign Missions, 1913.

Bavinck, Johan Herman. *The Impact of Christianity on the Non-Christian World.* Grand Rapids: Eerdman's, 1948.

Beach, Harlan Page, and Fahs, Charles H. (eds.). *World Missionary Atlas.* New York: Institute of Social and Religious Research, 1925.

Benedict, Ruth. *Patterns of Culture.* New York: Penguin Books, by arrangement with Houghton Mifflin Company, 1946.

Bertini, Ugo. *Pie XI el le Médecine au Service des Missions.* Paris: Librairie Bloud et Gay, 1929.

Bilheimer, Robert S. *What Must the Church Do?* (The Interseminary Series.) New York: Harper & Brothers, 1947.

Birtwhistle, Allen. *Colour, the Problem of Racial Discrimination.* London: Livingstone Press, 1949.

Bliss, Edwin M. *The Missionary Enterprise; A Concise History of Its Objects, Methods and Extension.* New York: Fleming H. Revell Company, 1908.

Boas, Franz, and Others. *General Anthropology.* Boston: D. C. Heath and Company, 1938.

Boas, Franz. *Race and Democratic Society.* New York: J. J. Augustin, 1945.

Brown, Arthur Judson. *The Foreign Missionary.* New York: Fleming H. Revell Company, 1907.

——. *Why and How of Foreign Missions.* New York: Eaton, 1908.

Buck, Peter H. *Anthropology and Religion.* New Haven: Yale University Press, 1939.

Burns, Sir Alan Cuthbert. *Colour Prejudice with Particular Reference to the Relationship Between Whites and Negroes.* London: G. Allen & Unwin, Ltd., 1948.

The Call, Qualifications and Preparation of Candidates for Foreign Missionary Service. New York: Student Volunteer Movement for Foreign Missions, 1906.

Calverley, Eleanor T. (M.D.) *How to Be Healthy in Hot Climates.* New York: Thomas Y. Crowell Co., 1949.

Carver, Wm. Owen. *The Bible, a Missionary Message; a Study of Activities and Methods.* New York: Fleming H. Revell Company, 1921.

Causton, Mary I. M. *For the Healing of the Nations: The Story of British Baptist Medical Missions 1792–1951.* London: The Carey Kingsgate Press Ltd., 1951.

Chesterman, Clement Clapton. *In the Service of Suffering: Phases of Medical Missionary Enterprise.* London: Edinburgh House Press, 1940.

Chirgwin, Arthur M. *The Bible in World Evangelism.* New York: Friendship Press, 1954.

——. *The Decisive Decade.* London: Livingstone Press, 1949.

Chollet, C. *Problemes de Races et de Couleurs, le Conflit, la Reconciliation.* Paris: Societé de Missions Evangelique, 1929.

Christian Council of South Africa. *Race—What Does the Bible Say?* Roodepoort, Transvaal; Christian Council of So. Africa, 1952.

Clark, C. A. "The Nevius Methods." *International Review of Missions.* 1935.

Clark, Charles Allen. *The Korean Church and the Nevius Methods.* New York: Fleming H. Revell Company, 1930.

Clarke, Wm. Newton. *A Study of Christian Missions.* New York: Scribners, 1900.

Clinchy, Everett Ross. *A Handbook on Human Relations.* New York: Farrar, Strauss, 1949.

Conservative Baptist Foreign Mission Society. *What a Missionary Costs.* Chicago: 1950.

Cook, Harold R. *An Introduction to the Study of Missions.* Chicago: Moody Press, 1954.

Counsel to New Missionaries from Older Missionaries of the Presbyterian Church, 1905.

Cox, Oliver Cromwell. *Caste, Class and Race; A Study in Social Dynamics.* Garden City; N.Y.: Doubleday, 1948.

Craig, Clarence Tucker, ed. *The Challenge of Our Culture* (The Interseminary Series). New York: Harper & Brothers, 1946.

——. *The One Church in the Light of the New Testament.* New York: Abingdon-Cokesbury Press, 1951.

Crawford, Mrs. E. M. (G.). *Called*. London: Church Missionary Society, 1915.

Cummings, Thomas Fulton. "Language Mastery: A Problem in Skill Mastery," *International Review of Missions*, July, 1935.

Davis, J. Merle. *The Economic and Social Environment of the Younger Churches*. London: Edinburgh House Press, 1929.

——. *New Buildings on Old Foundations; A Handbook on Stabilizing the Younger Churches in Their Environment*. New York: IMC, 1945.

Dawson, William James. *The Evangelistic Note*. New York: Fleming H. Revell Company, 1905.

Dennis, James S. *Christian Missions and Social Progress*. New York: Fleming H. Revell Company, 1897–1906, 3 vols.

Dillistone, Frederick Wm. *Revelation and Evangelism*. London: Lutterworth Press, 1948.

Dobson, J. *Why Christian Missions?* London: Student Christian Movement Press, 1930.

Dodd, Edward Mills. *How Far to the Nearest Doctor?* New York: Friendship Press, 1933.

Doig, Andrew Beveridge. *Missionary Motive and the Missionary Approach in the Light of the Fundamentals of the Christian Faith*. S.T.M. Thesis, 1939, Union Seminary.

Donohugh, Thomas Smith. *A Study of Salaries, etc.* Research Committee Foreign Missions Conference of North America, May, 1950.

Dougall, James Watson Cunningham. "The Reason for Medical Missions." *International Review of Missions*, July, 1946.

The Ecumenical Review (incorporating *Christendom*), Quarterly Journal issued by World Council of Churches, Geneva.

Edwards, M. R. *Work of the Medical Missionary*. New York: Student Christian Movement Press, 1909.

Fleming, Daniel J. *Devolution in Mission Administration*. New York: Fleming H. Revell Company, 1916.

——. *Living As Comrades: A Study of Factors Making for Community*. New York: Agricultural Missions, Inc., 1950.

——. *Ventures in Simpler Living*. New York: International Missionary Council, 1933.

——. *What Would You Do? When Christian Ethics Conflict With Standards of Non-Christian Cultures.* New York: Friendship Press, 1948.

——. *Whither Bound in Missions.* New York: Association Press, 1925.

Foreign Missions Conference of North America. *The Christian Mission Among Rural People: A Joint Study.* New York: Rural Missions Cooperating Committee of the Foreign Missions Conference of North America, 1948.

——. *The Family and Its Christian Fulfillment,* 1946.

——. *World Statistics of Christian Missions,* edited by Beach and St. John, 1916.

Foster, John. *World Church.* London: Student Christian Movement Press, 1945.

Fowler, Charles Henry. *Missionary Addresses* (1906).

Franklin, James H. *Ministers of Mercy.* New York: Missionary Education Movement of the U.S. and Canada, 1919.

——. *The Never Failing Light.* New York: Missionary Education Movement of the U.S. and Canada, 1933.

Garlick, Phyllis L. *The Wholeness of Man; A Study in the History of Healing.* London: Highway Press, 1943.

Glover, Robert Hall. *The Bible Basis of Missions.* Los Angeles: Bible House of Los Angeles, 1946.

Gordon, A. J. *Holy Spirit in Missions.* New York: Fleming H. Revell Company, 1893.

Grubb, Kenneth G., and Bingle, E. J. eds. *World Christian Handbook.* London: World Dominion Press, 1949, 1952.

Hamilton, Floyd E. and Cochrane, Thomas. *Basic Principles in Education and Medical Mission Work.* London: World Dominion Press, 1928.

Haughwout, Lefferd Merle Alexander. *The Missionary and His Work: An Evaluation.* Milwaukee, Wisc.: Morehouse Publishing Co., 1927.

Hering, Hollis Webster. *A World Wide Christian Outlook; A Selected Bibliography for Student Volunteer Movement,* 1935.

Herklots, Hugh Gerard Gibson. *For Such a Time As This.* London: Lutterworth Press, 1945.

Herskovits, Melville J. *Man and His Works.* New York: Alfred A. Knopf, 1948.

Hocking, William E., Chmn. The Commission of Appraisal. *Re-thinking Missions.* New York: Harper & Brothers, 1932.

Hogg, Wm. Richey. *Ecumenical Foundations.* New York: Harper, 1952.

Horton, W. M. *Toward a Reborn Church.* New York: Harper & Brothers, 1949.

Houghton, Frank. *George King, Medical Evangelist.* London: China Inland Mission, 1930.

Hovland, Carl I. *Experiments on Mass Communication.* Princeton, N.J.: Princeton University Press, 1949.

Hoyland, John Somervell. *The Race Problem and the Teaching of Jesus Christ.* London: Religious Tract Society.

Hume, Edward Hicks. *Doctors Courageous.* New York: Harper, 1950.

Hunnicutt, Benjamin Harris and Reid, Wm. Watkins. *The Story of Agricultural Missions.* New York: Missionary Educational Movement in U.S. and Canada, 1931.

Hutchings, Edith M. *The Medicine Man: Stories from Medical Missions in India, China, Africa, and Madagascar.* London: London Missionary Society, 1927.

International Missionary Council. *The Missionary Obligation of the Church.* London: Edinburgh House Press, 1952.

The International Review of Missions. Edinburgh, later London: The International Missionary Council, 1912 ff.

The Jerusalem Meeting of the International Missionary Council, March 24–April 8, 1928. New York: International Missionary Council, 1928. 8 vols.

Jones, Clarence W. *Radio, the New Missionary.* Chicago: Moody Press, 1946.

Kinne, C. J. *The Modern Samaritan: A Presentation of the Claim of Medical Missions.* Kansas City, Mo.: Pentecostal Nazarene Publishing House, n.d.

Kluckhohn, Clyde. *Mirror for Man.* New York: McGraw-Hill Book Company, 1949.

Kraemer, H. *The Christian Message in a Non-Christian World.* New York: Harper & Brothers, 1938.

Kroeber, A. L. *Anthropology*. New York: Harcourt, Brace & Co., 1948 (Rev. ed.).

Lambuth, Walter Russell. *Medical Missions: The Two-Fold Task*. New York: Student Volunteer Movement for Foreign Missions, 1920.

——. *Winning the World for Christ*. New York: Fleming H. Revell Company, 1915.

Lamott, Willis. *Committed Unto Us*. New York: Friendship Press, 1947.

——. *Revolution in Missions*. New York: The Macmillan Company, 1954.

Lankenau, F. J. *The World Is Our Field: a Missionary Survey*. St. Louis: Concordia Publishing House, 1928.

Lapham, Henry Alfred. *The Bible As a Missionary Handbook*. Cambridge: W. Heffer & Sons Ltd., 1925.

Lasker, Bruno. *Race Attitudes in Children*. New York: H. Holt & Co., 1929.

Latourette, Kenneth Scott. *The Christian Outlook*. New York: Harper & Brothers, 1948.

——. *The Christian World Mission in Our Day*. New York: Harper & Brothers, 1954.

——. *The Gospel, The Church and the World*. (Interseminary Series.) New York: Harper & Brothers, 1946.

——. *A History of Christianity*. New York: Harper & Brothers, 1953.

——. *A History of the Expansion of Christianity*. New York: Harper & Brothers, 1937–1945. 7 vols.

——. *Missions Tomorrow*. New York: Harper and Brothers, 1936.

——. "Pre-Nineteenth Century Evangelism; Its Outstanding Characteristics." *International Review of Missions*, July, 1937.

——. *Tomorrow Is Here*. New York: Friendship Press, 1948.

—— and Richey Hogg. *World Christian Community in Action: The Story of World War II and Orphaned Missions*. New York: International Missionary Council, 1949.

Laubach, Frank Charles. *Literacy as Evangelism*. New York: FMC Committee on World Literacy and Christian Literature, 1950.

——. *The Silent Billion Speak*. New York: Friendship Press, 1943.

——. *Teaching the World to Read.* New York: Friendship Press, 1947.

——. *Wake Up Or Blow Up.* New York: Fleming H. Revell Co., 1951.

Leber, Charles T., ed. *World Faith in Action: The Unified Missionary Enterprise of Protestant Christianity.* Indianapolis: The Bobbs-Merrill Co., Inc., 1951.

Leiper, Henry Smith. *Blind Spots: Experiments in the Self-Cure of Race Prejudice.* New York: Friendship Press, 1944.

Lerrigo, Peter Hugh James. "The Next Step in Medical Missions." *International Review of Missions,* July, 1938.

Lewis, L. "Visual Aids and the Churches Overseas." *International Review of Missions,* October, 1945.

Link, Henry Chas. *The Rediscovery of Morals.* New York: E. P. Dutton & Co. Inc., 1947.

Lipphard, Wm. B. *The Ministry of Healing; A Study of Medical Missionary Endeavor on Baptist Foreign Mission Fields.* Philadelphia: American Baptist Publication Society, 1920.

Lowe, John. *Medical Missions: Their Place and Power.* New York: Fleming H. Revell, 1896.

Mabie, Henry Clay. *Method in Soul Winning on Home and Foreign Fields.* New York: Fleming H. Revell Company, 1906.

MacDonald, J. I. *Redeemer's Reign: Foreign Ministers and the Second Advent.* London: Morgan, 1910.

McLean, Archibald. *The Primacy of the Missionary and Other Addresses.* St. Louis: Christian Board of Publication, 1920.

McLeish, Alexander. *Jesus Christ and World Evangelization; Missionary Principles, Christ's or Ours.* London: Lutterworth Press, 1934.

The Madras Series: "Presenting Papers Based Upon the Meeting of the International Missionary Council at Tamboram, Madras, India," December 12–29, 1938. New York: International Missionary Council, 1939. 7 vols.

Malden, R. H. *Foreign Missions; Being a Study of Some Principles and Methods in the Expansion of the Christian Church.* London: Longmans Green & Co., 1910.

The Amsterdam Assembly Series. *Man's Disorder and God's Design.* New York: Harper & Bros. 1949, vols. I–IV in one vol.

Martin, Chalmers. *Apostolic and Modern Missions.* New York: Fleming H. Revell Company, 1898.

Mennenga, Geo. H. *All the Families of the Earth.* Grand Rapids: Baker, 1950.

Miller, Randolph Crump. *The Church and Organized Movements.* (The Interseminary Series.) New York: Harper & Brothers, 1946.

The Missionary Obligation of the Church. International Missionary Council, London: Edinburgh House Press, 1952.

Missions Under the Cross: The Addresses, Statements, and Reports from the Meeting of the International Missionary Council, Willingen, Germany, July, 1952. ed., Norman Goodall, London: Edinburgh House Press, 1953.

Montgomery, H. H. *Service Abroad.* London: Longmans, 1910.

Moorshead, R. Fletcher. *The Appeal of Medical Missions.* New York: Fleming H. Revell Co., 1913.

——. *The Way of the Doctor: A Study in Medical Missions.* London: Carey Press, 1926.

Mott, John R. *The Evangelization of the World in This Generation.* New York: Student Volunteer Movement for Foreign Missions, 1900.

——. *Evangelism for the World Today as Interpreted by Christian Leaders Throughout the World.* New York: Harper and Brothers, 1938.

——. *Five Decades and a Forward View.* New York: Harper & Bros., 1939.

——. *The Larger Evangelism.* New York: Abingdon-Cokesbury, 1944.

——. *The Pastor and Modern Missions.* New York: Student Volunteer Movement for Foreign Missions, 1904.

——. *The Present-Day Summons to the World Mission of Christianity.* Nashville: Cokesbury, 1931.

Murdock, George Peter. *Our Primitive Contemporaries.* New York: The Macmillan Company, 1934.

National Council of the Churches of Christ in the United States of America, Division of Foreign Missions. *What Constitutes a Fair Basis of Missionary Support?* Pamphlet.

Northern Baptist Convention Board of Education. *The Triumph of the Missionary Motive.* 1920.

Newbigin, Leslie. *The Household of God.* New York: Friendship Press, 1953.

Nevius, John Livingston. *Demon Possession and Allied Themes.* Chicago: Fleming H. Revell Company, 1894–1896.

Nida, Eugene Albert. *Bible Translating.* New York: American Society, 1947.

——. *Customs and Cultures.* New York: Harper & Brothers, 1954.

——. *God's Word in Man's Language.* New York: Harper & Brothers, 1952.

——. *Learning a Foreign Language, A Handbook for Missionaries.* Committee on Missionary Personnel of the Foreign Missions Conference of North America, 1950.

Niebuhr, H. Richard. *Christ and Culture.* New York: Harper & Brothers, 1951.

Niles, Daniel T. *That They May Have Life.* New York: Harpers, 1951.

Nolde, O. Frederick. *Toward World-Wide Christianity.* (The Interseminary Series.) New York: Harper & Brothers, 1946.

Ockenga, Harold John. *The Spirit of the Living God.* New York: Fleming H. Revell Company, 1947.

Oldham, J. H. *Christianity and the Race Problem.* London: Student Christian Movement, 1924.

——. *Life Is Commitment.* New York: Harper & Brothers, 1952.

—— and others. *The Missionary Motive.* London, Student Christian Movement, 1913.

One World in Christ; A Program of Advance in Foreign Missions. New York: Foreign Missions Conference of North America, 1948.

Our Medical Task Overseas. Presbyterian Church, U.S.A., Board of Foreign Missions, 1949.

Paget, E. K. *The Claim of Suffering: A Plea for Medical Missions.* London: Society for the Propagation of the Gospel, 1918. 3rd edition.

Parker, Everett C. *Religious Radio; What to Do and How.* New York: Harper and Brothers, 1948.

Paton, David M. *Christian Missions and the Judgment of God.* London: Student Christian Movement Press, 1953.

Paton, William. "The Indigenous Church," in *The International Review of Missions,* Vol. XVI, No. 61: London and New York: January, 1927.

——. *Studies in Evangelism.* London: International Missionary Council, 1938.

Penrose, Valeria Fullerton. *Opportunities in the Path of the Great Physician.* Chicago: Missionary Campaign Library, 1903.

Phillips, Godfrey E. *The Gospel in the World.* London: Duckworth, 1939.

Pierson, A. T. *Crisis of Missions.* London: 1886 (N.Y.: Baker, 1886).

Price, Francis Wilson. *As the Lightning Flashes.* Richmond: John Knox Press, 1948.

Radin, Paul. *Social Anthropology.* New York: McGraw-Hill Book Company, 1932.

Ranson, Charles Wesley, Ed. *Renewal and Advance.* London: Edinburgh House Press, 1948.

——. *That the World May Know.* New York: Friendship Press, 1953.

Richardson, Henry Powell. *Shifting Trends and Emphases in the Missionary Enterprise, 1928–1939.* B.D. Thesis, Duke University, 1940.

Riebe, John R. *The Romance of Language.* Brooklyn, N.Y.: Africa Inland Mission, 1952.

Ritchie, John. *Indigenous Church Principles in Theory and Practice.* New York: Fleming H. Revell Company, 1946.

Rossman, Parker. *Ecumenical Student Workbook.* New York: United Student Christian Council, 1949.

Rowlands, Wm. Francis. *Indigenous Ideals in Practice.* London: World Dominion Press, 1932.

Rycroft, W. Stanley. *Indians of the High Andes.* New York: Committee on Cooperation in Latin America, 1946.

Sailer, T. H. P. *Christian Adult Education in Rural Asia and Africa.* New York: Friendship Press, 1943.

Schermerhorn, Wm. David. *The Christian Mission in the Modern World.* New York: Abingdon Press, 1933.

Schmidt, Otto Henry. *St. Paul Shows Us How*. St. Louis: Concordia Publishing House, 1950.

Smalley, William A., and Fetzer, Marie. "A Christian View of Anthropology," in *Modern Science and Christian Faith*. Wheaton: Van Kampen Press, 1950.

Shillito, Edward. *The New Christendom*. London: B.B.C., 1934.

Soltau, T. Stanley. *Missions at the Crossroads*. Wheaton: Van Kampen Press, Inc., 1954.

Soper, Edmund Davison. *Racism, A World Issue*. New York and Nashville: Abingdon-Cokesbury Press, 1947.

Speer, Robert E. *Christianity and the Nations*. New York: Fleming H. Revell Company, 1910.

———. *Church and Missions*. New York: Doran, 1926.

———. *Missionary Principles and Practice*. New York: Fleming H. Revell, 1902.

———. *Race and Race Relations*. New York: Fleming H. Revell, 1924.

Storm, W. Harold. *Whither Arabia? A Survey of Missionary Opportunity*. London: World Dominion Press, 1938.

Sturgis, W. C. *The Church's Life: A Study of the Fundamentals of the Church's Mission*, 1920.

Survey of the Training of the Ministry in Africa, Part II. New York and London: International Missionary Council, 1954.

Therapeutes. *Healing Art, The Right Hand of the Church; or Practical Medicine an Essential Element in the Christian System*. Edinburgh: Sutherland, 1859.

Tompkins, Oliver S. *The Church in the Purpose of God*. London: Student Christian Movement Press, 1952.

———. *The Wholeness of the Church*. London: Student Christian Movement Press, 1949.

Ure, Ruth. *The Highway of Print: A World-wide Study of the Production and Distribution of Christian Literature*. New York: Friendship Press, 1946.

Van Dusen, Henry Pitney. "United Strategy in Christian Missions—The Next Step," from *Theology Today*, July, 1949.

Van Kirk, Walter Wm. *A Christian Global Strategy*. Chicago: Willet, Clark & Co., 1945.

Warneck, Gustav. *Evangelische Missionslehre; Ein Missionstheoretischer Versuch.* Gotha, 1897–1903 (5 vols.).

Warren, Max Alexander Cunningham. *The Christian Mission.* London: Student Christian Movement Press, 1951.

Williamson, J. R. *Healing of the Nations; A Treatise on Medical Missions, Statement and Appeal.* New York: Student Volunteer Movement, 1899.

World Atlas of Christian Missions 1911. "Student Volunteer Movement" (Dennis, Beach & Fahs).

World Dominion: A Quarterly International Review of Christian Progress. London: World Dominion Press, 1923 ff.

Wright, Cora L. *The Enlarged Program of Modern Missions as Related to the Messengers, the Methods, and the Message.* M.A. Thesis, Duke University, 1927.

Young, Rev. Robert. *Suggestions for the Conversion of the World.* 1847.

Zwemer, Samuel Marinus. *Evangelism Today, Its Message, Its Motive, Its Dynamic.* Grand Rapids: Dept. of Evangelism, Board of Domestic Missions Reformed Church in America, 1948.

Index